THE ART OF DISCOVERY

THE ART OF DISCOVERY

Encounters in Literature and Science

Edited by
Margareth Hagen, Randi Koppen
and Margery Vibe Skagen

AARHUS UNIVERSITY PRESS |

The Art of Discovery
Acta Jutlandia. Humanities Series 2010/2
© The authors and Aarhus University Press 2010
Cover Design: Jørgen Sparre
Front cover: Wilhelm Heise, "Printemps fané". München, Städtische Galerie im
Lenbachhaus und Kunstbau, inv. G1955: Jean Clair, *Mélancolie – génie et folie en
Occident*, Paris, Galeries nationales du Grand Palais, 10/10 2005 -16/1 2006; Berlin,
Neue Nationalegalerie, 17/2 – 7/5 2006, 261, p. 475.

Printed by Narayana Press, Gylling
Printed in Denmark 2010

ISSN 0065-1354 (Acta Jutlandica)
ISSN 0901-0556 (Humanities Series/2)
ISBN 978 87 7934 5010

Aarhus University Press
Århus
Langelandsgade 177
8200 Århus N
Denmark

København
Tuborgvej 164
2400 Copenhagen NV
Denmark

www.unipress.dk

Fax 89 42 53 80

The book is published with the financial support of the University in Bergen and
The Research Council of Norway

CONTENTS

INTRODUCTION

MAPPING, BRIDGING, QUILTING: TRACING THE RELATIONS BETWEEN LITERATURE AND SCIENCE

Among the metaphors used to describe the complex and sometimes difficult relationship between literature and science, we find the topographical images of the abyss, the cleft, the labyrinth, all of which call out for building bridges, finding Ariadne's thread, drawing maps. Shortly before his death in 2002, the paleontologist and evolutionary biologist Stephen Jay Gould proposed a new, feminine metaphor to designate a potentially more productive stage in this fraught relationship, drawn from the art of quilting: "In our increasingly complex and confusing world, we need all the help we can get from each distinct domain of our emotional and intellectual being", Gould insists. Confronted by such a challenge, "*quilting* a diverse collection of separate patches into a beautiful and integrated coat of many colors, a garment called wisdom", offers itself as an appropriate metaphor for a new collaborative relation between the two (Gould 19).

Gould's image possesses a resonance that becomes all the more pronounced in its relation to other well-known invocations of the quilt metaphor, not least that made by the philosophers Gilles Deleuze and Félix Guattari in their book *Mille Plateaux* (1980). Here the quilt figures among the duo's "technological models" used to differentiate between two fundamentally opposed spaces, known as "smooth" and "striated", or, alternatively, "nomadic" and "sedentary"; "deterritorialised" and "territorialised". Where the striated space of *fabric* is constituted by intertwining opposed elements (the warp and the woof), the smooth space of the patchwork *quilt* "distributes a continuous variation", "in principle infinite, open, and unlimited in every direction" (Deleuze and Guattari 524-25):

> The striated is that which intertwines fixed and variable elements, produces an order and succession of distinct forms, and organizes horizontal melodic lines and vertical harmonic planes. The smooth is the continuous variation, continuous development of form; it is the fusion of harmony and melody in favour of

the production of properly rhythmic values, the pure act of the drawing of a diagonal across the vertical and the horizontal. (Deleuze and Guattari 528)

Significantly, in view of Gould's usage above, for Deleuze and Guattari the smooth space of the quilt serves to demonstrate that "'smooth' does not mean homogenous, quite the contrary: it is an *amorphous*, nonformal space (…) an amorphous collection of juxtaposed pieces that can be joined together in an infinite number of ways" (526).

Deleuze and Guattari's spatial typology brings into focus the idealism that marks Gould's rhetoric, but also helps to illuminate important principles behind the present book. Gould's "integrated coat of many colors" points us towards a project of unification rooted in the ideals of American democracy, the space of the sedentary rather than the migrant: a "joining of differences in a common goal"; "a diverse but common enterprise of unity and power", based on "goodwill and significant self-restraint on [all] sides" (Gould 8; 5). To the extent that the present collection of original essays attempts the quilting that Gould envisages, it identifies itself equally as an examination and unpicking of seams that neither promotes nor sets out to effect any homogenous intertwining of forms. Though inevitably mixed, the space it attempts to create tends towards the smooth rather than the striated.

Bringing together scholars from literature, natural sciences, the philosophy of science and information technology, while drawing on literatures spanning two centuries (the 19th and the 20th), as well as two continents (Europe and the Americas), the essays assembled here present diverse perspectives on the cultural and historical shifts, the continuities and discontinuities, the bridges and gaps that define the relations between literary and scientific communities at different times and in different places. The various contributors examine how science and scientists have been imagined from the perspective of literature over time – as challenge or opportunity, promise or scandal. The disturbance of science emanates perhaps from its association with a frightening future or its ability to change the appearance of the past; the scandal occurs as it recalls us to thresholds and hybrids: human and non-human, animal and machine. Science, however, also emerges as a source of metaphor and imaginative modelling; as myth and mythology. Less prominent, but no less important, is the view on how scientific cultures perceive literature or the literary academic, how science reflects on itself.

The range of perspectives presented in this book does not amount to a comprehensive history, perhaps not even a usable map of more than the outlines of a changing landscape viewed now close up, now from a distance.

The topography that does appear through this nomadic, quilt-like mapping offers several vantage points from which to view the conflicting lines of convergence and separation that seem to define the present moment in the relations between literature and science: the convergence identified by some in a postmodern "humanisation" of science; the separation opening up with the neo-positivist (biological or "evolutionary") turn in recent debates.

Though "science", as discussed in the essays of this volume, is chiefly invoked in its restricted contemporary sense, with reference to natural and physical science, the history and etymology of the term bear witness to its complex infiltration with other domains and methods of knowledge and inquiry – including that of literature. Gould's book, tellingly subtitled "Mending and minding the misconceived gap between science and the humanities", lists four stages of the modern antagonistic relationship: first, the dispute between ancient wisdom and the cult of scientific observation during the 17th and 18th centuries; second, the age-old struggle between religion and science, given new impetus by the claims of evolution in the 19th century and still surviving in today's Intelligent Design Movement; third, the "Two Cultures" debates during the years of the Cold War; and fourth and last, the challenges posed to science by postmodernism. While the Galileo case is often used to symbolise the conflict of science with religion, the 1996 Sokal affair stands out among the incidents in the controversy between postmodernist philosophy and the natural sciences. Despite the antagonism demonstrated by this infamous case, however, it may equally be observed that postmodernist theory (especially its notions of language, truth and subjectivity) has contributed, if not to Gould's quilting of knowledge, then at least to a degree of convergence between disparate discourses.

The questions surrounding the nature and status of language have been fundamental to the discussion about the two cultures since the mid to late 20th century. It is hardly surprising that in 1967 we find two French intellectuals at the centre of the controversy, as the debate between Roland Barthes and Raymond Queneau on the nature of scientific as compared to poetic language reached the pages of the *Times Literary Supplement*. Surprisingly, for a poststructuralist like Barthes, his essay, "Science versus Literature", takes a conservative view on the relationship between the two languages, maintaining that for science, language is merely an instrument; functioning at its best when presumably transparent and neutral. In opposition, Queneau's essay, "Science and Literature", disposes of the old dichotomy with a proposal for a new poetical rhetoric, based on the methods and languages of science (TLS September 1967). In subsequent years, as is well documented, positivist views on the language of science as rhetorically neutral, objective, constative, literal and so on have increasingly been losing ground. Gillian Beer, one of the authors in this book, was among the first to explore (and indeed to initiate a "wave" of studies into) the many ways in which scientific writing is embedded in culture and a shared language. Professor Andrea Battistini, another distinguished contributor to this volume, has likewise published incisive studies of the rhetorical and metaphorical features of writing in the sciences. In his contribution to the present collection, professor Battistini revisits the debate of the Victorian era as well as that of the 1950s and 1960s, concluding that it is no longer possible to contrast science and literature by means of the classic dichotomies between, for instance, subjective versus objective, or the world of values and that of facts. Science is indeed part of history, subjected to languages and instruments that are far from objective. Intuition and imagination, the use of metaphors and rhetoric, are the prerogative of the creative scientist as much as the poet. In the Italian literary tradition, to which Battistini turns, the work of Galileo demonstrates the grounding of science in aesthetic and rhetorical categories, while that of Primo Levi suggests how science may be put at the service of literature.

At the beginning of what may seem at times a post-humanist era, it may also be argued that postmodernism has contributed to a "humanisation" of science. If the death of the author has been a dream of literary theory since the 1960s, the subject seems to some extent to have been resuscitated in science – not simply as a scientist and a historical figure, but also as an instance whose influence on the object (his science) is undeniable. The figure of the scientist is present in some of the contributions in this book – a figure that literature has traditionally connected with hubris and madness, but which in our time (as Rasmus Slaattelid's essay reminds us) is as often embroiled in bureaucracy and questions of politically correct ethics. The broader historical perspective on the return of the subject in science is explored in Ragnar Fjelland's chapter on Goethe's theory of colours as distinct from that of Newton. Himself a physicist and philosopher of science, Fjelland opens up to renewed consideration and appreciation of Goethe's much-disputed theory, arguing – with the distinguished philosopher of science Stephen Toulmin – for the connections between premodern and postmodern science. If Toulmin was right in pointing to modern science as somewhat paradoxically founded on a refusal of the subject-perspective of Renaissance humanism, the implication for our reading of Goethe would be that what used to be considered a romantic, pre-modern theory, based on the acceptance of the observer role, in fact anticipates a postmodern, "humanised" science.

THRESHOLDS AND HYBRIDS: BETWEEN THE
ANTHROPOID APE AND THE ANDROID MACHINE

In his contribution to this collection, entitled "The Riddle of The Robots", the science-fiction writer and professor of information technology law Jon Bing ponders the early transition of the meaning of the word *robot*, by which an object's human characteristics came to be less dominant than those of an ingenious mechanical construction. Originally, the term *Robot* was introduced in 1920 by Karel Čapek to designate the completely human-looking, artificial creatures in his play *R.U.R.*, though only a few years later the word acquired its current meaning. As Bing suggests, this semantic riddle of the 1920s indexes a more fundamental one: what is the difference between a humanised machine and a machinised human? It also points to one of the most ancient and popular topoi where literature encounters science.

Sometimes picking up the magical and mystical Jewish tradition of the *Golem* (a slave automaton brought to life by cabbalistic conjuration), Renaissance alchemists dreamed of artificially breeding the *homunculus*; a tiny, fully formed individual supposed to be present in the sperm cell. This perilous ambition reappears in Goethe's *Faust*, and, in a different form, in Mary Shelley's *Frankenstein*, which imagines the contemporary scientist, inspired by Galvani's experiments, assembling graveyard body parts into a monster and reanimating this creature with electricity. Likewise, the mass production of babies in the hatcheries and assembly lines of Huxley's *Brave New World* contributed in preparing the ground for our present discussions on reproductive technology. From the myth of Prometheus, infusing the stolen fire of the gods into clay figures, to the biotechnological laboratories of today, the possibility of designing a creature in the image of man has been a tempting and frightening source of fictional and factual adventure, nourishing our collective imagination. The transgressive attempt to equal or exceed the divine creator, identified as the most deadly sin of pride, is a motif that mythology and literature have always indulged in – and punished. Since the beginning of modernity, however, the hero selling his soul to the devil to acquire godly knowledge and power is usually portrayed as an afflicted scientist or artist.

The early modern idea of the man-machine, given impetus by the vogue for mechanical inventions, was systematically applied by Enlightenment physiologists and philosophers, projecting onto the whole human being the Cartesian view of the human body as a clockwork and the animal as an automaton. The metaphysical conception of *homo duplex*, distinguishing the immaterial soul from the mechanical flesh – the "Cartesian Centaur" which Hugh Kenner has recognised in Beckett figures absurdly attached to their bicycle – existed alongside the materialist conception of the human individual as the function of exclusively physical processes. Since La Mettrie published *L'Homme machine* in 1747, the notion of mechanical man has reappeared in fictional monsters, robots and cyborgs, supplying powerful images of fear to the popular culture of the machine and computer age. Offering science-fictional perspectives of machines in the form of humans taking control of the universe, or visions of humanity in the form of linguistically and genetically programmed machines, these fearful images either exaggerate or erase the particularity by which we identify ourselves. The uncanny contamination of the living by the mechanical, or *vice versa*, brings out the eternal enigma of the specifically human.

The literary, technological and mass-medial concretisations of the man-machine over the last centuries are reminiscent of the scandalous outbreak of the "news" of man's descent, which is the topic of Gillian Beer's contribution to this collection, "Darwin's Filthy Heraldries". Reflecting on the profound disturbance caused by the publication of Darwin's theories, as well as the persistence of the scandal over the years, Beer observes that "it was not the *novelty* of what Darwin was arguing in his concept of 'natural selection' that first shook the foundation … It was as if a groundswell of half-formulated ideas had suddenly broken through into a flood. The breaking loose of the secret, or pseudo-secret, is key". In fact the human relationship to animals, like the affinity of humans to machines, expressed in "murmurs, hints and suspicions that have been suppressed", then shouted from the roof-tops, and then again familiarised to the point of invisibility, may still be disturbing to us. The irrational experience of the self, rendered in so much of the modernist literature concerned with problems of personal identity, is hardly compatible with science's rationalist objectification of the human subject. The proliferation of monsters in popular media, caricaturing aggressive living organisms at the threshold of hard technology, might seem to indicate some sort of obsession. Somehow the monsters and robots, threatening the individual experience of unity, development, choice, responsibility, compassion, respect and wonder, are also invading our language. Today the automatic tendency is to use technological and biological analogies when speaking of mental phenomena, whereas this was unheard of fifty years

THE ART OF DISCOVERY

ago. At the same time, the developing medical practice, implanting animal organs and technical devices in the human body, may seem to confirm that we are indeed at the beginning of a post-human era.

In his book *The Fourth Discontinuity: The Co-evolution of Humans and Machines* (1993), Bruce Mazlish claims that a fourth offence should be added to Freud's enumeration of scientific (or would-be scientific) blows to human self-centredness – the three major historical changes of perspective caused by helio-centrism, evolutionism and psychoanalysis, challenging anthropo-centrist assumptions of humankind's special position in the cosmos along with human rationality as our dominant and distinctive characteristic. The logical continuation of the series, according to Mazlish's argument, would be the recognition of a fourth fallacy: our discontinuity from the tools that have ensured our evolution from the Stone Age to the era of thinking machines and neural implants.

Reactions to the increasing convergence between humans and technology may vary from fear, culpability and nostalgia to utopian hopes of perfecting humankind by scientific means. For many, the idea of a continuum between humans and our mass-produced machines is incompatible with our culture's recognition of the inherent dignity and value of the human subject. And how do we come to terms with the ongoing recombination of man and beast in medical research? If we are getting used to the idea of baboon hearts in human bodies, we may still shudder to think of the progress of bioengineering, as scientists are already producing genetically humanised animals for medical experimentation *in vivo*. And when such possibilities arise from the biological affinities between animal and humankind, should the knowledge of these affinities not result in a more humane treatment of animals? Our cultural fear of the mechanical or animal alien suggests that the fundamental riddle remains unsolved. The Victorian bourgeoisie was said to be obsessed with repressed sexual desire; could it be that we are obsessed with some other unmentionable instinct which neither the animal nor the machine model of the human can account for? Some vital necessity of which the mechanised monsters serve as ironical reminders?

POST-HUMANISM OR A NEW HUMANIST POETICS?

From a literary point of view, the antagonistic affair between literature and science is often explained by the threat to the specifically human posed by scientific naturalism, materialism, determinism, utilitarianism or reduction-ism. On the other hand, literature may – and not only from the perspective of science – seem to lack serious legitimacy, perhaps because it is so often held to be a reason in itself. "Being a useful man has always appeared to me as something hideous", observed the poet Charles Baudelaire. For somewhere in-between the anthropoid ape and the android machine is the possibility of poetry: a surplus of imaginary worlds, intimate recognition and ethical, aesthetical, emotional reverberation of other personal existences, readings of enthusiasm and melancholy, mental wandering through time and space, useless to the illiterate animal or the dreamless machine.

The increasing power of science and technology to transform and dehumanise life presents a challenge to post-human or new humanist poetics. If science has provided the tools and machines from which we may now seem inseparable, literature has participated in our subjective adaptation to changing models of identification, anticipating and responding to science's unmasking of human presumption. Since the Renaissance, the humanist tradition of criticism, along with the development of modern literature, has contributed to the shaping of Western individuality. "This *I* that is so important to me", writes the French novelist and academic Pierre Jourde, "this freedom that I wish to make use of, are both largely literary productions." "We are formed by our literary conceptions", he affirms, but not in terms of "superficial imitation of cultural models". Now that we are constantly bombarded with the chattering slogans and stereotypes of the mass media, we are more than ever threatened by de-realisation. For some, Jourde's diagnosis of the present recalls the warnings of Italo Calvino twenty-five years ago, when, in *Six Memos for the Next Millennium*, he described the threat to the individual imagination of the postmodern proliferation of images and media: the risk of losing "our capacity of bringing visions into focus with our eyes shut" (Calvino 91). For Jourde, literature deepens and extends our feeling of existence, allowing us to multiply our lives and experiences by giving access to others, balancing individuality and inter-subjectivity:

> In the same way as literature has permitted the assumption of the individual, it is literature that prevents the individual from shutting itself inside its solitude, its own class, its own place, its own time, its own culture. Through literature the singular communicates with the universal. (Jourde, "À quoi sert la littérature?")

His lecture on the value of literature was improvised during the 2009 strike in French universities, a strike held to protest against the announcement of government reforms of the universities and against the fact that priority was being given to areas of research and knowledge which were thought of as financially profitable. Among the most resonant symbols of the protest movement was Madame de Lafayette's classical novel, *La Princesse de Clèves*, mocked on several occasions by President Sarkozy as a useless and imbecile object of study. Jourde's defence echoes Baudelaire's anti-utilitarian concept of literature as equally vital to the individual and to society. "Any healthy man can go without food for two days, is the poet's claim, but without poetry, – never." Jourde's lecture, delivered at the venerable Sorbonne and by internet blog, is a reminder of the humanising effect of classical literature and of the humanist challenge for future writers and readers.

SCIENCE, MYTH AND EVOLVING MYTHOLOGIES

Today's separation of literature and science into specialised activities is of comparatively recent times, alien to the myths and literatures of ancient Greece and Rome, as well as to medieval philosophy. Ancient instruments of knowledge, classical myths, may well be read as veiled science. This is exactly the approach taken by Holly Henry in her contribution to this volume. A literary scholar with a particular interest in the art and culture of space exploration, Henry returns to the mythical origin of science, stressing that myth, like language and art, is a technology: a tool for survival and a means of evolutionary adaption. Starting from *Oedipus*'s riddle of the Sphinx, considered through the theories of Claude Lévi-Strauss and Charles Darwin, Henry's reflections end in an enthusiastic embrace of the human conquest of space, a trajectory taking us, as it were, from amoeba to astronaut. The idea of humankind's shared ancestry with the barnacle, the scallop or the oyster, which Gillian Beer showed to be so scandalous to Victorian England, is turned to the adventure of potential future relatives with the theories of the planetary scientist Carl Sagan, speculating that the human species is genetically adapted to wander. Space travel would thus be natural to the human species. At the same time, it means stepping into myth: the first steps of man on the surface of the moon were an entry into this realm, the locus of knowledge prior to the development of natural philosophy and the emergence of science.

Placed in historical perspective, Sagan's visions for the future are in fact strikingly resonant of one of the most famous manifestos of humanism, Pico della Mirandola's *Oration on the Dignity of Man* (1486). Written in justification of the human desire for knowledge, the *Oration* posits man as his own creator, possessed of intellect and free will. Man has no particular place in the Chain of Being, Mirandola's Creator says, and yet:

I have placed you at the very center of the world, so that from that vantage point you may with greater ease glance round about you on all that the world contains. We have made you a creature neither of heaven nor of earth, neither mortal nor immortal, in order that you may, as the free and proud shaper of your own being, fashion yourself in the form you may prefer. It will be in your power to descend to the lower, brutish forms of life; you will be able, through your own decision, to rise again to the superior orders whose life is divine.

"Perhaps the myth of the Sphinx is deeply connected to our innate desire to discover what lies beyond our line of sight", reflects Holly Henry at the end of her contribution, pointing towards a distant future of human survival in space. The conclusion of her reflections, where man is seen as a conqueror of new spaces thanks to evolution and astronomy, suggests a fusion of Darwin and Galileo proper to the year that celebrated them both. Viewed in this light it is especially fitting that 2009 should be the international Year of Astronomy, designated to mark the four hundred years since the first recorded astronomical observations with a telescope by Galileo, as well as the year that celebrates the bicentenary of Darwin's birth.

Science creates new mythologies not only in the sense of being a treasure box for new literary topics and narrative forms, but also in an ontological, or even religious sense. The 20th century witnessed many discoveries that changed modes of thinking about time, space and matter. Gillian Beer has shown how evolutionary theory entailed a new myth of the past, replacing the garden with the sea and the swamp. A similar causality applies to the view of the cosmos, no longer eternal, but subject to violent changes. The process by which the new images of science encounter literature's nostalgia for the images of the past continues to fascinate. Kant referred to the eternal movement of the starry sky and the morals of man as two fundamental reasons of awe; we now have to contend with the discovery of the ever-changing and violent universe, in which stars explode and galaxies die, where nothing is stable and permanent. While these images, or objects, of past beliefs disappear onto the bookshelves of historians of science, etymologists and antiquarians, new scientific theories embark on their own, complex metamorphoses, turning into new myths and changing narrative plots.

INFLUENCE AND ADAPTATION: SCIENCE TO LITERATURE

The mastering of physical forces by science has existential, ethical, intellectual and metaphysical implications that literature responds to in many ways. The risk and thrill involved in unveiling the mysteries of creation, inventing new worlds and experimenting with living beings is the perilous privilege of literature as well as science. Several of the contributors to the present collection explore the literary and philosophical potential of newly discovered scientific principles. Two of the 19th century's major fields of scientific investigation, natural evolution and electricity, understood as universal explanatory models, had great impact on contemporary literature, as they proved applicable to aesthetic as well as natural processes, to mind and matter.

In his essay, "From Heredity of Acquired Traits to Atavism", the scholar of Scandinavian literature and the history of ideas Eivind Tjønneland considers how different interpretations of Darwin may explain the transition from naturalism to neo-romanticism and decadence in Scandinavian literature around 1890. Lamarck's belief in the heredity of habits suggested the possibility of improving future generations through the moral and rational conduct of present generations. Tjønneland's contention is that the optimism of the modern breakthrough was connected with the idea of directing evolution towards the "new human being". However, when the educational optimism of the 1880s was seen to have no effect on the human race, the more unpredictable side of evolution – the sudden rise of atavism – became more acceptable to the neo-romantics. Combined with Lombroso's theory of the genius, the criminal and the madman as different types of degeneration, atavism emerged as a new "ape energy" which could explain artistic creativity.

The essay by the scholar of French literature Margery Vibe Skagen, entitled "Baudelaire and the Poetics of Magnetism", examines how new discoveries and inventions within the field of electricity and magnetism, integrated into the popularised doctrine of Anton Mesmer, flowed through nineteenth-century literature, giving a distinct colouring to some aesthetic terms that today have lost their "magnetic" or hypnotic aura. Baudelaire renews the demiurge theme by introducing a figurative charge of galvanic electricity into the domains of poetry and aesthetics. Electricity or "animal magnetism" was perceived as a vital force to be manipulated at will, granting a seemingly supernatural ability to control the environment. But the conception of electricity as a universal fluid could also accommodate romantic nostalgia, the longing to return to an originary and unifying life force. Hypnotism and atavism have been associated as modes of regression to earlier stages of evolution, implying the idea of communion with the primitive and spontaneous forces of natural creation, or simply degeneration. The atavist could be a genius or a criminal according to Lombroso. In one Baudelairean context, the somnambulistic state may resemble poetic rapture; in another it evokes the alienating image of a human automaton's convulsive movements under the influence of electricity.

These are not the sole examples provided here of the remarkable adaptability – and at times radical implications – of scientific findings to very different literary discourses. With their focus on developments in the 20th century, the chapters by scholars of Italian and Spanish literature Margareth Hagen and Hans Jacob Ohldieck trace some consequences of the changed conceptions of space in recent Italian and Latin-American writing. The first steps of man on the moon – symbolic of the unreachable, ever-distant object of dreams and longing – were also representative of one of the most dramatic collisions between science and the domain of metaphor. Margareth Hagen's essay discusses how two contemporary Italian writers, Primo Levi and Italo Calvino, interpreted this event in quite different ways. Calvino's reaction to the lunar "conquests" was one of enthusiastic welcome. A true lover of the Moon, he says, rather than being content with the conventional image, will always strive to increase his/her knowledge of this satellite of the earth. Like Calvino, Primo Levi was a writer who kept up the dialogue with science, always treasuring the supply of metaphors provided by chemistry, a field in which he excelled because he was a chemist, and because he knew the elements from experience, from daily battles in the laboratory. Unlike Calvino, however, he thinks of the universe as poetically impoverished with increasing knowledge, threatening our capacity to marvel. To Levi the lunar conquest appears as an event that strongly underscores the challenges of poetry's dialogue with science: the call to create new metaphors and discard old ones, but first and foremost the need to maintain a common language.

Hans Jacob Ohldieck's chapter presents the great interwoven lines between scientific discoveries and literature in recent Latin American literature through the ideas of the Cuban author Severo Sarduy with regard to the Baroque and Neo-baroque traditions. Sarduy's book *Barroco* (1974) traces the undoing of Renaissance geocentrism by the German astronomer Johann Kepler, whose theory of the elliptical movement of the solar system supplanted the conception of circular movement around the sun, and with it the balanced structures of Classicism. In parallel to the connection made between the Baroque and Kepler's monstrous ellipse, Sarduy posits a link between Neo-baroque poetics and the theory of the Big Bang. The dispersing movement of the Big Bang is thus the new scientific metaphor, projecting a universe with black holes and objects forever out of reach. Focusing on two critical readings of Sarduy's novel *Maitreya* (1978), Ohldieck shows how different interpretations of the Big Bang metaphor lead to radically opposed conclusions regarding the implications of Sarduy's aesthetic project.

ENGAGING THE PRESENT, ENVISIONING THE FUTURE: ETHICAL AND POLITICAL PERSPECTIVES

The changing relations between literature and science – or, more generally, the humanities and science – partly take the form of disciplinary disputes, fought out on the territories of education or cultural politics. As such they find their place in a long-running debate whose British contenders, as Andrea Battistini points out in his discussion of the "Two Cultures" debates, have long since become established as international points of reference. The exchange in the 1880s between Thomas Huxley and Matthew Arnold famously discussed the relative merits of the arts and the sciences in education, with Huxley endorsing scientific education as a preparation for engagement with an increasingly complex and expanding world, and Arnold responding in defence of humane letters and a classical conception of education as a civilising, humanising process. While the initial dispute took place against a background of humanist dominance in British universities as well as government, this was hardly the case at the time of the second debate, initiated by C.P. Snow's 1959 Rede Lecture, taken to new levels of notoriety by F.R. Leavis's reply three years later, and continued over the following decade. As Guy Ortolano shows in a recent book on the Two Cultures controversy, Snow's insistence on the supposedly marginalised status of science, technology and expertise at a time of widespread public commitment to all three can only be described as flying in the face of facts. Ortolano refers to newspaper reports, broadcasts, government reports and political committees of the time, all of which present the scientist and a process of "scientific modernization" as the nation's best hope in a competitive decolonised world (Ortolano 20). Snow's critique, nonetheless, directs itself against an academic culture that takes the moral high ground outside the academic institution as much as inside it, dominating public debate as well as polite society, while representing an approach to the contemporary world which is not merely unequal to its challenges, but effectively counterproductive to their solutions. His main target is a theoretically minded academic culture – literary intellectuals and exponents of 20th-century modernism in particular, but also champions of "pure" science – whose hostility to the "scientific revolution" and "the application of real science to industry" (Snow 29) entails a hostility to the aims and hopes of modern society as such: the hopes of economic development, of industrial civilisation delivering material prosperity and social opportunity to the majority of the population. A literature whose aesthetic tenets (as Snow understands them) are those of autonomy, formalism, non-referentiality; that has abandoned the effort to produce narratives about society in favour of formalist experiment; and that "shudders away from" the technological basis of every social encounter, reflects a failure of engagement with the real world that is in effect a commitment to conservative and ultimately reactionary attitudes.

Leavis's reply refutes the charge of non-engagement, promoting literature as the exemplary adequate response to the challenges presented by the advances of science and technology. In a move that both anticipates and differs from the position to be taken by Pierre Jourde in a similar debate conducted more than half a century later, Leavis refuses science's claims on the reality of experience. Where Jourde was to evoke the depths of existence and inter-subjectivity opened up by literature in an era of increasing de-realisation, Leavis asserts the fundamental connectedness between literature and human *being*. Literature, for Leavis, the creative effort involved in writing and reading, embodies humanness; what it means to be human. It is the continuation and renewal of a work that precedes science and without which science would have been impossible: "the creation of the human world, including language" (Leavis 27). In the university he envisages, The English School will stand at the centre of that concerted, cross-disciplinary effort at "creative questioning", the "creative response to the new challenges of time" that is required to keep civilisation "human", as opposed to being mechanised and technocratic (Leavis 23; 27).

Grounded in disciplinary rivalries, both generations of the debate reveal the ideological stakes involved. "From Huxley in the 1880s to Snow in the 1960s", as Ortolano observes,

> figures who associated their positions with science frequently challenged their rivals from the left, branding them conservatives or reactionaries standing in the way of progress and reform. From the late 1960s, however, these positions came to be reversed, and the subsequent post-modern and post-colonial turns in literary studies fostered leftist critiques of scientific objectivity and Western hegemony (Ortolano 27).

In a more recent turn of events, given impetus not least by the flurry of media attention surrounding every occurrence of the word "evolution" in the year of the Darwin bicentenary, the attempt by some exponents of the "sciences" seems to be not so much to redefine the terms of the positions as to evict ideology from the domain of (true) science altogether. The lines of debate, properly speaking, should be drawn between scientific and non-scientific approaches to the world; science, the argument goes, is not about politics. Thus exponents of "biologism" in various disciplines challenge the cultural hegemony of a politically correct (left-oriented) humanism whose idealism results in a refusal of scientific truths; a commitment to social, cultural and discursive theories to the exclusion (and detriment) of scientific models and findings – indeed a branding of them as "reactionary". In a reenactment that is paradoxically both like and unlike the Snow-Leavis debate, the humanists are once more charged with turning away from reality, thus failing to engage with and present solutions to its problems.

If these are the terms of the current public debate, at least in a Scandinavian context, the situation within the academic institutions would seem to be very different, with humanities subjects fighting a losing battle against systems of selection and allocation of funds based on paradigms of natural science research. European education and research policies are at the centre of the philosopher of science Rasmus Slaattelid's ironic afterthoughts on the researcher ethos in Ibsen's *Hedda Gabler*, which bring the volume to a close. Slaattelid's contribution offers a playfully anachronistic, and ironic, staging of current policies through a classic of dramatic realism that does not seem to be addressing such issues at all. The author's reversal of foreground and background in Ibsen's play, however, produces some disconcertingly familiar conclusions: with the contest between empiricist and "imaginative" models of science parodically reduced to the principles of the Apollonian against the Dionysian, Ibsen's – and Slaattelid's – ironic conclusions hardly come as a surprise.

Re-opening the question of the relative merits of science and literature in an ethical engagement with the world, the biochemist and philosopher of science Roger Strand's chapter on the short fiction of American physicist Leo Szilard effectively reverses the terms of C.P. Snow's argument, asking whether fiction is indeed required to set straight the sins of science. Ironically, as Strand shows, at the time when Snow presents his ethically based critique of a society that allegedly gives too little space to science and the (technocratic) expert, the physicist Szilard is experimenting with his particular brand of "science fiction": short fictions in which science rules the day and the expert is always the man of the moment. Szilard's stories, however, turns into the most serious threat to the future of civilisation. What, Strand asks, in yet another twist to the Two Cultures debate, are the possibilities of a reflexive and ethically conscious position for science in the increasingly knowledge-driven capitalist economies that have dominated the world since World War II?

WHICH SCIENCE: MEDIATION AND POPULARISATION

With modernity's division of reason into distinct disciplines, and with increasing specialisation in all departments of knowledge, any "relation" between literature and science (apart from separation) must necessarily entail popularisation. From one perspective, at least, popularising theories and findings can be a way for science to hone its concepts, to test its theories in terms of applicability and relevance. Making knowledge intelligible across intellectual boundaries can be a way of creating cultural communities; sites of negotiation and exchange. Among the concerns of the contributors to this collection, nonetheless, has been the slightly more worrying question of what happens in the process: does popularised science cease to be science and become something different? What are the rhetorical and ideological frames of popular mediation, and what is the role and responsibility of literature (or the literary intellectual) in this process? Michael Whitworth's book *Einstein's Wake* (1998) drew attention to the institutional, ideological and strategic contingencies of mediation at a high point in science popularisation in British culture: the presentation of relativity and the "new physics" in best-selling popular science books, periodicals and radio broadcasts throughout the 1920s and 1930s. As Whitworth shows, British scientists in the early decades of the 20th century had an interest in presenting their discipline in a philosophical rather than a technological framework for at least three reasons: firstly, because universities and governments were dominated by graduates in the humanities; secondly, because of the practical (and nefarious) frame placed on science during the Great War; and, thirdly, as a means of differentiating 20th-century science from the perceived mechanist, materialist and utilitarian emphasis of its 19th-century counterpart. The new science, consequently, was presented as pure, abstract and non-mechanical; concerned with principles rather than mechanisms, and in possession of formal qualities that appealed to aestheticist lines of critical judgement. Such framing, suggesting that philosophical problems in literature and physics may be discussed within a common discourse, accounts for the success of popularisation at this time, including its embeddedness in elitist literary culture, though also for some less fortunate consequences of mis-construal and conflation: of physical relativity with philosophical relativity, empirical science with subjective idealism. It is the consequences of such convergences that concern Randi Koppen, scholar of British literature, in her chapter on Wyndham Lewis's critique of science popularisation in *Time and Western Man* (1927). Where Michael Whitworth describes the relations between science and literature in the interwar years as an "entente cordiale" (Whitworth 11), Lewis's perception of them is as unhealthily and destructively intimate, leading neither to individual nor social empowerment, but to loss of subjectivity and the grasp of the object world.

Pursuing the question of popularisation, though within a cultural and ideational context that seems far removed from Lewis's preoccupations during the 1920s, the scholar of Scandinavian literature Christine Hamm's chapter on the Norwegian Nobel laureate Sigrid Undset (1882-1949), addresses the author's concerns with the social and political consequences of the mediation of science to the general public through popular science journals in the early 1900s. Undset's critique was specifically directed against the emergent research in female biology and reproduction that was quickly being appropriated and redeployed in a range of ideological arguments, including those of feminists. Herself an ardent amateur biologist practised in the taxonomic systems of the Swedish botanist Carl von Linné, Undset was not one to doubt either the scientific data or their methods of discovery; she did, however, warn against the "quasi-scientific abracadabra" ensuing from popularisation and the modern privileging of the natural sciences over other epistemological paradigms. Undset's call, as Hamm elaborates it, is for models of understanding that are fundamentally embedded and relational, involving a conception of science as always culturally situated, placed in a network of relations. Undset formulates her critique of the ideological misuse of science most famously in a 1919 essay attacking contemporary feminists. As Hamm's chapter shows, however, it takes the form of the novel for the author to work out her own alternative epistemology.

THE LANGUAGES OF SCIENCE AND LITERATURE

If metaphors and other figures of speech are often thought of as having a potentially humanising effect on an essentially reductionist scientific language, the understanding that rhetorical figures play an important role in the *doing* of science is perhaps less well established. As John A. McCarthy shows in a recent book on the intersections among science, philosophy and literature, replacing the two cultures with a *ménage à trois* may help to bring about a fuller appreciation of the complex dynamics involved. Inquiring into the nodal points of the central scientific theories of chaos and complexity, McCarthy writes: "natural scientists rely almost as heavily on metaphor to achieve representation as do humanists. As an expression of the ability to find similarities in seemingly dissimilar things, metaphor is one of the tropes through which meaning is achieved … Metaphors, then, can be considered the building blocks of creative thought" (McCarthy 23).

As mentioned above, Gillian Beer was among the first to explore the many ways in which scientific writing is embedded in culture and a shared language, raising the fundamental question, with her seminal *Darwin's Plots* (1983), of what differences can be maintained between narrative and argument, between literary and scientific language, literary and non-literary instances of image, anthropomorphism and metaphor. Such questions are pursued by several of the contributors to this collection, most explicitly in the chapter on metaphor in science, theology and literature, written by the professor of Russian literature Jostein Børtnes. Addressing the re-evaluation of metaphor and analogy that has occurred within science and theology in recent decades, Børtnes shows by a number of examples how metaphors work as "disruptive cognitive acts" in all three fields, suggesting what the ultimate difference in their application might consist in.

A specialist of British poetry, Charles Armstrong brings the question of language to contemporary ecopoetry in his chapter. If poetry is the literary genre that traditionally has been the most resistant to instrumental uses of language, he asks, how does this square with ecopoetry's commitment to societal reform? How is this poetry to reconcile the objective, as the ecocritic William Howartz defines it, "of redirecting humanistic ideology through appropriation of ideas from the natural sciences", with a creative deployment of language capable of matching ecology as "the subversive science" that "undermines … science itself"? Armstrong's readings in British and American contemporary ecopoetry reveal some interesting cultural differences in the conception of the genre as well as the form of engagement with the natural sciences.

Unlike ecopoetry's "earnest" approach to natural science, the linguistic relation explored by scholar of American literature Željka Švrljuga in her chapter on Patricia Eakins's 1999 neo-slave narrative is that of a parodic transmutation. Ideationally and stylistically modelled on Comte de Buffon's master narrative of natural history, *Histoire naturelle* (1749-89), Eakin's text gives us the slave's parasitic *histoire*, effectively revealing the master/slave dialectic at work in Buffon's politics of observation and hierarchical structuring of nature.

TRACING THE SEAMS

In keeping with the metaphor that opened these reflections, the volume they introduce has the appearance of the quilt: a constellation of individual pieces composed to exhibit patterns of their own while contributing to a larger design. The principle of organisation involved, as with the quilt, is that of complementarity; juxtaposition rather than sequence. Following the opening section, containing essays by Andrea Battistini, Gillian Beer and Holly Henry, the arrangement of chapters is loosely based on the chronology of the literary texts under discussion by each author. Chapters may be read in the order in which they are placed, or non-sequentially, starting from any point in the composition. It is in the design of this particular quilt to let the seams show – the seams that serve to juxtapose science with literature, as well as those that align cultural moments and places. Letting seams show, as Berthold Brecht always insisted, puts work on display but also invites work: of unpicking and re-composition, removals and additions – or, as Deleuze and Guattari might say, "local operations involving changes in direction" (Deleuze and Guattari 528).

Based on papers originally read during a workshop on Literature and Science held at the University of Bergen in December 2008, this collection is the continuation of a dialogue begun between scholars representing a range of academic positions and fields – from physics to literature; from postgraduates to established scholars of international renown. The editors wish to thank the Department of Foreign Languages and the Faculty of the Humanities at the University of Bergen, as well as the Norwegian Research Council, for the means to initiate this dialogue and for generously supporting its publication.

Bergen, November 2009
Margareth Hagen   Randi Koppen   Margery Vibe Skagen

WORKS CITED

Calvino, Italo. *Six Memos for the Next Millennium*. London: Vintage, 1996.

Deleuze, Gilles and Félix Guattari. *A Thousand Plateaus*. London and New York: Continuum, 2004.

Gossin, Pamela, ed. *Encyclopedia of Literature and Science*. Westport, Connecticut and London: Greenwood Press, 2002.

Gould, Stephen Jay. *The Hedgehog, the Fox, and the Magister's Pox: Mending and Minding the Misconceived Gap between Science and the Humanities*. London: Vintage, 2004.

Jourde, Pierre. "À quoi sert la littérature?" *Confitures de culture*. http://bibliobus. nouvelobs.com/blog/pierre-jourde/20090303/10993/à-quoi-sert-la-littérature-1.

Leavis, F.R. *Two Cultures? The Significance of C.P. Snow*. London: Chatto & Windus, 1962.

Mazlish, Bruce. *The Fourth Discontinuity: The Co-evolution of Humans and Machines*. New Haven: Yale University Press, 1993.

McCarthy, John A. *Remapping Reality: Chaos and Creativity in Science and Literature*. Amsterdam and New York: Rodopi, 2006.

Mirandola, Pico della. *Oration on the Dignity of Man*. http://www.cscs.umich.edu/~crshalizi/Mirandola/.

Ortolano, Guy. *The Two Cultures Controversy: Science, Literature and Cultural Politics in Postwar Britain*. Cambridge: Cambridge University Press, 2009.

Snow, C.P. *The Two Cultures: And a Second Look*. Cambridge: Cambridge University Press, 1964.

Whitworth, Michael. *Einstein's Wake: Relativity, Metaphor, and Modernist Literature*. Oxford: Oxford University Press, 2001.

Williams, Raymond. *Keywords: A Vocabulary of Culture and Society*. Oxford and New York: Oxford University Press, 1983.

DISCOVERIES – STRUGGLE, SCANDAL AND ADAPTATION

THE LOVE-HATE RELATIONSHIP OF LITERATURE AND SCIENCE

Andrea Battistini, University of Bologna

Some have likened the periodical alternation with which, in time, moments of collaboration and moments of separation between literature and science have followed each other, to the quadrille – the old-fashioned square dance for couples – in which the dancers sometimes proceed in separate lines and then intertwine. Here, I will try to examine a few of these dance steps, dividing my essay into three parts. In the first part, I wish to set the statutes of literature and science against each other. I will then consider how literature can be put at the service of science, through Galileo's example. Finally, I will examine how science can be put at the service of literature, through the Italian author Primo Levi's example.

TWO STATUTES CONFRONTING EACH OTHER

In the relationship between science and literature, it is almost always literature which seeks to assimilate scientific discourse. Scientists may, of course, be acquainted with literary works, but it is unlikely that they can be used professionally in the scientist's research. In this sense, the cases of effective assimilation are, historically speaking, still far too rare. The idea that Greek tragedy with its concept of fate should be at the root of the modern natural order is no more cogent than the suggestion that the faith which animates medieval theology should be "behind" the faith in the possibility of scientific progress; both hypotheses, incidentally, belong to the mathematical logician Alfred North Whitehead. Who really believes nowadays that the techniques of the stream of consciousness could have influenced Einstein's theory of relativity?

The influence of science in literature is much more massive, given literature's welcoming attitude to experimentation, an attitude which is perhaps best summed up in the ancient Roman playwright Terence's saying: "homo sum: humani nil a me alienum puto" ("I am a man: what concerns man cannot be alien to me"). This is why the relationship between the two cultures is generally seen as one-way, from science to literature. Such a view obviously applies whenever the literati indulge in a fetishist worship of science, as at times in the 18th century, or in the Futuristic *Weltanschauung*. But it is also true in cases where poets categorically reject science, since even an apocalyptic condemnation (by Petrarch, Blake and Leopardi, for instance) shows a willingness to engage – a sort of dialogue, a sharing, albeit polemical or even antithetic – in the reasons of the "other" culture. The most fruitful attitude is, however, neither worship nor execration, but a critically focused gaze, receptive to other territories, and ready to re-elaborate their views.

We may say that literature can deduce contents, language and methods from science. If one thinks of Dante interpreting Aristotle as an astronomer or a naturalist, or of the 18th-century didascalic poets rendering Newton's optics or physics in verse, one may well understand how drastically the original content of these scientific works was changed. In these changes a kind of translation is carried out, sometimes not necessarily consciously, due to the unavoidable diversity of the codex. And this takes place even when terminology is transposed without modification from the scientific vocabulary to the literary lexicon. When the allegedly denotative and univocal terms of science are transposed to the literary field, layers of emotional nuance are added to them on account of literature's innate openness to interpretation. Where scientists need the rare technical term in order to concentrate the highest amount of information in a single word, authors make use of such precious linguistic material to create displacements and experimental verbal effects. When Marino, the Baroque Italian poet, in his *Adone* uses scientific terms such as "atom", "cartilages" and "telescope", or draws on the lexicon of anatomy, he does so to make his vocabulary take on an encyclopaedic effect and to surprise his readers, who find words they would not expect in poetry.

This is the connotative dimension of literature: its language contains a *surplus* of meanings, making it resemble a generator, charged by significations exceeding the mere literal meaning. In literature the message lives on echoes, suggestions, atmospheres. With a simple image one might visualise the word as a point around which a semantic halo of connotations is created, conferring on it a volumetric dimension where even what is unspoken takes part in the creation of the phenomenon usually called polyphony.

In order to convey the difference between the two languages, one need only see how the same word has different meanings in the two domains. The simplest case concerns the word "water." In chemistry it is designated H_2O, a formula that immediately quantifies its composition, unambiguously designating water – and only that. The word "water" in literature has quite another value, for example in the line written by John Keats for his tomb:

"Here lies one whose name was writ in water." In this phrase, water does not mean that it is composed of two atoms of hydrogen and one of oxygen, or perhaps it *also* means this, albeit with a totality of many other indefinite meanings: the meaning of the ephemeral, the precariousness of life, the weakness of man, the idea of fleeting existence, of melancholy, of death, of nothing that remains, and of so many impressions that form, so to speak, an open list, without excluding intertextual allusions to other lines from other poets.

On a syntactic level, the influence of science may be detected in a scrupulous rationality and causality of plot, as in the narratives by Primo Levi and Italo Calvino. The most profound and vital influence, however, affects authors' "vision of the world", their capacities as observers and interpreters, and consequently the organisation of their work, their methods and poetics. Even for those who do not practise it professionally, science inevitably modifies the way in which reality is perceived, multiplying interpretative and representational possibilities. Carlo Emilio Gadda would not have been able to write the *Pasticciaccio* (which, by the way, does not have any scientific contents) without his scientific knowledge which enabled him to elaborate a chaotic, or rather entropic conception of reality, similar to the uncontrollable trajectories of gas molecules, the literary equivalent of which is the cognitive "pasticcio" (muddle or tangle).

One common characteristic of writer scientists, or double talents (Carlo Emilio Gadda was an engineer, like Leonardo Sinisgalli; Primo Levi was a chemist; Giuseppe Bonaviri a cardiologist), and in general of those who are sensitive to the sciences, is the meta-discursive attitude, the tendency to reflect on the relationship between literature and science. At moments of acceleration in scientific and technological progress, such reflection tends to become more general. Recently, there have been two periods in which bibliography in literature and science has witnessed a steep rise: in England during the Victorian era and, globally, following the publication of Charles Snow's pamphlet "The Two Cultures" in 1959. In the first instance the confrontation was kept within the limits of constructive urbanity. In 1881 the Darwinist Thomas Henry Huxley intervened with a proposal for educational reform adjusted to the impressive progress undergone by science and technology, giving more significance to an area of knowledge which had been, in his view, underrated by an educational system dominated by *belles lettres* and a sterile and gratuitous aestheticism (Huxley 79-90). In 1883 Matthew Arnold replied, recognising the formative value of scientific texts, but assigning literature a guiding role. Its aesthetic and emotional features, according to Arnold, endowed literature with the ability to create a final synthesis of human knowledge, establishing correlations between the various disciplines. In this way the sectarian and unrelated knowledge of science could be reconciled to man's innate instinct for the good and the beautiful, permitting him to discover those educational and ethical values with which to overcome the mean utilitarianism, the arid determinism and the spreading agnosticism of Victorian society (Arnold 72-137).

The controversy ignited by Snow turned out to be of a considerably more embittered kind, as indicated already in the first, virulent response by Frank R. Leavis. The terms of the debate are too well known to merit repetition here. It is sufficient to recall, on the one hand, the general condemnation of humanists, supposedly guilty of an instinctual aversion to science and a consequent indifference to man's social ills (Snow); and on the other hand, Leavis's animated defence of the role of literature, all the more important in a highly technological society (Leavis 1962). There is some truth to Leavis's remark that, if literature tends to criticise science and those societies that make a fetish out of it, this is not because literature is necessarily conservative, but because it is constitutionally pervaded by an ideal tension; a perennial dialectic between what reality is and what it should be.

According to the Italian prose writer Claudio Magris, "one of the functions of literature consists in saying no, in defining oneself through negation, in not identifying oneself with the existing order but linking oneself closely to that which is not there yet, which does not exist. This does not mean to despise the world around us, to betray its values, its colours, its smell, its particulars" (Magris 25, my translation). So, the union between philosophy (or science) and literature may be compared, as did Italo Svevo, another novelist from Trieste, to a "legal marriage" where husband and wife "do not agree", yet "they beget very beautiful children". If the literati often express horror at the technological revolution, this is not because they are intrinsically averse to science, but because they reflect on the deterioration of the quality of life linked to a mere material bettering, often accompanied by alienation, egoism, intellectual blindness, the deadening of all critical sense reflecting profoundly on human existence, when a creative exploration of our nature might emerge.

Little by little, from this debate contributions developed that helped to clarify the operative distinctions of science and literature. Amongst the most significant outcomes are the differences undersigned by Aldous Huxley, Thomas Henry's grandchild, between "nomotetic" science, dedicated to the formulation of universal and univocal laws, and "idiographic" literature, exploring the most personal and intimate experiences, life's flow, its contradictions and otherwise ineffable aspects. Despite the different procedures, the two branches of knowledge are reconciled, for Huxley, as much as for Husserl, in the *Lebenswelt*, in the world of life, since both, albeit in different ways, address the same human experiences (Huxley 11-110). Giulio Preti's view that science and literature represent different scales of values is virtually complementary to this epistemological perspective. According to Preti, science is founded on "morality", with its absolute principles which transcend history and empirical circumstances, as well as its openness to being verified by intelligence, in a dialectic that coincides with liberty. Literature, on the other hand, is inspired by "ethics", instituted on the basis of persuasion, relativity, common sense and a restricted validity for definite groups.

Immersed in the Italian cultural tradition, the confrontation between science and literature seems again to propose the long debate between rhetoric, aiming at what is verisimilar and probable, and logic, which, like science, deals with what is real and universal (Preti). Thus a different operative dynamic descends, in the sense that the scientist must always verify his/her interpretative hypotheses against a real referent, confirming them, following the experimental vocation which, in fact, linked even Aristotle and Bacon, Ptolemy and Galileo. Differently, the man of letters, with the "poetic" text, creates a monad that finds the source of its reliability in itself. For this very reason, an Italian scholar in aesthetics, Galvano della Volpe, distinguished between science's "heteroverifiability" and literature's "autoverifiability" (Della Volpe 127-35).

Thomas Kuhn, who became popular with his book *The Structure of Scientific Revolutions* (1969), has rightly claimed that today it is no longer possible to contrast science and literature by means "of the classic dichotomies between, for example, the world of value and the world of fact, the subjective and the objective, or the intuitive and the inductive" (Kuhn 403). If then, up to about half a century ago, it was generally proclaimed that science proceeds rationally and literature imaginatively, today nobody any longer believes in this Manichean vision. With the affirmation of structuralism, in particular in its psychological version (the *Gestalt*), such a definite scission between the various spheres of cognitive activity is no longer accepted. In fact, using a scientific comparison, a process similar to that of electrolysis or osmosis has taken place, in the sense that as in an electrolytic solution positive ions migrate to the negative electrode and vice versa, in the same way literary scholars today claim for themselves qualities traditionally unique to scientists, and vice versa.

Today nobody believes in the myth of the platonic and romantic image of a possessed, instinctive poet, irrationally, and mysteriously inspired by heaven. Rather, it is acknowledged that the inventive freedom enjoyed by a writer or an artist is not unlimited. As the Italian writer and poet Carlo Emilio Gadda lets us understand with his habitual irony, "a xylographer, representing a locomotive, certainly will not draw it bolt by bolt, such as it is in the three orthogonal projections kept in the Technical Bureau's archives. The xylographer will be able to avoid seeing wheels, and instead see a Homeric nebula, wrapped up as he is in his drive to picture the fleeing run. He will not, nevertheless, be able to endow the machine with square wheels" (Gadda 77, my translation). In other words, the ways of reaching knowledge are different, but even the arts, and with them literature and the human sciences, must follow certain canons and respect certain rules.

Generalising this apologue, it can be added that in the area of literature procedures converge that, by tradition, were considered unique to the scientist. Writers, discussing their artistic actions, show the reflective awareness of working with rationality and intelligence on the realisation of a project, along the rigorous lines of a precise design, consistent throughout because they are subject to calculation. Literature too, beyond any mythology, is an engineered construction. It is reflection, study, research, because it has to face persistent technical problems which must be resolved in the pursuit of its craft.

In the same way, at the opposite pole of science, the positivist myth of the objective researcher, impassive in the photographing of reality with no subjective influence, has deceased. Science nowadays has drawn near literature's operative code because it has left its deterministic and homogeneous system, emanating from Newton, founded on the maximum predictability of phenomena and the presumption of the certainty of results. From this, it has moved on to a dynamic system that does not consider negative chaos, meaning the absence of order, but positively judges the richness of a chaotic universe, because being chaotic is no longer the synonym of chance, but of an indefinite number of variables, in which disorder is capable of creating structures. It is almost unanimously pointed out that nature is not only observed but also necessarily susceptible to interpretation. Intuition, imagination and fancy are thus judged as also pertaining to the scientist, and it has been realised that hypotheses are born from an imaginative flight, destined only later to be examined under the lens of logic.

If the literary metaphor consists in uniting things generally thought of as distant, its field of application can be widened to science, even more so since the mechanism of metaphor is not intended as a procedure by which a word is merely replaced by another that takes its place, but as a figurative meaning that establishes a dialectic tension with the proper term with which it interacts, to the point of proposing a sum of multiple connections.[1] When closely scrutinised, metaphor shows itself to behave in the way scientific laws do, since the latter, too, establish relations between phenomena. Besides, according to psychologists, those who wish to understand the relations between natural phenomena do not proceed by conceptual abstractions but by visual images, that is by metaphoric analogies. When Niels Bohr constructed a model of the atom, considering it as the solar system, he formulated a theory on the basis of an analogy, that is, a metaphor.

LITERATURE AT THE SERVICE OF SCIENCE: GALILEO'S EXAMPLE

Today even rhetoric is considered part of science because it is understood that scientific research is also a debate between different schools of thought that may engage the same phenomena in different ways. An example that proves how science uses rhetoric and the literary care for the aesthetic components of a text is given in the works of Galileo.

Until, to use Kuhn's terminology, science operates with a view to a "normal paradigm", it does not need to reinforce its voice by any particular attention to how its message is offered, focusing almost exclusively on "what" to say, and not on "how" to say it. In the case of a theorem (by way of a familiar example, we might think of Pythagoras), what really counts is what it demonstrates, the statement of its conclusion, whereas it matters little by which road it was reached. Usually we know what it wants to prove but not the proof that leads to that result. Things change in those revolutionary periods of science when, as Kuhn has it, "anomalies" and "puzzles" are no longer to be solved by using a normal paradigm and innovative scientists appear, acting in the light of paradigms that are alternative to any dominant one.

Discussing the nature of creative innovation in sciences, Kuhn's *Structure of the Scientific Revolutions* had the merit of treating such "topics as the role of competing schools and of incommensurable traditions, of changing

---

1   Umberto Eco rightly thinks that metaphor must be understood as an "instrument of *additive* and not *substitutive* knowledge". "Metafora". *Enciclopedia*, eds. Ruggiero Romano et al. Turin: Einaudi, 6 (1980): 192.

standards of value, and of altered modes of perception" (Kuhn 403). Topics like these have long been basic knowledge for the literary historian but are minimally represented in writings on the history of science. If one makes them central to science, one is led to deny, in consequence, that literature can be clearly distinguished from science.

In a phase of turbulence and epistemological conflict in which the old paradigms appear obsolete and the new ones are yet to develop objective and sure demonstrations, science tends to revert to rhetoric's persuasive resources and to typical literary tools in order to make its reasoning "better", more captivating or "pleasing". Galileo is fully aware of this when he confides to his friends that he also wants to attend to "the ceremonial introduction and the cues to the incipits of his dialogues with the following subjects, which are rhetorical and poetical, rather than strictly scientific", to give them "some spirit and beauty" (Galileo, *Letter to Federico Cesi*). Today we have an increasingly good understanding of how important the aesthetic component is in the texts of Galileo, a component which had already been recognised by his contemporaries. Kepler, in fact, upon receiving *Sidereus Nuncius* with amazing astronomical discoveries still to be proven, wrote: "Why shouldn't I believe in such a profound mathematician whose very style reveals clearly correctness of judgment?" (Kepler 23). What Kepler realised is confirmed today by Italo Calvino, who has written that "Galileo Galilei deserves as much fame for his felicitous invention of imaginative metaphors as he does for his rigorous scientific method" (Calvino 1977, 366).

Galileo does not only worry about demonstrating the truthfulness of the Copernican heliostatic hypothesis by physical experiments and astronomical observations – he also searches for the most elegant and effective way of presenting his assertions. To revert to old terminology, it may be said that the contents of science are melded with the forms of literature. One often hears of some mathematical demonstrations being more "elegant" than others for their better symmetry in symbolic expression. Naturally, even if science is not disdainful of the aesthetical care of its statements and makes good use of formulas that explain a chaotic group of elements with the greatest simplicity and economy, these are always tools, perhaps determining ones, as in Galileo's cultural policy, which enabled him to be listened to. They are simple means, nonetheless, of achieving the real aim, which is still the explanation of phenomena, with a definite prevalence of interest towards what is claimed, rather than how this is done. If science is enjoyed for the beauty of its results, these acquire an aesthetic value. This happened when two German physicists used fractals not to calculate real objects, but

THE ART OF DISCOVERY

to create abstract figures. The drawings became works of art, shown in an exhibition named "The Beauty of Fractals" (Peitgen & Richter).

The rhetorical or literary dimension of science has, in any event, definite relevance because, as we have seen, its results are always presented to a community which must examine and share them. In particular, in Galileo's case, the community was an alternative audience that required a special approach. It was not the academic world, composed mainly of peripatetic scholars, but educated intellectuals, passionate about science, amateurs lacking the preclusions typical of the university establishment. It is also for this reason he chose not only to write in Italian instead of Latin, but also to use the dialogue form instead of the treatise, which was the usual genre used by scientists. In Galileo the epistemological model of Plato's Socratic dialogues plays a great part; while on the structural and argumentative level, the influence of the scheme of Cicero's *De Oratore* is evident. Like the *Dialogo sopra I due massimi sistemi* (1632), *De Oratore* no longer presents the dialogue between a teacher and a pupil, but among three characters; not simple doctrinal voices but people; not larvae but men. In this way abstract theories are identified with particular people, assuming a concreteness well beyond the ordinary. Scientific research is not a simple two-handed game between "nature and the researcher who, thanks to the method, questions nature and reads it. Instead, it is a three-handed game: it requires nature, someone who questions it, and someone else (audience or community) who interrogates it as well and debates with the other questioners" (Pera 1991, *x*).

Galileo's epistemology, instead of being presented by philosophical disquisitions, is transmitted by means of the literary instruments of the apologue and the story. Typical, amongst so many, is the short story investigating the nature of sound inserted in his *Saggiatore*, which immediately acquires the allure of a romance. Upon closer inspection, scientists, when observing nature, are rather like *picaros* who, following their explorative instinct, confer on speculative investigation a sense of adventure, of itinerant quest, fitting snugly in the narrative scheme of the romance. The scientist's knowledge has a driving quality similar to that of a traveller, a picaro, experiencing life on the road, the chronotope of encounters and surprises, because of that element of casualness always underpinning all discoveries. Galileo, with the literary metaphor of the investigator of sounds, teaches us that scientific research follows the same diegetic logic as the novel. Thanks to his apologue, Galileo shows us that science writings not only exhibit wit and curiosity, which correspond to the rational and experimental moments, but are also endowed with *pathos*, intellectual anxiety, derived from the consciousness of the infinity of nature.

SCIENCE AT THE SERVICE OF LITERATURE: PRIMO LEVI'S EXAMPLE

Only a short-sighted and old-fashioned vision of literature can presume to be capable of doing without the teachings of science. Italo Calvino has said that we must "ask of literature more than a knowledge of the times or a mimesis of the external aspect of objects or of the internal aspects of the human soul. We want from literature a cosmic image" (Calvino 1962, 123). In the same way, Primo Levi has stated the will for a "mutual enthrallment" which allows for the widening of the capacity for observation typical of the technician and the scientist, from the world of nature to the world of men (Levi 1985, 632). By personal and direct experience Levi, who wrote a sort of autobiography based on the periodic system of elements, was able to claim that the "patrimony of mental habits deriving from chemistry and its environs" can easily find "vaster applications", allowing the writer "to never remain indifferent to the people that chance lets *him* come across", so that "human beings themselves can become 'samples', specimens in a sealed packet, to be recognised, analysed and weighted" (Levi 1986, 1102, my translation).

Precluding such possibilities of analysis, authentic and "formidable sources of literary inspiration" become, according to Levi, a type of "voluntary blindness" which loses the measure of the universe in which we live, "impregnated by technology and science". Again an ethical aspect comes to the fore, that of "humility", a key word often recalled by Levi in recognition of "crafts" that can no longer avoid integrating with experiences not exclusively of the same field. The continuous transit from one "culture" to the other is the manifestation of the "humility of looking around and noticing the fact that the prophet-artist, voice of a divine fountain of truth, is no longer valid: next to him a new culture is born, and is growing at dizzying speed. The poet who makes place for the physicist, the economist, the psychologist, will find himself in good company, and perhaps will have all the more to say" (Levi 1997, 112, my translation).

It is even better if all these varied competences live together in the same person, according to an ideal that Levi identifies with the heuristic figure of the centaurs. The balance in their double natures is certainly not stable, but as long as these double natures remain united, the centaur can mean less a "paranoid splitting" than a perceptive fullness. The centaur's soul, Levi said, is one without welding, and two souls are too many: "there is no contradiction between the nature of a chemist and the nature of a literary writer. On the contrary, there are reciprocal reinforcements" (1966, 505-16, my translation). That is why, in one of his last collections of writings, called *L'altrui mestiere* (*Other People's Trades*), Levi took recourse to a geological metaphor to protest against the absurdity of the "crevice" that exists between literature and science. What makes us wonder today about the gap diagnosed by Levi is certainly not the exhortation to throw a bridge over the abyss. What really counts is the observation that the cracks that we observe between the territories of science and literature are not the ineluctable result of a natural tectonic process, of an objective incompatibility of those involved, but the result of prejudice preventing us from knocking on a neighbour's door.

Levi identifies the common denominator in a statute made precarious for both cultures by the absence of certainties, although without giving in to scepticism. This is a thesis that has become most topical today after Ilya Prigogine, Nobel-prize winner for chemistry, published a book called *The End of Certainty*. This book is also an obituary to the determinism underpinning Newtonian and classical mechanics; the simplifications that transform the universe into a discreet, perfect machine. With a universe closer to chaos and entropy, the fluctuating rates of probability seem better suited, as is the consequent active role of the researcher's creativity – less distant, at this point, from the modus operandi of practitioners of the human sciences.

Even in this circumstance, the claim is certainly that of a realistic common utopia in which everyone, for his or her part, contributes to a "tension" which should not only be challenge and strife, but also "implication". The boundaries between the different jurisdictions are thus destined always to be forced, although with different moves. Scientific procedure is of a centripetal kind, because it aspires to include within the frames of already tried universal laws of behaviour, assigned to phenomena by rigorous rules, all that is unknown; what appears at first sight as particular and inexplicable. Literature and the arts, instead, with a centrifugal attitude, aspire to drive what is known and familiar, or even trivial, to deviation, to the limit of the unforeseeable, in a process that Russian formalists have called "*ostraneja*" ("estrangement", "defamiliarisation"). To express this cognitive difference between science and literature in the words of Musil, who was both a writer and an engineer, science adheres to the "dogmas of the law", to which it tends to steer all eccentricity; literature converts objective facts into subjectivity by narrating the "exceptions", "from Abraham's sacrifice to the beautiful woman who killed her lover yesterday" (Musil 245).

Naturally the degree of *"ostraneja"* varies from poetics to poetics and from text to text. It will be greatest in avant-garde poetry or in the theatre of the absurd, less in realistic works or in those that seek verisimilitude and *decoro*; but it is valid nonetheless because literature so often flees from banality and the suffocating and petrified laziness of everything that is taken for granted, seeking any kind of surprise to react to the most mechanical aspects of life. This is a logic Levi is fully aware of when he brings to mind his amusement in "watching the world under unusual light, inverting, so to speak, the instrumentation, and visiting things belonging to technique with the literary eye, and literature with the technical one" (1985, 631). Hopefully this proposal by Primo Levi will serve as a suitable conclusion to my essay as well as a constructive beginning for the interfacing of sciences, literatures and the humanities that is the aim of this book.

WORKS CITED

Arnold, Matthew. "Literature and Science". *Discourses in America*. London: Macmillan, 1894.

Calvino, Italo. "La sfida al labirinto." 1962. *Saggi 1945-1985*. Ed. Mario Barenghi. Milano: Mondadori, 1995: vol. 1.

—. "La penna in prima persona." 1977. *Saggi 1945-1985*. Ed. Mario Barenghi. Milano: Mondadori, 1995: vol. 1.

Della Volpe, Galvano. "Discorso poetico e discorso scientifico." 1956. *Crisi dell'estetica romantica e altri saggi*. Roma: Samonà & Savelli, 1963.

Gadda, Carlo Emilio. *I viaggi la morte*. Milano: Garzanti, 1977.

Galilei, Galileo. "Letter to Federico Cesi 24 Dec. 1629. *Opere*. Ed. Antonio Favaro. Firenze: Barbèra, 1890-1909: vol. 14.

Huxley, Aldous. *Letteratura e scienza e altri saggi*. 1963. Ital. trans. Corrado Pavolini. Milano: Il Saggiatore, 1965.

Huxley, Thomas Henry. "La scienza e la cultura." *Scritti pedagogici*. Ital. trans. Giuseppina Dilaghi. Milano-Roma: D. Alighieri, 1904.

Kepler, Johannes. *Dissertatio cum Nuncio Sidereo*. Ital. trans. Elio Pasoli and Giorgio Tabarroni. Torino: Bottega d'Erasmo, 1972.

Kuhn, Thomas S. "Comment [on the Relations between Science and Arts]." *Comparative Studies in Philosophy and History* 11 (1969).

Leavis, Frank Raymond. "Two Cultures. The Significance of C.P. Snow." *Spectator* 9 (March 1962).

Levi, Primo. *Storie naturali*. 1966. *Opere*, vol. 1, Torino: Einaudi, 1990.

—. *L'altrui mestiere*. 1985. *Opere*. Ed. Marco Belpoliti. Torino: Einaudi, 1997: vol. 2

—. *I sommersi e i salvati*. 1986. *Opere*: 1997: vol. 2.

—. *Conversazioni e interviste 1963-1987*. Ed. Marco Belpoliti. Torino: Einaudi, 1997.

Magris, Claudio. "L'Europa vista da Trieste." *Lettera internazionale* 9, Roma, 1992.

Musil, Robert. L'uomo senza qualità. Ital. transl. Anita Rho. Torino: Einaudi, 1978. Trans. of *Der Mann ohne Eigenschaften*.

Peitgen, Heinz-Otto and Richter, Peter-Hans. *The Beauty of Fractals: Images of Complex Dynamical Systems*. Berlin-New York: Springer Verlag, 1986.

Pera, Marcello. *Scienza e retorica*. Roma-Bari: Laterza, 1991.

Preti, Giulio. *Retorica e logica. Le due culture*. Torino: Einaudi, 1968.

Enciclopedia. Ed. Ruggiero Romano and others. Torino: Einaudi, 6 (1980).

Snow, Charles Percy. *The Two Cultures, And a Second Look*. Cambridge: Cambridge University Press, 1959.

Whitehead, Alfred North. *Science and the Modern World*. 1926. Ital. trans. Antonio Banfi. Milano: Bompiani, 1945.

DARWIN'S "FILTHY HERALDRIES"[1]

Gillan Beer, University of Cambridge

Darwin was a most pacific man. After his return from the five-year voyage of the Beagle round the world in the 1830s, he soon left London to live in the country with his wife and growing family. He remained at Down House for the rest of his life, writing, observing, tending plants in his garden and greenhouse; and thinking more and more radical thoughts. The contrast between the life lived and the profound upheavals caused by his publications is striking indeed. But what caused the shudder? And in what sense can we read him as scandalous? What can the scandals then tell us about our reactions now?

Scandal is always a matter of "other people". It is a reaction to something that, at least on the surface, is alien to us. What may be perfectly acceptable among one group makes another aghast. The prime source of scandal is secrets that burst into the open. Such abrupt change exhilarates. Scandal gives a frisson of pleasure. Retrospect and revision are part of scandal too: our judgments of people, our understanding of affairs, or sense of ourselves as knowledgeable and in control, all turn out to have been faulty. Things *were not as they seemed*. The relish of scandal is picking up the hints early, being in the know. But the danger is being found guilty of connivance, or even involvement. Scandal is a spectator sport, deeply wounding to those trapped inside the plot but a great source of jokes to everyone else. The secrets that erupt may have to do with political corruption, chicanery, family romance, sex and sexuality, ethnicity, faith, social class, money: any or several of these.

In Victorian fiction one of the main plots is inheritance, which tangles most of these together: the writing and re-writing of wills, the re-appearance of lost heirs, the insurgence of lower-class characters with claims on the great family are the stock-in-trade of novelists. This plot nearly always includes secret marriages or adultery. George Eliot makes considerable use of the inheritance plot, for example in *Felix Holt* and *Middlemarch*, where the creeping power of past actions, obliterated but not expunged, comes

---

1 A somewhat different version of this essay was first included in *Search: a Church of Ireland Journal*, vol. 38, 2008.

to overwhelm present fortune. In *Middlemarch* the assertive banker and churchman Bulstrode has a hidden past of trickery and sexual misconduct that entraps him. Or in Dickens's *Bleak House* Lady Deadlock's lost, illegitimate daughter proves to be one of the two narrators of the book, Esther. Perhaps the most famous of all these works, as novel and as play, was *Lady Audley's Secret*, with its never-forgotten line: "Dead, dead, and never called me mother". Low connections can prove to be the undoing of high families, although as Dickens and George Eliot both suggest, the child who is the issue of such unions can prove redemptive too. But only after a profound shaking and re-ordering of relations.

All this would have been very familiar to Darwin, an addicted novel-reader even when all other forms of aesthetic pleasure had waned for him. In his autobiography addressed privately to members of his family towards the end of his life, in 1876, Darwin acknowledges that his earlier passion for poetry and music has deserted him:

> But now for many years I cannot endure to read a line of poetry; I have tried lately to read Shakespeare, and found it so intolerably dull that it nauseated me. Music generally sets me thinking too energetically on what I have been working on, instead of giving me pleasure.

This, from the man who in his youth felt the hairs rise on his back as he listened to choristers, who thrilled to Shakespeare as a child, and who carried Milton's poems everywhere with him on the Beagle sea and land voyage. But not quite all is lost:

> On the other hand, novels, which are works of the imagination, though not of a very high order, have been for years a wonderful relief and pleasure to me, and I bless all novelists.

With a certain defensive self-mockery he then declares his taste in fiction:

> A surprising number have been read aloud to me, and I like all if moderately good, and if they do not end unhappily – against which a law ought to be passed. A novel, according to my taste, does not come into the first class unless it contains some person one can thoroughly love, and if a pretty woman all the better. (Darwin 1958, 53-54)

The plot of descent and inheritance, of the great family and secret offspring, so familiar from Victorian fiction permeated Darwin's thinking too. And he radically re-thought it in ways that perturbed human grandeur and self-aggrandisement.

A key paradox of the Origin and its reception is that Darwin deliberately avoided discussing humankind – mankind in 19th century parlance – for what he called "diplomatic" reasons. His hope was that he would thus evade religious controversy and that his readers would be able to approach his ideas in a more temperate way, without getting fixated on the implications of his theories for human prestige and centrality. But in fact that avoidance proved to be not calming but explosive. Darwin's refusal to separate human beings from the class of "higher primates" or to give them special discussion, or a bit of space for the soul, was the major challenge. To his enemies it seemed like effrontery. He simply took for granted the animal nature of the human. He failed to ally the human with godhead or to position us over against animals, what were then called "the brutes".

We, the readers, found no special niche assigned to our species. Were we, then, implicated in the animal kingdom by descent? Were we the jumped-up progeny of monkeys? – low in the social scale of creation, instead of the specially chosen of God? When Darwin talked about "the great family" he thought inclusively, not hierarchically. We have no armorial bearings, he remarked; we are not part of the high chivalric world. Instead "we have to discover and trace the many diverging lines of descent in our natural genealogies" (Darwin 1859, 486). In his Conclusion Darwin seeks to hearten and reassure the reader:

> When I view all beings not as special creations, but as the lineal descendents of some few beings which lived long before the first bed of the Silurian system was deposited, they seem to me to become ennobled. (Darwin 1859, 488-489)

We are part of the grandest of all families, he suggests, because we are part of the oldest family (that criterion by which the grandeur of aristocratic families is judged). But according to his argument, all organic beings, present and extinct, are part of the same family. This doesn't leave much room for special pride in being human. We are kin, promiscuously, with all other organic forms, present and extinct. His theory challenged apartheid in all its forms.

His story gave a new twist to the anxiety about illegitimate progeny declaring themselves and upsetting the family apple-cart. Indeed, the concept of illegitimacy itself is threatened by the inclusiveness of his family tree. Instead of the hidden illegitimate child it was the realisation of the low status of our ancestors that burst out and caused the shock. Dickens explored the hidden sources of wealth and the tangling effects of illegitimacy in *Great Expectations*, where the hero Pip's benefactor turns out to be not the superior Miss Havisham but the convict crept back from the hulks. But socially even worse than being "in trade", or a felon, was being a monkey. Darwin himself avoided making any such overt connection, but his readers rapidly put things together. The secret was out: our close relations were not aristocrats but chimpanzees. That blow to pride was one element in the scandal. Worse, within it, was a creeping suspicion of miscegenation: how did we get from being monkeys to being human? Were there intermediate forms – and what happened to our grandmothers?

THE DESCENT OF MAN.

Figurative Party. "So long as *I* am a Man, Sorr, what does it matther to me whether me *great-grandfather* was an Anthropoid Ape or not, Sorr!"
Literal Party. "Haw! wather disagweeable for your *gwate gwand-mother*, wasn't it!"

The figure of the grandmother becomes an uneasy presence in the jokes about evolution (the mother would be too agonisingly close). Punch, for example, shows two smartly dressed men at a club, one of them with distinctly ape-like features:

THE ART OF DISCOVERY

Figurative Party: "So long as *I* am a man, Sorr, what does it matther to me whether me *great-grandfather* was an anthropoid ape or not, sorr!

Literal Party: Haw! Wather disagreeable for your Gwate-Gwandmother, wasn't it?" (May 24, 1873)

The second man speaks with the effete drawl of the aristocrat, the first with the voice of the Irish: racial and class politics become tangled with sexual scandal too. The smutty joke at the core of the cartoon – sexual congress between human and ape: bestiality – touches the nub of what seemed scandalous to many of Darwin's contemporaries. It has in it, though more cheerfully, the same disgust that Ruskin expressed when in *Love's Meinie* he wrote scornfully of Darwin's "deciphering of the filthy heraldries which record the relations of humanity to the ascidian and the crocodile" (Ruskin 59). The family tree had been perverted. It was not a matter of a few loose branches, of natural children denied, but of the whole root of the matter. Human beings were not exiles from the Garden of Eden but denizens of the swamp.

This is where the seemingly separate strands of the scandal around Darwin's ideas converge for his contemporaries: kinship, descent, class, gender, sex, privilege, race, faith, all come under debate. And religious belief, if reliant on the account of creation offered in Genesis, was fundamentally challenged too. Belief in the radiant body of man issuing direct from the will of God in the garden, and woman from Adam's desire, had to be relinquished. Of course, much of this argument was already underway among theologians of the new historical school before Darwin, but Darwin's work, as George Eliot remarked on first reading the *Origin* "made an epoch", because here was a well-regarded scientist arguing with much evidence on topics that had already been under discussion among theologians, and had been broached in a popular form by the author – at first anonymous, in fact the journalist Robert Chambers – of the immensely popular *Vestiges of Creation* (1844). So in one sense it was not the *novelty* of what Darwin was arguing in his concept of "natural selection" that first shook the foundations – and that seems to me typical of scandal. It was as if a groundswell of half-formulated ideas had suddenly broken through into a flood. The breaking loose of the secret, or pseudo-secret, is key: indeed, I would suggest that scandal most often occurs *not* when something is unknown but when the murmurs, hints and suspicions that have been suppressed are suddenly authenticated and spoken out.

It is worth emphasising that the cartoon I discussed just now was published after *The Descent of Man* in 1871, and there is a sense in which the appearance of that work cracked open Darwin's earlier pseudo-secret. The very title announced that this time Darwin was not going to be circumspect about the position of the human in nature. Huxley had already in 1863 published his set of anthropological essays on "Man's Place in Nature". Now Darwin himself was taking on the question of how human beings descend, and how they form themselves into cultures. The *Descent* extended the reach of the *Origin* and provoked further anxieties. But the first level of scandal generated by Darwin's theories had already blown itself out during the 1860s.

Scandal breeds *tribes*: friends and enemies gather their gangs. Bystanders find themselves corralled into one group or the other. Probably the most famous encounter between the pro- and anti-Darwinians immediately after the publication of the *Origin* was that between the Bishop of Oxford, Wilber-force, and Thomas Henry Huxley at the meeting of the British Association for the Advancement of Science in Oxford in 1860. Since no notes were kept on the occasion, various versions of what happened were immediately abroad and there is no single authoritative account. No matter. What all agree is that Bishop Wilberforce gave a rather brilliant half-hour discourse maintaining that evolution by natural selection was unphilosophical and (I quote here Darwin's biographer Janet Browne, vol II *The Power of* Place, 2002) that "The line between humanity and animals was obvious and dis-tinct". There was no tendency on the part of lower organisms to become self-conscious intelligent beings. "Is it credible that a turnip strives to become a man?" (Browne 120). You will notice that this is a Lamarckian reading, with its embedded idea of self-help, and of intermediate forms, rather than of the process of natural selection which requires variability, survival and the bearing of progeny with the potential for further variation. That is, Wilberforce had not grasped what was distinctive in Darwin's argument, but then neither did many of his scientific fellows.

The previous day, in response to Owen, Huxley had jokingly remarked that churchmen would have little to fear even if it were shown that apes were their ancestors. The next day some in the audience set up a chant of "mawnkey, mawnkey". And Wilberforce, relishing his own command, turned to Huxley near the end of his speech to ask "was Huxley related on his grandfather's or his grandmother's side to an ape?" (or, in another ver-sion, he registered his "disquietude" at the thought that he might be shown a monkey in a zoo as his ancestress). Huxley at this point apparently mur-mured "The Lord hath delivered him into mine hands". He spoke tellingly against the intellectual arguments that Wilberforce had used but at the crisis of his speech he produced a ringing condemnation that remained famous throughout the century.

> If I would rather have a miserable ape for a grandfather or a man endowed by nature and possessed of great means and influence, and yet who employs those faculties for the mere purpose of introducing ridicule into a grave scientific discussion – I unhesitatingly affirm my preference for the ape.

Notice how Huxley takes the high ground – this is about the sacredness of knowledge not about imputed sexual liaisons, however fanciful. He evades the grandmother joke, substituting the grandfather, though the joke still lurks there and is turned back upon the man of religion who can descend to such demeaning jests.

This is the amusing side of that BAAS debate and its relish of scandal. The more tragic side is the intervention of Robert Fitzroy, who had been captain of the Beagle during Darwin's five-year voyage and who had, even at that time twenty years before, engaged in tempestuous arguments with him about religious faith. Fitzroy was a profoundly religious man, and also one who suffered from depression. Now, in excoriating terms, he spoke of his dismay at having nurtured such theories by providing the opportunity for Darwin to collect the facts which – in Fitzroy's view – did not justify his theories. He begged the assembled company to believe God's word in the Bible rather than that of a mere human on the matter of creation.

One of Darwin's correspondents – for Darwin was not present – later wrote to him: "I shall never forget that meeting of the combined sections of the BAAS when at Oxford in 1860, where Admiral Fitzroy expressed his sorrow for having given you the opportunity of collecting facts for such a shocking theory as yours". The company there fell silent. Several years later, driven by mental and financial problems, Fitzroy committed suicide. Darwin was probably not at the core of his disquiets by then, but the sense of betrayal, the shattering of faith that came from his dismay at Darwin's use of the opportunities he had provided, played its part. This is where scandal finds its victims: often not in the protagonists, but in the bystanders, in those half-implicated.

Darwin had to bear the brunt of reviews hostile and unfair as well as taking comfort from the support of his scientific allies. For example, in Dickens's journal, *All the Year Round* (no 63, Sat Jul 7 1860), an apparently friendly assessment shifted as it went on into a more and more threatening temper, concealed beneath a joking tone. It opened:

It is well for Mr. Charles Darwin, and a comfort to his friends, that he is living now instead of having lived in the sixteenth century; it is even well that he is a British subject, and not a native of Austria, Naples, or Rome. Men have been kept for long years in durance, and even put to the rack, or the stake, for the commission of offences minor to the publication of ideas less in opposition to the notions held by the powers that be. (*All the Year Round* 293)

The review ends by commiserating with the likely outcome: that his will prove to be a life spent chasing a will-o-the wisp, a fruitless idea that eventually comes to nothing. Perhaps, the reviewer allows, someone else will find their way through the maze; perhaps there really is something in it. But the impression left is that Darwin is almost certainly chasing a figment of his own imagination. (The review, incidentally, is placed in the magazine immediately after an instalment of Wilkie Collins, *The Woman in White*.) Darwin had already experienced this tone, in a more extreme form in the *Athenaeum* review which appeared just before the *Origin* was published. Darwin was bitterly upset by its sensationalising tone and responded with nightmare intensity:

The manner in which he drags in immortality, & sets the priests on me, & leaves me to their mercies, is base. He would on no account burn me; but he will get the wood ready & tell the black beasts how to catch me. (Darwin 1958 b, 224)

The sinister black beasts are part-priest, part-brute, in Darwin's uneasy fantasy here. For him, this scandal is no spectator sport; it is, in the night-hours, the bearing-out of his fears, when he wrote in one of his notebooks that it felt as if he were confessing to a murder.

The possible martyrdom of scientists – the image of the inquisition – does sometimes haunt the first reception of Darwin's ideas. It helps to give us back some understanding of the scale of the disquiet that his views produced among his contemporaries. Indeed, we are now experiencing a resurgence of that disquiet in the highly funded and felt pressure of creationism. Scandal usually generates a flurry of attention that dies away quite fast. But in the case of Darwin's theories, the profound difficulty that many have in relinquishing the high history of a created race of mankind specially designed by God for his own pleasure still surfaces. That view simply cannot be reconciled with Darwin's own and all that flows from it. Another conciliation must be found.

One of Darwin's contemporaries and valued colleagues, Philip Gosse, was beset by the difficulties produced by geological evidence for the long history of the earth. A little before the publication of the *Origin* he wrote a work called *Omphalos*. How could it be that Adam was a full-grown man from the start, and how had the trees in Paradise grown to their full height? Gosse disliked the idea of God as a conjuror who could simply make things be, in their present state. He had to find a place for the past in creation. By a series of agonised and ingenious argumentative moves, he ended up with the idea that God had put the fossils in the rocks to test our faith, and that Adam's navel – if he had one – similarly acted as an aesthetic rather than a functional nod to descent. Adam had no mother, no womb had contained him, no cord needed to be cut: did he therefore have a navel?

Such troubled debate may seem to us now like the arguments among medieval theologians as to how many angels could fit on a pin head. And even at the time the publication of *Omphalos* was greeted with more mirth than sober agreement. But such extremes of ingenuity bear witness to the intensity of need felt by many at the time of Darwin to reconcile the immense tracts of time, and the anonymity of the "single progenitor" (unsexed, outside gender) necessitated by Darwin's argument, with humankind's sense of special fate, of centrality, of meaning. Nor has that contention gone away. Darwin himself struggled with the agency inevitable in human language. "Natural Selection" even is haunted by the ghostly selector – who or what selects – and Darwin endlessly returned in later editions to the problems of words like Nature.

But there are two other elements in Darwin's theory that are problematic for us now and that have nothing to do with creationism or intelligent design. One disturbing perception in his theory is that he gives little room to memory, save as survival habit within the lifetime of an organism. Samuel Butler and Freud have both in their time attempted to put right what they saw as that lack, insisting on behaviour as the expression of unconscious memory stretched across aeons of time. Some current theorists have taken up Butler's hints and formed the idea of "memes": ideas that can form and endure over manifold generations, not necessarily to the advantage of those who pass them on (selfish memes operate like selfish genes in Dawkins's economy).

But there is another disturbing perception in Darwin's theory, particularly troubling for our own time. So troubling is it that recent commentators have blanked out what Darwin wrote and thought, since it is out of kilter with our own current fears and desires. This is Darwin's acceptance of extinction as fundamental to his theory. The concept of extinction was still relatively new when Darwin wrote, emerging in the late 18th century and seen then as threatening to the fundamental order of God's creation. But Darwin saw extinction as ordinary, humdrum, indeed necessary to the process of evolutionary growth. In a world of so much variety, some variet-

MONKEYANA.

ies must inevitably perish. Moreover, their vanishing would give space to newer "improved" forms. This matter-of-fact view contrasts perturbingly with our present panics about species-extinction. The implicit assumption of an eventually benign order that encompasses change and extinction is at the core of Darwin's thinking, even though he recognises the destructive powers of life and struggle. That emphasis on "improvement", like the hierarchy of human races, is an element that Darwin draws from his own society's assumptions and might well seem scandalous to us now.

Let me end with some poems by Darwin's contemporaries that bring home, as tragedy, or as comedy, or as scandal, the struggle to believe in the new world that Darwin offered. Strikingly, it was in the main women poets who responded to the implications of Darwin's theories, in verse sombre and satiric. Scandal generates salves for itself: one of the most powerful of these is mockery. Another is nostalgia. We hear both mockery and nostalgia in these poets, alongside mourning for the losses that evolution entails.

Mathilde Blind in "The Ascent of Man" produces an epic of evolution that focuses its attention on those neglected or spurned by the insistence on evolutionary success. Emily Pfeiffer mourns the substitution of force and machine for the maternal in the figuring of nature now. In her sonnet "Evolution", she figures evolution as hunger:

Hunger that strives in the restless arms
Of the sea-flower, that drivest rooted things

To break their moorings, that unfoldest wings
In creatures to be rapt above thy harms. (Pfeiffer 1886, 51)

In the next sonnet in the sequence, "Nature", hunger has become machinate force:

Dread Force, in whom of old we loved to see
A nursing mother, clothing with her life
The seeds of Love divine, – with what sore strife
We hold or yield our thoughts of Love and thee!
Thou art not "calm", but restless as the ocean,
Filling with aimless toil the endless years –
Stumbling on thought, and throwing off the spheres,
Churning the Universe with mindless motion. (Pfeiffer 1886, 29-30)

Instead of the succouring and familial image of the mother as nature, all that is left is this "Cold motor of our fervid faith and song,/Dead, but engendering life, love, pangs, and fears". Pfeiffer reaches beyond scandal into tragedy.

Constance Naden and May Kendall satirise current society and the new forms of faith demanded by Darwinian thought. In "The New Orthodoxy" Naden, herself well-educated scientifically, suggests that faith in science has usurped religious faith as a mark of respectability: the young woman speaker in the poem – a college girl at Girton – berates her suitor for his backsliding from belief (in science, not religion):

Things with fin, and claw, and hoof
Join to give us perfect proof
That our being's warp and woof
We from near and far win.
Yet your flippant doubts you vaunt,
And – to please a maiden aunt –
You've been heard to say you can't
Pin you faith on Darwin! (Naden 1887, 141)

In "Solomon Redivivus, 1886" she figures the story of evolution as the gradual separating of male and female from each other – both a joy and a loss:

We were a soft Amoeba
In ages past and gone,
Ere you were Queen of Sheba,
And I King Solomon.

Unorganed, undivided,
We lived in happy sloth,
And all that you did I did,
One dinner nourished both:

Till you incurred the odium
Of fission and divorce –
A severed pseudopodium
You strayed your lonely course.

The poem wends its agile course through all the stages of evolution:

But now, disdaining trammels
Of scale and limbless coil,
Through every grade of mammal
We passed with upward toil.

Till, anthropoid and wary
Appeared the parent ape,
And soon we grew less hairy,
And soon began to drape.

So, from that soft Amoeba
In ages past and gone,
You've grown the Queen of Sheba,
And I King Solomon. (Naden 1887, 145-146)

Darwin's "filthy heraldries", in Ruskin's phrase, his emphasis on our kinship with all forms of life, whether at the level of the organism or the molecule, may no longer shock us. But, as I argue here, there are still deeply disquieting elements to his theory: not only its emphasis on competition and its Victorian assumption that advanced races will prosper and other races fail, but – more fundamentally – his acceptance of the inevitability, even the need for, extinction and the loss of all remembrance. For most of the history of the planet, he makes clear, humanity was not there, and in the future almost certainly will be gone again, along with most forms now alive. The past will be forgotten, as will our present too. This sombre and discomfiting insight plays over against his insistence on "improvement" and the good of each organism through natural selection. Both aspects of his thinking, loss and generation, are in equipoise in his theory.

SONNETS.
EMILY PFEIFFER.

I.–EVOLUTION.

HUNGER that strivest in the restless arms
    Of the sea-flower, that drivest rooted things
    To break their moorings, that unfoldest wings
In creatures to be rapt above thy harms;
Hunger, of whom the hungry-seeming waves
    Were the first ministers, till, free to range,
    Thou mad'st the Universe thy park and grange,
    What is it thine insatiate heart still craves?

Sacred disquietude, divine unrest!
    Maker of all that breathes the breath of life,
No unthrift greed spurs thine unflagging zest,
    No lust self-slaying hounds thee to the strife;
Thou art the Unknown God on whom we wait:
Thy path the course of our unfolding fate.

II.–TO NATURE.

DREAD Force, in whom of old we loved to see
    A nursing mother, clothing with her life
    The seeds of Love divine,—with what sore strife
We hold or yield our thoughts of Love and thee!
Thou art not "calm," but restless as the ocean,
    Filling with aimless toil the endless years—
    Stumbling on thought, and throwing off the spheres,
Churning the Universe with mindless motion.

Dull fount of joy, unhallowed source of tears,
    Cold motor of our fervid faith and song,
Dead, but engendering life, love, pangs, and fears,
    Thou crownedst thy wild work with foulest wrong
When first thou lightedst on a seeming goal,
And darkly blundered on man's suffering soul.

EVOLUTIONAL EROTICS.
CONSTANCE NADEN.

THE NEW ORTHODOXY.

So, dear Fred, you're not content
Though I quote the books you lent,
And I've kept the spray you sent
    Of the milk-white heather;
For you fear I'm too "advanced"
To remember all that chanced
In the old days, when we danced,
    Walked and rode together.

Trust me, Fred, beneath the curls
Of the most "advanced" of girls,
Many a foolish fancy whirls,
    Bidding Fact defiance,
And the simplest village maid
Needs not to be much afraid
Of her sister, sage and staid,
    Bachelor of Science.

Ah! while yet our hope was new
Guardians thought 'twould never do
That Sir Frederick's heir should woo
    Little Amy Merton:
So the budding joy they snatched
From our hearts, so meetly matched–
You to Oxford they despatched,
    Me they sent to Girton.

Were the vows all writ in dust!
No–you're one-and-twenty–just–
And you write–"We will, we must
    Now, at once, be married!"
Nay, you plan the wedding trip!
Softly, sir! there's many a slip
Ere the goblet to the lip
    Finally is carried.

Oh, the wicked tales I hear!
Not that you at Ruskin jeer,
Nor that at Carlyle you sneer,
    With his growls dyspeptic:
But that, having read in vain
Huxley, Tyndall, Clifford, Bain,
All the scientific train–
    You're a hardened sceptic!

Things with fin, and claw, and hoof
Join to give us perfect proof
That our being's warp and woof
    We from near and far win;
Yet your flippant doubts you vaunt,
And–to please a maiden aunt–
You've been heard to say you can't
    Pin your faith to Darwin!

Then you jest, because Laplace
Said this Earth was nought but gas
Till the vast rotating mass
    Denser grew and denser:
Something worse they whisper too,
But I'm sure it *can't* be true–
For they tell me, Fred, that you
    Scoff at Herbert Spencer!

Write–or telegraph–or call!
Come yourself and tell me all:
No fond hope shall me enthrall,
　　No regret shall sway me:
Yet–until the worst is said,
Till I know your faith is dead,
I remain, dear doubting Fred,
　　Your believing
　　　AMY.

WORKS CITED

All the Year Round: a Weekly Journal. London: Chapman & Hall, 1859-1895.

Braddon, Mary. *Lady Audley's Secret.* London, 1862. 1 September 2005 <http://www.gutenberg.org/etext/8954.

Browne, Janet. Charles Darwin: *The Power of Place.* New York: Knopf, 2002.

Darwin, Charles. *On the Origin of Species by Means of Natural Selection or the Preservation of Favoured Races in the Struggle for Life.* London. John Murray, 1859.

—.*The Autobiography of Charles Darwin and Selected Letters.* Ed. Francis Darwin. New York: Dover, 1958.

—. *Selected Letters on Evolution and Origin of Species.* Ed. Francis Darwin. New York: Dover, 1958.

Naden, Constance. *A Modern Apostle: The Elixir of Life: The Story of Clarice and other Poems.* London: Kegan Paul and Co., 1887.

Pfeiffer, Emily. *Sonnets.* London: Field & Tuer; New York: Scribner & Welford, 1886.

Ruskin, John. *Love's Meinie. Lectures on Greek and English Birds.* Keston, Kent: G. Allen, 1873.

SCANDAL AND OBLIVION: SOME THOUGHTS ON DARWIN, OEDIPUS AND ADAPTATION

Holly Henry, California State University, San Bernardino

I am pleased to reflect on "Darwin's 'Filthy Heraldries,'" Gillian Beer's deeply insightful and compelling analysis of Victorian poetry and Darwin's findings.[1] Gillian's contribution clearly demonstrates that we have not yet fully mapped the interconnections between Darwin and Victorian literature and culture. As Gillian brilliantly argues, "The plot of descent and inheritance, of the great family and secret offspring, so familiar from Victorian fiction permeated Darwin's thinking". The paper sent my mind reeling in multiple directions regarding the intersection between "scandal", Darwin's troubling over the term "nature," and the probability of human extinction. Darwin supposed, Beer eloquently observes, that "[h]uman beings were not exiles from the garden of Eden but denizens of the swamp". And therein, she explains, lies the scandal.

In thinking about the term "scandal", I couldn't help but recall Jacques Derrida's groundbreaking essay "Structure, Sign, and Play in the Discourse of the Human Sciences", in which Derrida recounts the "scandal" Claude Levi-Strauss found at the heart of his research in anthropology and mythology. Derrida notes that "in the very first pages of the *Elementary Structures* Levi-Strauss... encounters what he calls a *scandal*, that is to say, something which no longer tolerates the nature/culture opposition he has accepted..." (283). That scandal, Levi-Strauss confesses in the introduction to his first book *The Elementary Structures of Kinship*, was the fact that incest aversion among humans appeared to be both innate, or biologically inbred, as well as learned via culture. Levi-Strauss had written, "We are then confronted with a fact, or rather, a group of facts... not far removed from a scandal: we refer to that complex group of beliefs, customs, conditions and institutions described succinctly as the prohibition of incest... in which we recognize

---

1   I am very grateful to Randi Koppen and Gillian Beer for making possible this wonderful dialogic opportunity. Without Gillian's inspired research, I would not have wandered through the various trains of thought suggested in this essay.

the conflicting features of two mutually exclusive orders" (Levi-Strauss 1969, 8). Incest aversion, it seemed, was a product of culture and of nature.

Like Darwin, who, Gillian reports, "endlessly returned... to the problems of words like Nature", Levi-Strauss throughout his career troubled over the term "nature" in attempts to definitively distinguish the innate from the learned, the uncivilized from the civilized – the raw from the cooked as Levi-Strauss would say. Yet, human communities he viewed as primitive and closer to nature largely adhered to, and were structured by, incest taboo. This was an unexpected find that collapsed cultural anthropology's most heavily weighted binary: nature versus culture.[2] Alan Richardson comments that in *Elementary Structures* Levi-Strauss considered incest prohibition as the determining characteristic of culture (Richardson 553). In that text, Levi-Strauss cited incest prohibition as "the fundamental step because of which, by which, but above all in which, the transition from nature to culture is accomplished" (Levi-Strauss 1969, 24). He suggested, though, that "any incipient stage" to incest avoidance might be found among "the superior animals, and more especially the anthropoid apes" (Levi-Strauss 1969, 5). Actually, as celebrated biologist and entomologist Edward O. Wilson notes, nonhuman primates, including baboons, lemurs, the large part of monkey species, gorillas and chimpanzees "tend to practice the equivalent of human exogamy" and, like humans, generally display an instinctual incest avoidance (Wilson 174). Mark Erickson writes:

> The first study to examine whether incest was common in nature was not carried out until the mid-1960s... Research now suggests that incest is uncommon between mature mother-son, father-daughter, or sibling pairs in a variety of primate species. In a complete reversal of earlier opinion, it is now thought that incest is rare throughout the animal kingdom. (Erickson 412)

PRIMATES, MYTH AND "SCANDAL"

In *The Raw and the Cooked*, Levi-Strauss analyzed a series of myths of the Bororo people of central Brazil by randomly designating one as the "key myth" (1983, 2). His so-called "key myth" was a tale of incest in which a

---

2   Derrida claims the presumed absolute opposition of nature and culture is "at least as old as the Sophists" (283).

young man rapes his mother and later kills his father (1983, 35).[3] Given his research focus on, and uncertainty about, incest aversion, it is not surprising that Levi-Strauss also addressed Oedipus, one of the most powerful myths to shape western culture and the myth *par excellence* that deals with the topic of incest. Also a tale about "descent and inheritance," the Oedipus myth clearly involves scandal. In "The Structural Study of Myth", Levi-Strauss contends that Labdacos, Oedipus's grandfather, his father Laios, and Oedipus himself, all have names that refer to difficulty in walking. Labdacos translates as "lame", Laios as "left-sided", and Oedipus as "swollen-foot" (214).[4] The names, Levi-Strauss asserts, "have a common feature" in that they all "refer to *difficulty in walking straight and standing upright*" (215; italics in original text). According to Jean-Pierre Vernant and Pierre Vidal-Naquet, "Levi-Strauss is the first to have noticed the importance of [this] characteristic feature of all three generations of the Labdicid lineage: a lopsided gait, a lack of symmetry between two sides of the body, a defect in one foot" (Vernant and Vidal-Naquet 207). Interestingly, difficulty in walking, or stumbling, is directly associated with the term "scandal", derived from the Latin word *scandalum* and the Greek word *skandalon*. The Latin *scandalum* translates as "that which causes one to stumble, a stumbling-block", while the Greek word *skandalon* translates as "stumbling-block".[5] The *Oxford English Dictionary* also lists "stumbling-block" as one definition for the term "scandal".

"[S]candal," as Gillian contends, "most often occurs not when something is unknown but when the murmurs, hints and suspicions that have been suppressed are suddenly authenticated and spoken out". Certainly this is Oedipus's problem. It is as if the Oedipus myth, with its riddle of the Sphinx and its multiple male characters who have difficulty in walking straight or upright, suggests that our prehominid ancestors were more like nonhuman primates, maybe even knuckle-walkers like chimpanzees or gorillas. Athenaeus, apparently, provides the "most famous, most detailed, and most relied-upon version of the riddle" of the Sphinx (Statkiewicz 47).

---

3 Levi-Strauss additionally argued that "cooking mark[ed] the transition from nature to culture", and that this transition is articulated in myths on the origin of fire used in preparing cooked meat (1983, 164).

4 Levi-Strauss used Latinised-Greek spellings for the characters' names.

5 I am very grateful to my colleague Lawrence Beaston, of the Pennsylvania College of Technology, for kindly pointing out the connection between the term "scandal" and the Greek and Latin words for stumbling or stumbling-block, as well as the Latin term *scandere*, to climb or to rise. Sources for the Greek and Latin terms are listed under Works Cited.

As it happens, Athenaeus's version, as translated by John Tressider Sheppard, strikingly evokes the notion of the mutability of species:

> A thing there is whose voice is one;
> Whose feet are two and four and three.
> So mutable a thing is none
> That moves in earth or sky or sea.
> When on most feet this thing doth go
> Its strength is weakest and its pace most slow!
> (*The Oedipus Tyrannus of Sophocles* xvii)[6]

Oedipus solves the riddle, Willis Regier explains, with the term "*anthropon* in noble Corinthian Greek – man the species, rather than man the gender" (Regier 75). The answer, of course, has to do with recognizing humankind as first going on all fours, then walking upright, and later in life walking with a cane. Yet, the hint of another reading is palpable. "Early Greek versions of the riddle consistently count four, two, and three feet" (Regier 72). As if to further suggest that our most immediate progenitor was a knuckle-walking primate, the riddle specifically emphasizes the slow pace of going on all fours. One thing seems certain to Peter Stallybrass: the riddle of the Sphinx, one of the oldest in western culture, focuses our attention on "the *strangeness* of walking", by which he means walking upright (Stallybrass 571; italics in original text).[7] Levi-Strauss noted in his discussion of the Oedipus myth that many Amerindian myths involve primordial humans having difficulty in walking. He writes, "In mythology it is a universal characteristic of men born from the Earth that at the moment they emerge from the depth they either cannot walk or they walk clumsily" (1963, 215). These chtho-

---

6   An original literary version of the riddle does not exist, though an epic poem titled *Oedipodeia*, no longer extant, may have been a source. As Levi-Strauss argues of all myths, "There is no single 'true' version of which all the others are copies or distortions. Every version belongs to the myth" ("The Structural Study of Myth" 218). Sheppard's translation appears in the introduction to his edition, *The Oedipus Tyrannus of Sophocles* (1920). See also Athenaeus, *The Deipnosophists* X, 456. I am grateful to Edwin Floyd, at the University of Pittsburgh, for directing me to both Athenaeus and Sheppard.

7   Stallybrass highlights the appropriateness and irony of the swollen-footed Oedipus solving a riddle that "stages the strangeness and difficulty of the balancing act that walking presupposes" (572). Dinosaurs and birds, of course, are upright walkers, but with less efficiency than humans.

nian characters are described as emerging from underground as lame, with "bleeding-foot" or "sore-foot", so that when they reach the Earth's surface "they limped forward or tripped sideways" (1963, 215-16).[8]

What made Darwin so scandalous, as Gillian Beer demonstrates, is that he revealed what no-one was willing to openly say. Could the Victorian aversion to evolution also have somehow deeply drawn on one of western culture's most entrenched myths with its hint at humans' difficult adaptation, among all the primates, to walk upright? Because in appearance humans are so similar to other primates, biologist Dorothy Cheney and psychologist Robert Seyfarth point out that even in ancient times "the Greeks, Romans, and Japanese all knew that [nonhuman primates] were somehow involved in fundamental questions about the origin of human beings... But the revulsion that arose in each of these cultures whenever monkeys and apes were compared to humans apparently prevented scholars from recognizing that their own legends might be more than just mythical accounts" (Cheney and Seyfarth 20).[9] Though Cheney and Seyfarth's field research on baboon cognition does not address the Oedipus tale, their point regarding nonhuman primates in myth makes one wonder about the Sphinx's riddle. Perhaps Darwin simply confirmed what has always been intimated in every recounting of the Oedipus myth.

BIPEDALISM VERSUS KNUCKLE-WALKING

"The chimpanzee 'knuckle-walks', placing its forward body weight on one set of knuckles curled under the hand and so moves in an odd, modified form of quadrupedalism" that requires chimpanzees to "keep all four limbs on the ground", notes primatologist Craig Stanford, co-director of the Jane

---

8   The term "scandal" is also derived from the Latin term *scandere* (to climb or to rise), which is suggestive of Levi-Strauss's point about chthonian characters' difficulty in walking. See the *Merriam-Webster Dictionary* online at <http://www.merriam-webster.com/dictionary/scandal>.

9   Cheney and Seyfarth offer an apt example of our anxiety about being classified as primates: "Carolus Linnaeus... lumped the apes as they were then known together with humans in the group Anthropomorpha. This provoked an outraged response from – among many others – the French naturalist Georges-Louis Leclerc, Comte de Buffon, who strongly objected to Linnaeus' exclusive reliance on anatomical features... Twenty-three years later, in the 1758 edition of the *Systema*, Linnaeus responded to his critics by separating the various members of the genus Homo from all other animals..." (Stanford 23).

Goodall Primate Research Center at the University of Southern California (Stanford 12, 173). Gorillas likewise "spend most of their time walking on the ground on all fours" (Stanford 34). At the turn of the 20th century there developed an ongoing debate regarding whether hominids evolved into upright walkers from arm-hanging primates like the tree-dwelling gibbon or from knuckle-walkers like *Pan troglodytes*, the chimpanzee.[10] Stanford posits that the progenitors of hominids and all other primates may have attempted upright walking via any number of combinations and as a result of a variety of environmental pressures; the debate, he admits, "remains wide open" (121, 28).

Darwin, apparently, offered "the first cogent writings about upright posture since Aristotle" (Stanford 7). Aristotle, like Darwin, was a serious naturalist interested in marine invertebrates. Besides his important analysis of Sophocles' *Oedipus Rex*, Aristotle offered rigorous classification of plants and animals.[11] Stanford claims it was Darwin who recognized upright walking as one of our most important adaptations. Stanford explains, "Becoming upright, he decided, allowed our newly freed hands to make and use tools, which in turn placed an evolutionary premium on being a clever craftsman" (8).[12] For Stanford, our bipedal ability *is* our most important adaptation. Upright walking, along with the opposable thumb, afforded humans the opportunity to develop and use tools key in garnering a higher protein diet that eventually contributed to a larger brain. In fact, "bipeds have a potential advantage over quadrupeds in decoupling their breathing from their loco-motion" that may have contributed to "the co-option of the adjustable flow

---

10 Stanford reports that Arthur Keith initially theorised that a progenitor of the arm-hanging gibbon eventually began using its legs, which ultimately led to hominids walking upright; however, "arm-swinging is… more adapted to hanging under tree limbs" to gather fruit than for the kind of extensive and "rapid travel" humans developed (Stanford 11). Sherwood Washburn and other paleontologists have argued that the immediate prehominid progenitor was instead a knuckle-walker (Stanford 13).

11 According to the University of California Museum of Paleontology, "Though Aristotle's work in zoology was not without errors, it was the grandest biological synthesis of the time, and remained the ultimate authority for many centuries after his death" See < http://www.ucmp.berkeley.edu/history/aristotle.html>.

12 Darwin apparently imagined upright walking and tool-use emerging at approximately the same time. But bipedalism and tool use occurred millions of years apart with tool use beginning 2.5 million years ago, while walking upright began roughly three million years prior to that (Stanford 110).

THE ART OF DISCOVERY

of air for speech" (Stanford 52). And nearly limitless standing and walking set the stage for migrations, argues Stanford, so that "upright walking, not expanded brain size, became the key to humanity's conquest of the [E]arth" (155).

BARNACLES, MUTABILITY, AND OBLIVION

In *Darwin and the Barnacle*, Rebecca Stott asserts that Darwin came to his conclusions about the mutability of species, in part, based on his extensive research on barnacles and his detailed investigation of a previously unclassified barnacle he found on a Chilean beach in January 1835. When Darwin returned from the *Beagle* expedition, he off-loaded 1,529 species of preserved barnacle specimens and determined to thoroughly classify and catalogue the world's barnacles, though at the time he could not have known "that this extremely diverse genus would be the very epitome of mutability" (Stott xvi, 82). Darwin's particular research of the unknown barnacle variety he later classified as *Cryptophialus minutus*, which does not create its own shell, demonstrated its shared common ancestry with barnacles that do.[13] By 1844, Stott points out, Darwin had drafted a manuscript that would eventually become *On the Origin of Species* but delayed publication of his conclusions about evolution and the mutability of species so that he could rigorously confirm his findings (xxi). His barnacle research consumed the intervening years and, Stott argues, did just that.

As Gillian Beer explains in *Darwin's Plots*, Victorian England was unnerved by the idea of humankind's probable shared ancestry with the barnacle, scallop, or oyster. "Erasmus Darwin's dictum 'Omnia ex Conchis' (All from Oysters) continued to irritate and disturb later generations," writes Beer; "They found it particularly offensive to figure themselves as the descendants of such mute and grudging organisms as shellfish. Darwin, having spent several years of his life in the concentrated study of cirripedes, the parasitic crustacea, which 'coat the rocks all over the world in infinite numbers'[,] did not share this hubris" (Beer 2000, 120). His contemporaries were equally averse, as Beer's seminal presentation illustrates, to Darwin's calm acceptance that humankind, like all species, faces probable extinction. Indeed, among the other hominids Darwin speculated once existed, besides the Neanderthal,

---

13 What shocked Darwin about a shell-less barnacle was that, at the time, barnacles were classified as organisms that made their own shell. Of the zoological notes Darwin kept while on the *Beagle*, "more than half concern marine invertebrates" (Stott 57).

and one of which was much later identified as *Homo habilis*, the only extant species is *Homo sapiens*.[14]

In the early 20th century, British biologist J.B.S. Haldane took up the question of human extinction in a parable he relates in his essay "Possible Worlds". Clearly inspired by Darwin, the parable describes humans as barnacles stuck to a rock, most likely Earth, that third rock from the sun. Haldane's imaginary *Lepas sapiens*, with its sea-anemone tentacles, barnacle-like jointed appendages, and scallop eyes, has extremely limited brain development due to its restricted visual and physical reach. Such rudimentary intellectual ability could lead to extinction, Haldane suggested. "Man is after all only a little freer than a barnacle", Haldane declared; "Our bodily and mental activities are fairly rigidly confined to those which have had survival value to our ancestors during the last few million generations" ("Possible Worlds" 291, 292). Yet, despite his biting depiction of humans as the hapless barnacles of the parable, Haldane thought humanity might potentially find a way to avert extinction. In an essay titled "Man's Destiny," Haldane speculated that we would "certainly attempt to leave the earth" and would most likely settle on "other planets of our [solar] system, and ultimately the planets, if such exist, revolving round other stars than our sun" ("Man's Destiny" 305).[15] However, he warned that humankind would have to evolve, presumably physically and in intelligence, if we are to ultimately escape extinction, what he referred to as "oblivion and darkness" ("Man's Destiny" 305).

MYTH AS SURVIVAL TECHNOLOGY

Like Haldane, planetary scientist Carl Sagan also envisioned humans someday evolving into a spacefaring species and eventually living on other planets. Sagan speculated that humans are genetically adapted to wander, to explore, and that the appeal of exploration "has been meticulously crafted

---

14 Darwin was well aware of *Homo sapiens neanderthalensis,* the Neanderthal (Stanford 8). Humans are actually *Homo sapiens sapiens.*

15 While Haldane's essay "Possible Worlds" is dated in its eugenic overtones, Haldane was prescient with regard to space flight and the possible necessity of humans migrating to other planets. Mars would be our most immediate option should the Earth become unable to sustain human life. To date, astronomers have identified over 400 extra-solar planets, or exoplanets. Of those, at least 257 are gas giants, 82 are Hot Jupiters, neither of which are suitable for human life. One is nearly Earth-sized; but none so far are Earth-like. See NASA's Jct Propulsion Laboratory website "Planet Quest: Exoplanet Exploration" at <http://planetquest.jpl.nasa.gov/>.

by natural selection as an essential element in our survival" (Sagan xii). In our primordial past, Sagan asserted, it was this innate drive to wander as well as our ability to collaborate that assured our survival:

> We were wanderers from the beginning. We knew every stand of tree for a hundred miles. When the fruits or nuts were ripe, we were there. We followed the herds in their annual migrations... Through stealth, feint, ambush, and main-force assault, a few of us cooperating accomplished what many of us, each hunting alone, could not. We depended on one another. Making it on our own was as ludicrous to imagine as was settling down. (Sagan xi)

Our curiosity as wanderers, Sagan argued, caused humans to evolve an upright posture that ultimately made possible space flight to the Moon. But it was also our myths, particularly our myths about the Moon, he intimates, which sparked imaginative journeys that culminated in the Apollo missions. "We knew the Moon from our earliest days", wrote Sagan; "[The Moon] was there when our ancestors... learned to walk upright, when we first devised stone tools, when we domesticated fire... The word 'month' and the second day of the week are both named after the Moon... Especially when we lived out-of-doors, it [the Moon] was a major – if oddly intangible – presence in our lives" (Sagan 205-6). When in 1969 Apollo 11 astronauts Neil Armstrong and Buzz Aldrin took those first steps on the lunar surface, Sagan posits, "humans had entered the realm of myth and legend" (Sagan 205).

Myth, like language and art, is a technology, a tool for survival. Scientists and literary scholars alike maintain that these human preoccupations are as much evolutionary adaptations as upright walking or the opposable thumb. Biologist Edward O. Wilson, literary scholars Joseph Carroll and Brian Boyd, and multiple others cogently assert that the arts, including narrative, emerged via natural selection.[16] Boyd explains, "In evolutionary theory, an 'adaptation' is a biological trait, physiological, psychological or

---

16 See Edward O. Wilson's *Consilience* (1998), Joseph Carroll's *Literary Darwinism: Evolution, Human Nature, and Literature* (2004) as well as Brian Boyd's "Evolutionary Theories of Art" and Ian McEwan's "Literature, Science, and Human Nature" in *The Literary Animal: Evolution and the Nature of Narrative* (2005), edited by Jonathan Gottschall and David Sloan Wilson. Edward Wilson eloquently cites evidence that suggests the arts are biological adaptations. Carroll surveys a range of scholars and disciplines that have contributed to this area of scholarship. As a short introduction to the topic, Boyd in *The Literary Animal* surveys various theories that specifically identify how art emerged as an adaptation. Boyd's book-length discussion of his own

behavioral, shaped by natural selection to enhance the fitness of members of a species" (*The Literary Animal* 150). Boyd emphasizes that an evolutionary adaptation must specifically enhance reproduction or survival. Music, dance, narrative, actually all art, these scholars assert, are adaptations that Boyd explains "natural selection has designed into humans over time because they led to higher rates of survival and reproduction".[17] Storytelling, myth, and narrative, Boyd contends, are forms of cognitive play that "help train us to explore possibility as well as actuality, effortlessly and even playfully..." (*On the Origin of Stories* 188). Through storytelling, fiction and myth we learn from the past, anticipate future possibilities, and can more easily problem-solve. And, communities that developed such arts as storytelling, song, cave painting, and myth could better socialize and collaborate to survive. Boyd asserts, "[W]e have evolved to engage in art and in storytelling because of the survival advantages they offer our species" (*On the Origin of Stories* 209).

Darwin, himself, regarded metaphysics as an evolutionary adaptation, according to scientists Cheney and Seyfarth, who note that, in 1838, in a notebook labeled "M" for Metaphysics, Darwin had written: "He who understands baboon would do more towards metaphysics than Locke".[18] Cheney and Seyfarth argue, "Darwin's goal was to link metaphysics with survival and reproduction" (Cheney and Seyfarth 273). Darwin realized that human cognition must have evolved like any biological trait, Cheney and Seyfarth write, and that "metaphysics must be the product of evolution. And just as the key to reconstructing the evolution of a whale's fin or a bird's beak comes from comparative research on similar traits in closely related species, the key to reconstructing the evolution of the human mind must come from comparative research on the minds of our closest animal relatives" (Cheney and Seyfarth 4). Following Darwin's lead, Cheney and Seyfarth's investigation of baboon cognition, as a means of understanding how language emerged

---

bio-cultural theory of art is titled *On the Origin of Stories: Evolution, Cognition, and Fiction* (2009).

17 "The Art of Literature and the Science of Literature." *The American Scholar* (Mar. 1, 2008) <http://www.theamericanscholar.org/the-art-of-literature-and-the-science-of-literature/>. This Phi Beta Kappa Society journal does not list page numbers for online articles.

18 Charles Darwin, Notebook M: Metaphysics on morals & speculations on expression, 1838. The Complete Work of Charles Darwin Online. Cambridge University Library. DAR 125, Paragraph 84e <http://darwin-online.org.uk/content/frameset?viewtype=text&itemID=CUL-DAR125.-&pageseq=1>. Also qtd. in Cheney and Seyfarth, *Baboon Metaphysics* 4.

in hominids, demonstrates that the tools for socializing and communicating enhance survival among all primates (Cheney and Seyfarth 270).[19]

If narrative, and particularly myth, is an evolutionary adaptation, then Gillian Beer's adept insight that Darwin powerfully reworked our myths of origin takes on new and important significance. Beer writes in *Darwin's Plots:* "Evolutionary theory implied a new myth of the past: instead of the garden at the beginning, there was the sea and the swamp. Instead of man, emptiness – or the empire of the molluscs. There was no way back to a previous paradise: the primordial was comfortless" (118). Nevertheless, Beer is quick to point out, "It was possible in evolutionary theory to trace a new form of quest myth" (Beer 2000, 106). Darwin saw a noble story of humans evolving from the simpler life forms of barnacles, scallops, and sea squirts. Beer especially notes in *Darwin's Plots* and in the seminar presentation that with his idea of a common progenitor Darwin supposed, and deliberately emphasized, not only our interconnectedness with all species but also the absolute equality of all people. Darwin's rewriting of our origin narrative challenged us to rethink what some researchers believe is a biologically inbuilt heightened attention to difference that can contribute to prejudice. For early hominids, recognizing those in and outside one's group may have been genetically inbred as a survival mechanism as is the case in animals and insects. As Boyd explains, "In many social species from ants to hyenas, dolphins and chimpanzees, recognition of out-groups, of others from the same species who belong to different groups" can provide a survival mechanism against possible predators but also "can trigger fierce antagonism and conflict" ("Literature and Evolution" 11).[20] If Boyd is correct that "the cognitive play of art – from tribal work songs to tradesmen's transistors to urbanites' iPods – allows us to extend and refine the neural pathways that produce and process pattern... especially in sociality", then Darwin's narra-

---

19 Cheney and Seyfarth argue that baboons display "a system of mental representations" for understanding "other individual's mental states, and...the causal relations between one social event and another" (270). They claim this system of mental representations gave rise to language in hominids and that "the discrete, compositional structure we find in spoken language" occurs in thought processing observed in baboons (272).

20 Boyd cites John Tooby and Leda Cosmides' research on evolutionary psychology and issues of prejudice.

tive of humankind's shared origin has led the way in refining our response to cultural and physical difference.[21]

Maybe Haldane was right that humans eventually must adapt to the extreme rigors of space if we hope to survive millions of years into the future. In the conclusion to *Upright*, Stanford presents a scene of simultaneous human exploration:

> Cloaked in an oversized white suit and reflective glass helmet, an astronaut floats high above blue Earth. His gloved hands fumble with the tools he uses to do the most simple tasks... Two hundred miles below, a scuba diver explores a coral reef in deep blue waters. His feet are rubber finned, his body is wrapped in neoprene, and his head is bottled up in a mask and air hose... A few miles away, a rock climber is plastered against a naked cliff face. Her hands seek the smallest crevice for support... (177)

This compact image makes the point that humans inhabit all regions of the planet despite the fact that our bodies are ill fitted for most of the Earth's environments. Perhaps the myth of the Sphinx is deeply connected to our innate desire to explore in extreme environments, even beyond the horizon. The Sphinx in Giza specifically draws our attention to the horizon. According to astronomer Ed Krupp, ancient Egyptian texts indicate that the Great Sphinx of Giza portrays "Horemakhet ('Horus of the Horizon')[,] the divine personification of the rising disk of the Sun, fully poised on the eastern horizon" (Krupp 86).[22] In those five years on the *Beagle* with the ocean skyline and the starry night ever immediate, Darwin must have wondered whether humans might venture beyond Earth's horizon. In part, what allowed him to conceptualize his theory of evolution was Darwin's ability to envision Earth whirling on through space over the long eons of astronomical time. In the final line of *On the Origin of Species*, he reflected on the "grandeur" of the process of evolution, "whilst this planet has gone cycling on accord-

---

21 "The Art of Literature and the Science of Literature." <http://www.theamerican-scholar.org/the-art-of-literature-and-the-science-of-literature/>.

22 While Egyptian sphinxes are not coincident with Greek sphinxes, Levi-Strauss would read them as synonymous in his structural analysis of myth. Boyd theorises the ways the arts powerfully engage human attention in his book *On the Origin of Stories* (2009). Krupp is director of the Griffith Observatory, operated by the City of Los Angeles, California.

THE ART OF DISCOVERY

ing to the fixed law of gravity" through the black interstellar abyss (760).[23] We have always been drawn to the horizon, the limb of the Earth. Natural selection, after all, has given us the ability to walk upright, to travel, and to take our tools (jets, satellites, laptops, GPS devices, Blackberries) with us into the most extreme of environments, namely outer space. However, I suspect that if our species is to have even the slightest chance of escaping extinction and oblivion, it will take everything we have: our animal and plant partners, our science and technology, and, of course, our literature and our myths.

WORKS CITED

"Aristotle 384-322 B.C.E." Accessed 13 Feb. 2000 <http://www.ucmp.berkeley.edu/history/aristotle.html>.

Athenaeus. *The Deipnosophists. Vol. 4.* 1930. Trans. Charles Burton Gulick. London and Cambridge, MA: Harvard UP, 1961.

Beer, Gillian. "Darwin's 'Filthy Heraldries.'" Presented at Literature andScience: The Two Cultures. Multi-disciplinary seminar sponsored by the Department of Language, Literature and Culture, University of Bergen, Norway. 11-12 December 2008.

—. *Darwin's Plots: Evolutionary Narrative in Darwin, George Eliot and Nineteenth-Century Fiction.* 2nd ed. Cambridge: Cambridge University Press, 2000.

Boyd, Brian. "The Art of Literature and the Science of Literature." *The American Scholar* (March 2008). Accessed 4 Apr. 2009 <http://www.theamericanscholar.org/the-art-of-literature-and-the-science-of-literature/>.

—. "Evolutionary Theories of Art." *The Literary Animal: Evolution and the Nature of Narrative.* Eds. Jonathan Gottschall and David Sloan Wilson. Evanston: Northwestern University Press, 2005. 147-76.

—. "Literature and Evolution: A Bio-Cultural Approach." *Philosophy and Literature* 29.1 (2005): 1-23.

—. *On the Origin of Stories: Evolution, Cognition, and Fiction.* Cambridge, Mass and London: Belknap/Harvard University Press, 2009.

---

23 Commenting on Darwin's ability to see the big scientific picture, Jason Lindquist notes that in *The Descent of Man*, Darwin suggested, in order to understand human courtship, that his readers should imagine being "an inhabitant of another planet" observing young men "'quarrelling over a pretty girl, like birds at one of their places of assemblage'" ("'The Mightiest Instrument of the Physical Discoverer': The Visual 'Imagination' and the Victorian Observer" 188). Darwin understood the age of the Earth had to number in billions of years long before astronomers accepted this fact. His son George Darwin became a serious astronomer who profoundly changed our understanding of planetary science, the Sun-Earth-Moon system, and our solar system in general.

Carroll, Joseph. *Literary Darwinism: Evolution, Human Nature, and Literature*. New York and London: Routledge, 2004.

Cheney, Dorothy L. and Robert M. Seyfarth. *Baboon Metaphysics: The Evolution of a Social Mind*. Chicago: University of Chicago Press, 2007.

Darwin, Charles. Notebook M: Metaphysics on morals & speculations on expression, 1838. DAR 125. *The Complete Work of Charles Darwin Online*. Cambridge University Library. Accessed on 11 Nov. 2009 <http//Darwin-online.org.uk/content/frameset?viewtype=text&itemID=CUL-DAR125.-&pageseq=1>.

—. *On the Origin of Species*. 1859. Reprinted in *From So Simple A Beginning: The Four Great Books of Charles Darwin*. Ed. and Intro. Edward O. Wilson. New York and London: W.W. Norton, 2006. 445-760.

Derrida, Jacques. "Structure, Sign, and Play in the Discourse of the Human Sciences." *Writing and Difference*. Trans. Alan Bass. Chicago: University of Chicago Press, 1978. 278-93.

Erickson, Mark T. "Rethinking Oedipus: An Evolutionary Perspective of Incest Avoidance." *American Journal of Psychiatry* 150.3 (March 1993): 411-16.

Gottschall, Jonathan and David Sloan Wilson. eds. *The Literary Animal: Evolution and the Nature of Narrative*. Evanston: Northwestern University Press, 2005.

Haldane, J.B.S. "Man's Destiny." *Possible Worlds and Other Papers*. New York and London: Harper & Bros., 1928. 300-305.

—. "Possible Worlds." *Possible Worlds and Other Papers*. New York and London: Harper & Bros., 1928. 272-99.

Krupp, Ed. "The Sphinx Blinks." *Sky and Telescope* (March 2001): 86.

Levi-Strauss, Claude. *The Elementary Structures of Kinship*. Rev. ed. James Harle Bell, John Richard von Sturmer, and Rodney Needham. Boston: Beacon P, 1969.

—. *The Raw and the Cooked: Introduction to the Science of Mythology, Volume 1*. Trans. Johns and Doreen Weightman. Chicago: University of Chicago Press, 1983.

—. "The Structural Study of Myth." *Structural Anthropology Vol. 1*. Trans. Claire Jacobson and Brooke Grundfest Schoepf. New York and London: Basic Books, 1963. 206-31.

Lindquist, Jason H. "'The Mightiest Instrument of the Physical Discoverer': The Visual 'Imagination' and the Victorian Observer." *Journal of Victorian Culture* 13.2 (Autumn 2008): 171-199.

McEwan, Ian. "Literature, Science, and Human Nature." *The Literary Animal: Evolution and the Nature of Narrative*. Eds. Jonathan Gottschall and David Sloan Wilson. Evanston: Northwestern UP, 2005. 5-19.

"Planet Quest: Exoplanet Exploration." Jet Propulsion Laboratory, California Institute of Technology. Accessed 9 Nov. 2009 <http://planetquest.jpl.nasa.gov/>.

Regier, Willis Goth. *Book of The Sphinx*. Lincoln: University of Nebraska Press, 2004.

Richardson, Alan. "Rethinking Romantic Incest: Human Universals, Literary Representation, and the Biology of Mind." *New Literary History* 31 (2000): 553-72.

Sagan, Carl. *Pale Blue Dot: A Vision of the Human Future in Space*. New York: Random House, 1994.

"Scandal/Scandere." Merriam-Webster Dictionary online. Accessed 25 Mar. 2009 < http://www.merriam-webster.com/dictionary/scandal>.

"Scandalum." *Charlton T. Lewis, Charles Short, A Latin Dictionary*. Accessed 13 Feb. 2009 < http://old.perseus.tufts.edu/cgi-bin/ptext?doc=Perseus%3Atext%3A1999.0 4.0059%3Aentry%3D%2342857>.

Sheppard, John Tressider, Intro. and Trans. *The Oedipus Tyrannus of Sophocles*. London: Cambridge University Press, 1920.

"Skandalon." Henry George Liddell, Robert Scott. An Intermediate Greek-English Lexicon. Accessed 13 Feb. 2009 <http://www.perseus.tufts.edu/cgibin/ptext?doc=P erseus%3Atext%3A1999.04.0058%3Aentry%3D%2329669>.

Stallybrass, Peter. "The Mystery of Walking." *Journal of Medieval and Early Modern Studies* 32.2 (2002): 571-80.

Stanford, Craig. *Upright: The Evolutionary Key to Becoming Human*. Boston and New York: Houghton Mifflin, 2003.

Statkiewicz, Max. "The Master of Riddles and the Mystery of Truth," *Mystery In Its Passions: Literary Explorations*. Ed. Anna-Teresa Tymieniecka. Chichester, UK: Springer, 2004. 47-63.

Stott, Rebecca. *Darwin and the Barnacle: The Story of One Tiny Creature and History's Most Spectacular Scientific Breakthrough*. New York and London: W.W. Norton, 2003.

Vernant, Jean-Pierre and Pierre Vidal-Naquet. *Myth and Tragedy in Ancient Greece*. New York: Zone Books, 1988.

Wilson, Edward O. *Consilience: The Unity of Knowledge*. New York: Alfred A. Knopf, 1998.

ENCOUNTERS – BORDERS AND CROSSINGS

GOETHE'S THEORY OF COLOUR: PREMODERN OR POSTMODERN?

Ragnar Fjelland, University of Bergen1

Although Goethe was universally recognised as one of the leading poets, playwrights and novelists of his time, he himself regarded his theory of colour as his main accomplishment. His most important work on colour is *Zur Farbenlehre*, published in 1808. At the end of this voluminous book of more than one thousand pages, under the heading "Konfession des Verfassers" ("Confessions of the Author"), he recounts the story of how colours caught his interest. Having started a career as a writer, he wanted to study an art that was not too closely related to the art of writing, and selected painting. During his journey to Italy he had the opportunity to study many great paintings. However, it struck him that in contrast to the form and composition of the paintings, which was obviously well planned and could be accounted for, the use of colour appeared entirely arbitrary. It looked as if it was based on a certain taste, a taste that had been formed by habit or preconception (*Zur Farbenlehre* 905). He found no valuable written accounts, and the painters themselves were unable to account for any rules or principles that they applied to the use of colours in their paintings.

Goethe understood that to learn something about colours in the arts, he had to study colours as physical phenomena. Although he had graduated from university as a lawyer, he had been interested in natural science as a student, and had frequently attended lectures on topics from the natural sciences. But he could not recollect having ever attended any demonstration of Newton's experiments on colour. However, it turned out that one of his friends happened to be in possession of the prisms that were required to carry out Newton's experiments, and allowed Goethe to borrow them. To carry out the experiments a beam of sunlight must shine into a dark room, and at the time Goethe did not have a suitable room available. The equip-

---

1 Most of the research for this article was carried out when I was a visiting scholar at Max-Planck-Institut für Wissenschaftsgeschichte in Berlin. I want to thank the institute in general, and its director, professor Hans-Jörg Rheinberger in particular, for generous support. I also want to thank the editors for useful comments.

ment was therefore kept in its box, and left there until his friend wanted it back. When the friend sent a servant to pick up the box, Goethe took a prism out of the box to try it. He was in a room with white walls, and looked at the wall through the prism. He had expected to see Newton's spectrum of colours, but the only thing he saw was white. After a few trials he found that a boundary was required to produce colours, and at that very moment he was convinced that Newton's theory was erroneous (*Zur Farbenlehre* 920).

Goethe immediately persuaded his friend to let him keep the prism for a little longer, and started his investigations into colours. He carried out his investigations for years, and gradually developed an alternative to Newton's theory of light and colour. At the time, fifty years after Newton's death, Newton was regarded as probably the greatest scientist of all time, and his theory of light and colour had acquired the status of scientific orthodoxy. Challenging the theory was therefore a daring – not to say foolhardy – venture. And it is the general view that Goethe failed. He was not taken seriously by many scientists, and even his followers regarded his theory of colour as a blunder on the part of the great master. Goethe's main objection to Newton's theory was that it could not give an adequate account of the colours we perceive. Hence, the theory was not a complete theory of light and colour. If he had restricted himself to criticising Newton's theory of colour perception, posterity's assessment of his contribution would probably have been more positive. However, Goethe went further. Although he did not challenge Newton's experimental facts, he challenged the interpretation of the facts. According to Goethe, they did not have the status that Newton attributed to them.

A distinguishing mark of modern science is a sharp division between the subjective and the objective. The first to introduce this division in modern times was Galileo, when he introduced the distinction between primary and secondary qualities in *The Assayer* (1623). The properties of the world that we perceive with our senses, such as colours, taste and smell, are not properties of the objective world. They are merely created in our sensory organs and transmitted to our consciousness. The really existing properties are the primary qualities, such as location, extension and impenetrability. Descartes took over this division, and made it the basis of his own philosophy (cf. Mittelstrass 330). The task of science is to investigate the objective world, Galileo's primary qualities. It follows that this science cannot be based on sensory perception, because the world that we perceive is only subjective. Both Galileo and Descartes emphasised the unreliability of our senses. To compensate for this, we must use measuring instruments, mathematics and experiments to obtain access to the objective world.

In contrast to Newton, who, along with Galileo, Descartes and Boyle, may be regarded as one of the founders of modern science, Goethe's conception of science was closer to that of Aristotle (cf. Hegge). Goethe did not accept the absolute division between subjective and objective. On the contrary, the subject plays an important part in his science. It has been argued that he therefore did not understand the abstract character of modern science. There may be some truth in this, but we should not jump to the conclusion that his theory of colour is simply based on ignorance. Although his investigations of colour phenomena were originally initiated by a misunderstanding – that not seeing the spectrum when looking at a white wall through a prism was in accordance with Newton's theory – he had studied Newton carefully, and was probably the one among his contemporaries with the best knowledge of Newton's theory. Nevertheless, he challenged the very foundation of Newton's theory, Newton's view of science and nature in general, and therefore, it may be argued, the very foundation of modern science. Because Goethe's own theory of colour and conception of science is closer to the Aristotelian tradition, it is natural to call his theory premodern.

The scientific revolution, and therefore the birth of modern science, took place during the first half of the 17th century, and Galileo is usually seen as a key figure. Given Galileo's many important predecessors and contemporaries, however (for example Kepler), it would perhaps be more correct to consider him a part of a movement that had started one or two centuries earlier. Nonetheless, in his book *Cosmopolis: The Hidden Agenda of Modernity* (1990), Stephen Toulmin[2] argues that this traditional view is problematic. He agrees that the birth of modern science, and of modernity, can be dated to the first part of the 17th century. However, he argues that modernity has two different roots. One is the scientific revolution of the 17th century, with people like Galileo, Descartes and Newton, while the

---

2   Although Toulmin is not as well known as his contemporary Thomas Kuhn, he was one of the most influential philosophers and historians of science in the second half of the 20th century. In his first book, *The Philosophy of Science* (1953), he anticipated many of the arguments that later made Kuhn famous. He published books on the history of science, in particular on astronomy, matter and time. And he made important contributions to logic, to the uses of argument, and to the theory of ethics. In this paper I refer to his second-last book, *Cosmopolis*. However, his later book, *Return to Reason* (2001), is also relevant.

other is the Renaissance humanism of the 15th century, with people like Erasmus and Montaigne. As the term "humanism" indicates, it was based on a human perspective, characterised by an awareness of the limits of one's own perspective, the acceptance of uncertainty and the imperfection of man, and, therefore, a tolerance towards other opinions. However, the scientific revolution was not a continuation of Renaissance humanism. According to Toulmin it was rather a counter-Renaissance. The human perspective was replaced by the ideal of an absolute perspective, which defined objectivity in modern science.

When Toulmin published his book in 1990, the term "postmodern" had gained popularity. The prefix "post" indicates that modernity is not regarded as the final stage in human history, and denoted a position that was critical of some aspects of modernity. Sometimes it was associated with nihilism and relativism, as a reaction against modernity's emphasis on reason and objectivity. Toulmin used the term "postmodern" in a related, but slightly different sense.[3] According to Toulmin the transition from modernity to postmodernity, which is already well underway, basically involves a return to the lost ideals of Renaissance humanism. Of course, it is not just a return to the premodern, it is rather a new synthesis, between Renaissance humanism and modernity. Toulmin called this "humanising modernity".

Toulmin's theory of modernity and postmodernity has consequences for our view of contemporary science, and for our visions of future science. And it has consequences for our classification of Goethe's theory of colour as premodern or postmodern. However, before I address this question I will give an outline of Newton's theory of light and colour, and then Goethe's theory of colour. I will then compare the two theories, and show that Goethe's theory of colour had some merits from the very beginning. But in view of the development of modern science that Toulmin calls "postmodern", we shall see that Goethe was more postmodern than premodern.

NEWTON'S THEORY OF LIGHT AND COLOUR

Newton subscribed to Robert Boyle's "experimental philosophy", and the opening sentence of the first book of *Opticks* is: "My Design in this Book is not to explain the Properties of Light by Hypotheses, but to propose and prove them by Reason and Experiments...." (Newton 1) True to this prom-

---

3   However, his project has many similarities to Lyotard's as it is described in "Rewriting Modernity" (Lyotard 1993).

THE ART OF DISCOVERY

ise, he based his theory of light and colour on experiments, most of them carried out with prisms. The first experiments were carried out in 1666, when Newton was twenty-three, but the complete version of his theory was published in *Opticks* as late as 1704.

The best known experiment is known as the "crucial experiment", because Newton regarded it as the most convincing demonstration of his theory. Somewhat simplified, the experiment may be described as follows: A beam of sunlight passes through a small chink in the window shutters and into a dark room. It is refracted through a prism, and projected onto a screen, which reveals the colours of the spectrum. Although there is a continuous transition from one colour to another, and the division of the spectrum into distinct colours to some degree is arbitrary, Newton distinguished between seven different colours: red, orange, yellow, green, blue, indigo and violet. Violet at one end of the spectrum is refracted most, and red at the opposite end is the least refracted.[4]

The crucial experiment is supposed to prove the core of Newton's theory, which may be formulated in what is usually called *the thesis of differential refrangibility*: White light is composed of rays with a varying degree of refrangibility. Newton held a corpuscular view of light, but when the wave theory of light became dominating, refrangibility was replaced by wavelength.[5] Newton followed Galileo and Descartes in maintaining that no colours exist in the objective world. He is careful in pointing out that when he uses the word "colour", he does not speak "philosophically and properly, but grossly, and accordingly to such Conceptions as vulgar People in seeing all these Experiments would be apt to frame" (Newton 124).

But Newton also treats colours in *Opticks*. The subtitle of the book is "A Treatise of the Reflections, Refractions, Inflections & Colour of Light". We may call this the subjective part of the theory, and it explains colour phenomena as an effect of light that hits the retina. In addition to demonstrating the relationship between refrangibility (wavelength) and colour, Newton demonstrated that all colours can be composed from three elementary colours: red, green and blue. Young, and after him Helmholtz, showed that the three colours correspond to three different colour receptors of the human

---

4   As mentioned in the text, this is a simplified version of the experiment. Newton only used the term "crucial experiment" ("Experimentis Crucis") a couple of times. It is experiment 6 in *Opticks* (Newton 45ff). See also (Sepper 10).

5   It is easy to demonstrate that refrangibility is a function of wavelength. Where the historical context is not important, I shall use wavelength instead of refrangibility.

retina (the cones): These are sensitive to red, green and blue respectively. The core of the subjective part is that the colours we perceive only depend on the local properties, that is, the wavelength distribution of the light that hits the retina. Although Newton did not possess the required physiological knowledge to give a detailed description, the account is reductionist: Colours do not exist in the objective world, but are effects of external stimuli of our senses. In a more modern terminology we could say that there is a direct transmission of wavelength information from the retina to the brain, and a direct conversion of this information into colour.

GOETHE'S ALTERNATIVE

Unlike Newton, Goethe insisted that colours in fact exist in the objective world. At the same time he emphasised the active part of the eye, as an integrated part of any colour phenomenon. Instead of Newton's division into subjective and objective, he argued that there are three indispensable elements in colour perception: The object, a medium (for example air or water), and the observer. He also insisted that colours must be systematically described in their familiar settings, in all their aspects, variations and appearances: The colours of trees, flowers and insects, the bright sky of daylight, the sky at dawn, shadows etc. (Sepper 59). In studying colour phenomena, context is therefore important. For example, a grey surface on a dark background looks much lighter than the same surface on a white background. Even if we compare them, we will have problems in determining that it is the same grey surface (*Zur Farbenlehre* 36).

A typical result of Goethe's empirical research is the systematic investigation of after-images. If we look at a blue square for half a minute, and then look at a white surface, a red-yellow area with the same shape as the original blue square will appear. This after-image is created by the original colour. The paper remains white, and there is no doubt that the colour is created in the eye. On the other hand, this is not just something that we imagine; it is "real". A similar phenomenon can be observed with shadows: An opaque object is placed at a distance from a white wall. It is illuminated by two light sources that cast two shadows on the wall. Let one light source be white, and the other red. The shadow from the white light is illuminated by the red source, and hence has a reddish colour. The other shadow is cast by the red light, and is illuminated by the white light. We should expect it to be white, or grey. However, it turns out to be green. Green is the complementary colour of red, and it is created by the eye in order to obtain balance. The retina forms a whole by adding the opposing element to create harmony (*Zur Fahrbenlehre* 40).[6] Goethe calls it an example of "the laws of vision": "The eye exhibits an exacting need for wholeness in this connection; it completes the circle of colours within itself" (*Zur Farbenlehre* 45[7]).

But Goethe was not content with just finding empirical laws of colour perception. In one passage he describes the acquisition of scientific knowledge as an ascent and a descent: We start with empirical phenomena, which are based on everyday observations. They are unsystematic and scattered, and cannot be the basis of scientific theories. The next level is scientific phenomena. Scientific phenomena are obtained by systematic observations, in particular experiments, where the conditions can be systematically controlled and changed.

As related in the introduction, Goethe performed experiments with prisms. He varied the conditions systematically, and simplified and idealised until he obtained the "minimal conditions" that produce colour (Sepper 72). The simplest case is a white and a black area separated by a straight line. Let us start with the black area above the white. If we look at the two areas through a prism with its edge down, we will see a red colour closest to the black area, and then a broader yellow stripe below that, closest to the white area. If we turn the figure upside down, with the white on top, we will see a blue stripe on top (closest to the white) and a broader violet stripe below (closest to the black area). According to Goethe, these are the two simplest conditions that produce colour, and he concluded that colours arise when light meets darkness. Therefore, darkness is as important as light in producing colour. This is the essence of all colour phenomena. Phenomena that reveal the essence of all related phenomena Goethe called archetypical phenomena ("Urphaenomene") (*Zur Farbenlehre* 74).[8]

Goethe was not the first to hold the view that both light and darkness are required to produce colour. It was in fact a widespread view among philosophers at the time of Boyle that colours are created from light and darkness (Crombie Vol 1, 1038). Some authors have argued that

---

6   This result is similar to the findings of Gestalt psychology a hundred years later.

7   Quotation from the English translation of *Zur Farbenlehre* (Goethe 2006, 16); p. 45 in the original.

8   The terminology "empirical phenomena", "scientific phenomena" and "archetypical phenomena" is used in a letter to Schiller in 1798 (Zajonc 231 and Sepper 70).

one major difference between Newton and Goethe concerns the way they performed their experiments. One alleged difference is that while Newton's experiments were "objective" (in most of his experiments light rays passed through his prisms and were projected onto a screen), Goethe's experiments were "subjective" (he looked through the prism). However, Goethe performed many of his experiments as "objective" as well, and they gave the same results. There are two major differences, though. The first is that Newton used narrow beams of light, whereas Goethe used boundaries between light and darkness. The second major difference is the following: Newton regarded the processes in nature as governed by deterministic mathematical laws. To be able to describe these laws we have to reduce complex processes to simple and idealised cases. In the crucial experiment he was allegedly able to decompose a beam of light into its "atomic" constituents.

Goethe, on the other hand, took quite a different view of his archetypical phenomenon. A key to this view is an ambiguity in Goethe's own determination of the phenomenon. Apparently, there is an alternative candidate to the prismatic experiments as archetypical phenomena: the sun and the sky seen through the atmosphere. The light from the sun is in itself white. But seen through the atmosphere as a turbid medium, it looks yellow. When the turbidity increases, it changes from yellow to orange, and to red. These changes can be observed from dawn to sunset. When the sun rises above the horizon, it passes through a thicker layer of the atmosphere, and hence looks red. When it rises higher in the sky, it turns more and more yellow. When it has reached its highest point, the process is reversed, until the sun sets. In the same way, darkness seen through an illuminated turbid medium looks blue. The blue colour becomes lighter and paler if the medium becomes more turbid, and darker and deeper if it becomes more transparent. Therefore, the sky has its deepest blue colour in the middle of the day. At dawn and sunset it is paler (*Zur Farbenlehre* 68).

Which of these phenomena is archetypical – the prismatic or the atmospheric? According to Goethe's own characterisation, an archetypical phenomenon explains other phenomena and he explicitly says that the prismatic experiments explain the atmospheric phenomena (*Zur Farbenlehre* 73). Therefore, in my opinion there can be no doubt that the prismatic phenomenon is the archetypical one. On the other hand, the two types of phenomena are closely related, but Goethe does not explain how. I see only one possible relationship: The prismatic experiments relate to the atmospheric phenomena as the part to the whole, and there is a relationship of similarity between them: The black area above the white seen through a prism with the edge down corresponds to the white sun seen through the atmosphere (in both cases the white is darkened by the black), and the white area above the black corresponds to the dark sky seen through the lit atmosphere (the black is lit by the white).

To show the similarity relation between the two phenomena, we have to show how we get from one phenomenon (the prismatic experiments) to the other (the atmospheric phenomena) through a series of successive transformations. As far as I know, Goethe does not say anything like this about the relationship between the two phenomena. However, if we go to his morphology, the idea that the relationship between two phenomena can be demonstrated by a series of transformations is a central topic. It is the basic idea behind the archetypical plant ("die Urpflanze"). Goethe's archetypical plant is neither a concrete plant nor an idealised, abstract plant. It is rather a generative principle that determines the transformations and differentiations of the parts of the plant into the whole plant. (cf. Brady; Bohm & Peat 162f).

WHERE GOETHE WAS RIGHT

Let us start with what I have called the subjective part of Newton's theory: colour perception. Newton's theory allegedly gives a causal explanation of colour phenomena: The light rays are the cause, and the perceived colour the effect. This was regarded as an explanation of colour perception, and at the same time it was regarded as one of the shortcomings of Goethe's theory that it does not give a similar explanation. However, one may legitimately ask if reference to the refrangibility of light rays, wavelength or corpuscles really explains the sensation of a colour. I will not address that question here. Instead, I will take a critical look at the premise that there is a well-defined correspondence between wavelength distribution and perceived colour.

As pointed out in the introduction, the initial response to Goethe's theory was that it was simply an error. However, it was gradually recognised that Newton's theory was insufficient in accounting for the colours we perceive. In the 19th century Helmholtz argued that "an act of judgement" was involved in colour perception, and at the beginning of the 20th century Albert H. Munsell studied colours in the tradition of Goethe. His system for describing and classifying colours is widely used today by artists and in industry. However, the decisive arguments against the subjective part of Newton's theory were produced more than fifty years later. Starting around 1950 Edwind Land carried out a series of experiments which showed that there is no well-defined relationship between wavelength distribution and perceived colours.[9]

I shall give a short summary of an article in which Land presented some important results from his investigation. He starts by pointing to the apparent paradox that modern colour photography has reinforced Newton's theory that there is a unique correspondence between wavelength distribution and perceived colours. However, the very same technology demonstrates that there cannot be such a correspondence. A colour photograph of objects taken in a room illuminated by artificial light (tungsten filament lamps) will look red compared to the same objects photographed in daylight. Nonetheless we see approximately the same colours in daylight as in a tungsten-lit room. If the eye had not been able to deal with this problem, we would be confused all the time: Objects would change colour under various conditions. This contradicts the everyday fact that objects retain their colours under a great variety of light conditions (Land 108).

Some of Land's most spectacular experiments were carried out with what Land called "colour Mondrians" (alluding to the painter Mondrian). These were squares consisting of a hundred rectangles of different colours which were illuminated by three different light sources, emitting light of well-defined wavelength: long wave (red), middle wave (green) and short wave (blue). The intensity of the three light sources could be varied, and the intensities of the light reflected from the various areas of the Mondrians were functions of the intensity of the light sources. In the experiments Land used a simplified Mondrian of seventeen colour areas. The left eye of the subject in the experiment was exposed to the simplified Mondrian, and the right eye was exposed to a square with a colour under standard "white" illumination. This colour was selected by the subject from a standard reference book (The Munsell Book of Colour) to match the colour seen with the left eye. Five colours from the Mondrian were used: grey, red, yellow, blue and green. The experiments were performed five times, focusing on each of the five colours. The intensities of the three light sources were adjusted so that each time the light reflected from the colour selected was exactly the same. In other words, the light reflected from the grey, red, yellow, blue and green areas respectively was the same. Therefore, the light that hit the retina of the experimental subject was the same in all cases, but it was perceived as

---

9   Edwind Land was the inventor of the polaroid camera, and founder and president of the Polaroid Corporation. The series of experiments spanned several decades.

THE ART OF DISCOVERY

different colours: grey, red, yellow, blue and green respectively. This is, of course, contrary to Newton's theory.

I will not go into the technical details of Land's theory. The core of the theory is the observation that boundaries are important, and that in determining a specific colour the eye uses the whole perceptive field and compares different areas. The perception of colour is thus a complex process in which context and wholeness are important. In current terminology we could say that colour is an emergent complex phenomenon. Land himself was not able to determine where in the visual system this integrating process took place, but it had to be somewhere along the path from the retina to the cortex. He therefore he called his theory the retinex theory of colour vision.

GOETHE'S CONCEPTION OF SCIENCE AND TOULMIN'S POSTMODERNISM

Land did not refer to Goethe, but his theory supports Goethe's on two important points: 1) Colour cannot be reduced to the wavelength distribution of the light that hits the retina. 2) Wholeness and context are imperative for the perception of colour.

However, Land probably regarded his own theory as a correction of that part of Newton's theory that deals with colour perception. In fact, Land developed a theory which in many ways is a precursor of neural network theories. But as far as I know, he always retained a traditional view of science. We may, therefore, argue that Goethe's criticism of Newton, and of science in general, was more radical than Land's. As an alternative to what Goethe regarded as Newton's mechanistic conception of nature, he called his own theory "organic". However, to decide if Goethe was more radical (or more conservative) than Land, we must have an idea of the present (and future) development of science, and this is where we return to Toulmin.

According to Toulmin, the process of humanising modern science has already started, and he points to certain tendencies in contemporary science. Among them is a change in the concept of objectivity. Modern science's ideal of objectivity left no place for ethical norms and values, and the result was the separation of "ought" from "is", and values from facts. Ethical norms and values had to be justified outside the sciences (for example in religion or in a theory of human nature), or else they might be regarded as mere conventions. Of course this did not prevent them from being relevant in the application of science. However, the scientific and technical development has precluded the separation between facts and values. One example is modern medicine. Previously, medical doctors could take it for granted that the goal of their activity was to save lives. But when medicine enables us to extend the life processes beyond any realistic hope of regaining a meaningful life, this goal no longer makes sense. According to Toulmin, the fact that the oxygen level in the patient's arterial blood is at a life-threatening level is on a par with, for example, the fact that the patient does not want to be resuscitated by technical means. A second example is physics. The invention of the atomic bomb changed the consciousness of physicists, who now understood that it was impossible to do physics without taking the wider, societal context into consideration. Toulmin's third example is engineering. Previously any technical project would be carried out if it was technically feasible and useful in a narrow sense. Now it is unthinkable to initiate a technical project without taking a much broader set of factors into consideration. The common denominator of these examples is that today it is impossible for scientists to carry on their activities solely pursuing truth, disregarding the societal context and implications of their activities. The central topics of Renaissance humanism are therefore returning.

Of course, returning to the past is out of the question. We cannot (and we do not want to) ignore modern science and technology. The only possible alternative is to "humanize modernity" (Toulmin, *Cosmopolis* 180). One consequence of this is that the idea of finding one fundamental, all-comprising theory (sometimes called a "theory of everything") – as well as the "absolute" status of modern science – should be given up. Toulmin was not the first to argue this. In the middle of the last century Edmund Husserl argued in a similar way (Husserl 1962), and more recently Nancy Cartwright has used the term "scientific fundamentalism" to indicate that she regards this position as being just as untenable as religious fundamentalism (Cartwright 1999). The human perspective must be integrated into the sciences, or, rather, the sciences must be submitted to the human perspective. The best example is quantum mechanics. The "observer" as an integrated part of the theory was a central topic in the debates between Bohr and Einstein.[10] Einstein never accepted quantum mechanics as complete because it violated the modern idea of objectivity. Einstein himself advocated the idea of objectivity that we have inherited from Galileo and Descartes. Bohr, on the other hand, called this "God's Eye View", and argued that we are always limited to a

---

10 It should be pointed out that according to Bohr the "observer" includes the body and instruments of the agent that performs the experiments, and not just his or her consciousness. If only consciousness is included, mysticism is just one step away.

human perspective. Although this is sometimes called "the Copenhagen interpretation" of quantum mechanics, it is important to keep in mind that it is in fact the standard interpretation.[11]

While one might argue that I am now turning science on its head, it is more a case of putting it back on its feet. As Husserl pointed out, even the most abstract science must be grounded in the lifeworld. It follows that we have "to limit the scope of even the best-framed theories" (Toulmin, *Cosmopolis* 193). This is exactly what Goethe did to Newton's theory. Therefore, the relationship is in fact the opposite. Goethe's theory (or an improved version of it; Goethe was himself aware of many shortcomings of his theory) is the primary theory, whereas Newton's theory is more an abstraction that is highly useful for many purposes, in particular constructing optical instruments.

We may conclude that Goethe's theory was just as postmodern as it was premodern. However, when we use "premodern", "modern" and "postmodern" to denote successive epochs in the history of science (or the history of mankind), we tacitly presuppose a linear conception of time. Even Thomas Kuhn, who destroyed the simple accumulative view of science, retained a linear view: Science develops through a succession of paradigms. Although the paradigms, according to Kuhn, are incommensurable, and we cannot speak about progress in any simple sense, there is no way we can turn back. A more adequate description of the development of science – compatible with Toulmin's view – is the theory of "styles of scientific thinking" developed by the historian of science Alistain Crombie. His styles of scientific thinking have some similarities to Kuhn's paradigms. But in contrast to Kuhn's paradigms, which succeed each other through history, Crombie's styles coexist. He distinguishes between six styles of scientific thinking in the European scientific tradition: 1) The method of postulation, 2) the experimental method, 3) hypothetical modelling, 4) taxonomy, 5) probabilistic and statistical analysis, and 6) historical derivation. Newton and Goethe represent different styles of scientific thinking: Newton is an example of the experimental method, and Goethe is an example of the taxonomic method.

Each style arises at a certain time in history, it is more or less widespread

---

11   I have written about this in more detail in Fjelland 2001 and Fjelland 2002. Toulmin does not mention Bohr or quantum mechanics, and according to his characterisation of postmodern science, he would not classify quantum mechanics as postmodern. However, I think he would classify it as the beginning of the development that leads to postmodern science.

at different times, and it changes through history. For example, the experimental method has its roots back in Greek science, but it was fundamentally transformed during the scientific revolution in the 17th century, not least due to the contributions of Galileo, Descartes, Boyle and Newton. After this, it gradually colonised the other sciences. The taxonomic style was also invented by the Greeks (in particular Plato, Aristotle and Theophrastus). It was rediscovered in the 13th century, and carried further until now. Among those who contributed to developing the method, Crombie mentions Linnaeus, Lamarck, Cuvier, Goethe and Darwin (Crombie Vol. 3, 1259ff).

More important in this context is that although the taxonomic style of thinking came under pressure after the scientific revolution, due to the success of the experimental method, the taxonomic style has prevailed, and is being revived. Today it is associated with key words like "holism" and "complexity". To the list of names above we may add d'Arcy Thompson, Kauffman and Gould, all of whom invoke Goethe as a source of inspiration (Thompson 41, Kauffman 4, Gould 281). Although they refer to Goethe's contributions to morphology, the same would apply to Goethe's philosophy of science. I have already indicated that it is not important to conclude one way or the other. Having said as much, I tend towards concluding that Goethe's theory of colour should be classified as postmodern.

WORKS CITED

Bohm, D. & Peat, F.D. *Science, Order, and Creativity*. New York: Bantam Books, 1987.

Brady, R. "Form and cause in Goethe's morphology". In F. Amrine, F.J. Zucker, & H. Wheeler, eds., *Goethe and the Sciences: A Reappraisal*. Boston Studies in the Philosophy of Science Vol. 97 (257-305). Boston: D. Reidel Publishing Company, 1987.

Cartwright, N. *The Dappled World. A Study of the Boundaries of Science*. Cambridge: Cambridge University Press, 1999.

Crombie, A.C. *Styles of Scientific Thinking in the European Tradition*. London: Duckworth, 1994.

Fjelland, R. "Niels Bohr on Physics, Biology and Psychology". Teorie & Modelli, n.s., VI(1), 2001. 87-101.

—. "The Copenhagen interpretation of quantum mechanics and phenomenology". In Babich, B. ed., *Hermeneutic Philosophy of Science, van Gogh's Eyes, and God*. Boston Studies in the Philosophy of Science, vol. 225 (53-65). Dordrecht: Kluwer Academic Publishers, 2002.

Galilei, G. *The Assayer* (*Il Saggiatore*, 1623). Ed. S. Drake, *Discoveries and Opinions of Galileo*. New York: Doubleday & Company, 1957.

THE ART OF DISCOVERY

Goethe, J.W. *Zur Farbenlehre* (1808). *Sämtliche Werke*. Vol. 10. München: Carl Hanser Verlag, 1989.

—. *Theory of Colours* (1840, English trans. of *Zur Farbenlehre*). New York: Dover Publications, 2006.

Gould, S.J. *The Structure of Evolutionary Theory*. Cambridge, MA: Belknap, Press of Harvard University, 2002.

Hegge, H. *Theory of Science in the Light of Goethe's Science of Nature*. In F. Amrine, J.F. Zucker, & H. Wheeler, eds., *Goethe and the Sciences: A Reappraisal*. Boston Studies in the Philosophy of Science. Vol. 97. Dordrecht: Reidel Publishing Company, 1987.

Husserl, E. *Die Krisis der Europaischen Wissenschaften und die transzendentale Phaenomenologie*, vol. VI. *Husserliana*. Haag: Martinus Nijhoff, 1962.

Kauffman, S.A. *The Origins of Order*. Oxford: Oxford University Press, 1993.

Land, E. (1977). "The retinex theory of color vision". *Scientific American*, 237(6), (1993): 108-128.

Lyotard, J.-F. "Rewriting Modernity". *In the Inhuman. Reflections on Time.* Cambridge: Polity Press, 1993, 24-35.

Mittelstrass, J., *Neuzeit und Aufklärung*, Berlin: Walter de Gruyter, 1970.

Newton, I. *Opticks, or a treatise of the reflections, refractions, inflections and colours of light* (4th ed. London 1730). New York: Dover, 1952.

Sepper, D.L. *Goethe contra Newton. Polemics and the Project for a New Science of Color.* Cambridge: Cambridge University Press, 1988.

Thompson, D W. (1992). *On Growth and Form* (1917). Cambridge: Cambridge University Press, abridged edition (1961) edition, 1992.

Toulmin, S. *Cosmopolis. The Hidden Agenda of Modernity*. New York: The Free Press, 1990.

—. *Return to Reason*. Cambridge, Massachusetts: Harvard University Press, 2001.

BAUDELAIRE AND THE POETICS OF MAGNETISM

Margery Vibe Skagen, University of Bergen

Throughout the 19th century the widespread popularisation of Anton Mesmer's therapeutic use of hypnosis – explained as an effect of "animal magnetism" – was an important source of experimentation, writing, wonder and controversy. Carrying on hermetic conceptions developed by Paracelsus and Swedenborg, the mesmeric doctrine of animal magnetism fertilised a flowering tradition of philosophical speculation and pseudo-scientific fantasy. As a therapist Mesmer inaugurated a widely used medical practice, which remains devoid of any consensual explanatory theory (Roustang 8). He also opened the door to a new domain of psychological enquiry, the unconscious, which became a generally accepted factor in our understanding of the human.

Hypnotism is known from ancient ritual and occult magic. It evolved through the open debate of the Enlightenment, and from idealist philosophy to romantic and naturalistic literature and psychiatry. It was the starting point of psychoanalysis, and became a popular technique of surrealistic experimentation and a commonplace of fantastic fiction. Today hypnosis is a key topic for alternative therapies as well as for neuroscientific research. Its multifaceted history demonstrates in many ways how hypnotic phenomena are a constant challenge to understanding the relation between psyche and soma, mind and matter, within the conventionally opposed realms of literature and science.[1]

According to Mesmer, hypnotical states were caused by the literally understood *influence* of an animate and "magnetic" force, which could be canalised by the hypnotiser into the bodies of his subjects. By metonymy, "animal magnetism" came to denote not only the occult energy and its therapeutic uses, but also its mysterious psycho-physiological effects in the individual.

In the following I will examine how Charles Baudelaire applies to poetry and aesthetics supposedly mesmeric concepts of *sympathy, imagination,*

---

1   On the history, controversies and actuality of hypnosis, cf. Waterfield, *The Hidden Depths – The Story of Hypnosis*, 2002.

suggestion and *suggestiveness,* often in connection to figures of electricity and magnetism. In connection with 19th century literature and (pseudo) science, hypnosis will be referred to as a continuum of trancelike states ranging from profound reverie to somnambulism. A network of concepts associable with "animal magnetism" can be traced in Baudelaire's writings as in the vocabulary of many of his contemporaries. But the French poet is less explicit in his literary use of this doctrine than for example Poe, Balzac or Gautier. The verb *magnétiser* in French or *electrify* in English may still mean *fascinate* or *mesmerise.* Like the adjective *suggestive,* these terms may be used today in an aesthetical context, but hardly in the literal sense of inducing hypnosis. By revisiting certain fields of association related to mesmerism in 19th-century literature, this essay will try to restore some of the "magnetic" colouring to faded figures of Baudelaire's supernaturalism.

ANIMAL MAGNETISM

Mesmer (1734-1815) postulated the existence of a mutual influence between the celestial bodies, the earth and animate bodies, provided by a universal agent that was believed to have many of the characteristics of magnetism and electricity. *Animal* magnetism, as opposed to *mineral* magnetism, to which it was said to have an analogical likeness, may be understood in relation to "animal spirits", originally "the supposed 'spirit' or principle of sensation and voluntary motion; answering to nerve fluid, nerve force, nervous action" (*Oxford English Dictionary*). Animal spirits are described by Descartes as "a very subtle wind" or "a pure flame" flowing through the nervous system (Descartes 49-50). They were believed to transmit will impulses to muscles as well as sensory information to the brain through the pineal gland, known as the Cartesian point of intersection between soul and body. More than a century later, the electric nature of nerve impulses was suggested by Galvani's frog experiments, and the animal spirits or fluids tended to be redefined in terms of electricity or some analogical and "imponderable fluid". Jean Starobinski notes the disposability of the fluid metaphor, facilitating not only the assimilation of the animal or nervous principle with electricity and magnetism, but also generating universal principles of explanation – too universal to be scientific (Starobinski 196-213).

Mesmer himself defined animal magnetism as a "universally distributed fluid, a fluid which surrounds all that exists and which serves to maintain the equilibrium of all the vital functions" (Mesmer 81). He believed that this harmonising principle permeated all animate and inanimate things, and had the capacity of being intensified and channelled at will through the nerves of the therapist or "magnetizer" and into those of the entranced patient. By certain followers of Mesmer, animal magnetism was identified not only with the vital principle of nerves and electricity, but likewise with the spiritual principle of thought and love. As an effect of this original principle and accommodated to romantic nostalgia, hypnosis could be explained as a state of regression to earlier stages either of the individual or of humankind, implying the idea of a communion with the spontaneous forces of natural creation.[2]

Stefan Zweig has described the extravagances of Mesmer's famous hypno-therapeutic practice with magnets and "electrified" tubs. As *mesmeromania* reached its climax in pre-revolutionary Paris, Louis XVI appointed Benjamin Franklin to a committee that discredited Mesmer's theory as pure imagination and his practice as dangerous. But in spite of the academic hostility to mesmerism, there soon appeared different schools of hypnosis, making it a well reputed remedy for patients and medical practitioners in the first half of the 19th century. As magnetism or mesmerism was transformed into hypnotism it became more acceptable to the medical establishment. To the Scottish physician James Braid, who experienced the effects of mesmerism in 1841, it appeared to be a natural psycho-physiological mechanism which he named "neuro-hypnotism", after the Greek god of sleep, Hypnos.[3]

Meanwhile, among French literary writers of this period, the influence of German idealism, and especially the popularity of Hoffmann's tales, enforced the romantic conception of mesmerism. "Le magnétisme animal" is a recurrent reference in the writings of Balzac, Dumas, Hugo, Stendhal, Gautier and Flaubert, and is often assimilated with widely accepted conceptions of the mesmerist's supernatural power to project thoughts, control by means of thoughts or read thoughts. In Gautier's fantastic novel *Avatar* (1856), one of the characters, mastering animal magnetism, is able to transfer souls from one body to another. But since Mesmer's days, the reading public had been no less dazzled by news of the technical wonders of magnetism and electric-

---

2 According to hypnotherapist and theorist Francois Roustang, hypnosis liberates an innate, prelinguistic potential to organise and configurate a consistent world, a power which seems to be active in the infant and which manifests itself through the free deployment of the imagination in the entranced subject. (Roustang 17-53).

3 Littré's French dictionary defines Hypnotism in 1863 as follows: "physiological term. A kind of magnetic state induced by making someone look at a bright object held near the eyes."

ity: Leyden jars producing powerful sparks, and transmitting the force with lightning speed over great distances; Benjamin Franklin's experiments with thunderstorms, demonstrating how it is possible to charge a Leyden jar from a kite-string; Galvani's frog experiments, causing contractions of the muscles under the influence of electrical discharge; Volta's great electrochemical pile constructed in Paris by the order of Napoleon. To an adept of animal magnetism, witnessing the short span of time from the invention of telegraphy in the 1830s to the first realization of a transatlantic telegraph cable in 1858, the idea of mesmeric communication regardless of the distance ("mental telegraphy") must have seemed close to fact.

POE AND BALZAC: HYPNOTIC REVELATIONS

The rush of scientific and pseudo-scientific studies, pondering the mysterious mental, physiological and physical mechanisms of magnetism and electricity, had a special appeal to authors admired by Baudelaire. In Hoffmann, Balzac and Poe, the French poet recognises the same "manie de l'unité" and supernaturalism, nourished by scientific progress: "Animal unity, fluid unity, unity of the primary matter, all these recent theories have sometimes, by a singular coincidence come into the heads of poets and scientists at the same time".[4] It is in these terms that Baudelaire introduces his own translation of Poe's "Mesmeric Revelation" in 1848, speaking obligingly of the excessive ambition in visionary poets that would also be scientists and philosophers. Poe's story, published in 1844, presents animal magnetism through the words of a scholarly mesmerist, responding to the usual attack on mesmerism as unscientific:

> Whatever doubt may still envelop the *rationale* of mesmerism, its startling *facts* are now almost universally admitted... There can be no more absolute waste of time than the attempt to *prove*, at the present day, that man, by mere exercise of will, can so impress his fellow, as to cast him into an abnormal condition, of which the phenomena resemble very closely those of *death*, or at least resemble them more nearly than they do the phenomena of any other normal condition

---

4   When citing Baudelaire, if nothing else is mentioned, the translations are my own. "Unité de l'animal, unité de fluide, unité de la matière première, toutes ces théories récentes sont quelquefois tombées par un accident singulier dans la tête de poètes, en même temps que dans les têtes savantes." Introduction to Baudelaire's translation of Poe's story "Mesmeric Revelation" (Baudelaire II, 248).

within our cognizance; that, while in this state, the person so impressed employs only with effort, and then feebly, the external organs of sense, yet perceives, with keenly refined perception, and through channels supposed unknown, matters beyond the scope of the physical organs; that, moreover, his intellectual faculties are wonderfully exalted and invigorated; that his sympathies with the person so impressing him are profound; (Poe 587).

To suit the story – where a dying man, who has been placed in a trance, hypnotised by the narrator, reveals secrets of the after life – the mesmeric condition is presented in the form of catalepsy. This psycho-physiological state (well known to Poe's readers), which may be induced by hypnosis or hysteria, is characterised by a corpselike rigidity and mental dissociation. Catalepsy exemplifies the general or partial immobility of the hypnotised subject's body, as he or she may appear to be physically "dead" to the outside world. Dissociation is the term currently used in relation to hypnosis to designate, among other things, the typical hypnotic absorption in one inner activity to the exclusion of all other activity, or the entranced subject's sole perception of the hypnotiser's voice to the exclusion of all other external stimuli. Subjective accounts of hypnosis confirm a certain distortion of the sense of time. The "deepening" of the inner perceptions of time and space generally experienced in trance, together with the increased ability to re-call, may explain the popular assimilation of hypnosis with supernatural intuition. Characteristic of deeper trance is also the tendency to experi-ence imaginary conceptions, perceptions or memories with the impressive evidence of real life, and to accept without questioning conceptions that to normal logic would seem contradictory. Referring to the Poe citation above, one might agree that among the cognitive faculties, the *imagination* at least is "wonderfully exalted and invigorated" by hypnosis. The responsiveness of the hypnotised subject to the hypnotiser's suggestions has facilitated the acceptance of their *rapport* as a profound form of *sympathy* or telepathy. Still, not considering the claim that the somnambulist perceives "matters beyond the scope of the physical organs", the definition Poe's narrator gives of the trance is not so different from the *Encyclopaedia Britannica's* current definition of hypnosis:

special psychological state with certain physiological attributes, resembling sleep only superficially and marked by a functioning of the individual at a level of awareness other than the ordinary conscious state. This state is characterized by a degree of increased receptiveness and responsiveness in which inner experiential perceptions are given as much significance as is generally given only to external reality.

In Balzac's most mesmeric novel, *Ursule Mirouët* (1842), "le magnétisme" (because of its presumed healing properties) is characterised by the narrator as "the favourite science of Jesus and one of the divine powers transmitted to the apostles" (Balzac 821-822). At a decisive point in the novel, an uneducated woman under trance impresses the most sceptical of doctors with her precise and intelligent account of the mental activity of a person miles away, which should be completely inaccessible to her (Balzac 837-838). Needless to say, the doctor, when experiencing this, turns to the Lord and to mesmerism. In the *Avant-propos* to *La Comédie humaine*, Balzac speaks of his literary project as a contribution to the progress of natural science into the realms of metaphysics. In this context he compares the past fifty years of research on "the prodigies of electricity" – meaning the psycho-physiological, "cerebral and nervous" effects attributed to mesmerism as well as the physical phenomena – with the controversial discoveries of Columbus and Galilei. To Balzac mesmerism is no illusion; it should be regarded as a confirmation of religion, and among the "sciences of imponderable agents", its mysterious and incontestable power to control body and mind seemed prophetic of the coming unity of all sciences. Electricity in the form of light, studied by opticians, and electricity in the form of thoughts, studied by mesmerists, are "quasi-semblable" or almost the same according to Balzac (16-17).

This philosophical ambition to unite literature with scientific and metaphysical speculation is perhaps immodest and naïve, writes Baudelaire, but it is nevertheless a mark of greatness characteristic of some of his favourite authors, namely the ones who manage to surprise us as a result of their "perpetual supernaturalism" and innate *curiosity* concerning the first things (Baudelaire II, 248).

MAGNETIC SYMPATHY AND IMAGINATION

Sympathy is a key word to Mesmer's world picture as well as to Baudelaire's poetics of magnetism; in fact, the sympathetic *rapport* between mesmeriser and mesmerized seems to have been a model for aesthetical expressiveness and receptivity. When speaking of universal analogy, musical harmony, symbolism or correspondences, whether in a literal or figurative sense, Baudelaire implicitly refers to the hermetic and idealistic conception of the cosmos, which includes the idea of a spiritual or vital *sympathy* between all elements.[5] The identification of the sympathy principle with magnetism can at least be traced back to Paracelsus, who saw the human being as the miniature magnet or *magnes microcosmi*, having, like the macro-cosmos, its poles and magnetic properties. The law of sympathy implies that by secret affinities between different things within the Great Chain of Being, they affect or influence each other correspondingly. The rhythm of the universe was believed to be governed by "magnetic" attraction and repulsion, sympathy and antipathy, flux and reflux, determining the mutual influence and interaction of all things. In this dynamic and dialectical rhythm, all oppositions or polarities – in likeness to the negatively and positively loaded poles of the magnet – affect each other interdependently within the whole.

In the same way as Balzac understood electricity as thought and light, the sympathy principle connects physical to spiritual phenomena and the individual to cosmos. The imagination is thus seen as a universal structure of cognition and creation, governed as everything else by the laws of sympathy and magnetism. Baudelaire's definition of the imagination as "the Queen of the faculties", in the *Salon* of 1859, is indebted to Catherine Crowe's mediation of German natural philosophy and this tradition's combining of hermetism, pantheism and mesmerism. It is by virtue of imagination, he states, that analogies and correspondences, the secret relations between things, can be perceived immediately. In his *Salon*, Baudelaire cites (not without condescension) Catherine Crowe's *The Night Side of Nature* to maintain his understanding of the imagination as the highest of human mental capacities, resembling the power with which the divine creator projects and upholds the universe (Baudelaire II, 624).

> It is imagination that has taught man the moral significance of colour, contour, sound and scent. In the beginning of things, imagination created analogy and metaphor. It decomposes all creation, and, with the wealth of materials amassed and ordered according to rules whose origins can be found only in the deepest recesses of the soul, it creates a new world, it produces the sensation of something new. Since imagination created the world (I think we are entitled to say

---

5   A rather explicit use of these notions is found among other places in Baudelaire's article on Théophile Gautier from 1859 (Baudelaire II, 117-118); in *Les Paradis artificiels* from 1860 (Baudelaire I, 430); in his article on Victor Hugo from 1861 (Baudelaire II, 133); and in his article on Richard Wagner from 1861, where he also cites his early poem "Correspondances" (Baudelaire II, 784).

that much even in a religious sense), it is right that imagination should govern the world. (Trans. Warner I, 201)

According to Schelling, who adopts the notion from Paracelsus, nature is "a poem in mysterious signs"; Baudelaire in turn echoes Novalis when characterising the world as "un dictionnaire hiéroglyphique" and varying the same theme in the poem "Correspondances", where nature is pictured as "forests of symbols". Through the constructive and all-comprehending imagination, the poet may find his way back to the original principle of creation and recognise the world's poetry as well as the "sweet native tongue" of the soul.[6] Crowe formulates the same idea: "The whole of nature is one large book of symbols, which, because we have lost the key to it, we cannot decipher". There is a hidden poet in the depth of the human soul, it is obscured by the noise and dissipation of modern civilisation. Nonetheless, traces of the original poetic language may be recognised in the symbolism produced in dreamlike or somnambulistic states of immersion into "the deeper self".[7]

MYSTERIOUS MOMENTS OF PROFOUNDNESS: SYMPATHY AND "CORRESPONDANCES"

The "sympathetic" or symbolic reading of the world in entranced states of the mind is also a topic in Baudelaire's study of different kinds of drunkenness or *artificial paradises*. In his first article on stimulants, "Du vin et du hachisch comparés comme moyens de multiplication de l'individualité", he conclusively quotes a certain philosopher and musical theorist named Barbereau, who assimilates "artificial" intoxication with "poetic rapture" or "natural" means of attaining "a supernatural existence":

"I just don't understand why rational and spiritual men use artificial means to attain supernatural existence. Great poets, philosophers, prophets are people who by the sheer and free use of will power, are able to attain a state of mind in which they are, at the same time, cause and effect, subject and object, magnetizer and somnambulist." I think exactly like him. (Baudelaire I, 398)

---

6 The expression "sa douce langue natale" is used in the poem "L'Invitation au voyage" (Baudelaire I, 53).

7 C. Crowe quoted by Cl. Pichois (Baudelaire II, 1394).

Following the same logic in "The Poem of Hashish", Baudelaire compares the drunkenness caused by hashish and opium to "natural" (or supernatural) states of altered consciousness like "hieroglyphic" dreaming, aesthetical admiration, poetic frenzy, mystical ecstasy, contemplation, poetic melancholy and somnambulism. To Baudelaire, all these forms of trancelike absorption or exaltation are similar means of satisfying the human thirst for infinity or "multiplication of the individuality" (Baudelaire, I, 337). The most interesting parts of this essay, as regards understanding Baudelaire's poetics, are the drug experiences of a character with which he obviously identifies himself, possessing all the artistic, intellectual, moral and temperamental dispositions of a modern poet and man of nerves. The impressions of the "homme sensible" under the influence of drugs, illustrate what Baudelaire calls the beautiful instants of the soul, which, according to him, ought to come naturally to any poet. These instances occur when a world of associations is released by the sudden strangeness of the most insignificant object, revealing the mysterious depth of life amidst the usually dreary "desert of existence". It is a feeling of musical connection with the rhythm of the universe, and most importantly, a feeling of recognition in all things, sensations and thoughts, symbolically echoing through time and space: "profundity of space, allegorical of the profundity of time".[8]

Baudelaire's most famous poem, "Correspondances", can be read as a celebration of the spiritual and sensory resounding of analogies, occurring in these "almost supernatural states of the soul" (Baudelaire, I, 659), understood as the sudden revival or recollection of the principle of creation. The poem is generally known as a lesson in synaesthesia, using metaphorically a phenomenon described in Baudelaire's accounts of intoxication with opium and hashish, as a mind-expanding experience of paradoxically meaningful "sympathies" between normally separate sense perceptions. In his *Salon of 1846*, Baudelaire refers to the hypersensitive musician, the narrator in Hoffmann's *Kreisleriana*, explaining how special inner states – like the delirious phase just before falling asleep, and when he is under the influence of music – let him experience an intimate reunion of colour, sound and scent.[9] The sense of smell, known as a particularly powerful means of mental travelling, has a privileged position in "Correspondances". The use of perfumes

---

8   "profondeur de l'espace, allégorie de la profondeur du temps", *Le Poème du hachisch* (Baudelaire I, 430-431).

9   *Salon de 1846*, (Baudelaire II, 425). Recent studies have shown that synesthesia may be induced by hypnosis. www.physorg.com/news143994178.html.

is in fact mentioned by Baudelaire, among other hallucinating artificial stimulants, as capable of granting their user a "taste of the infinite". It may be noted that the first of the aromatic substances enumerated in the final tercet of "Correspondances" ("Having the expansion of infinite things, / That sing the transports of the spirit and senses.") is *amber*. Amber, *elektron* in Greek, appeals to many senses; it is not only a sparkling, polished jewel and a substance producing a sweet smell when burned, it has also been associated with electricity and magnetism since Antiquity, because it becomes perceptibly loaded with static electricity when rubbed.[10] Like a discharge of energy finding its way through invisible connections between remote things, the metaphorical transference from scent to sound, from thing to thought, from finite to infinite, lights up lines of cohesion in "the tenebrous and profound unity" of correspondences.[11]

"Correspondances" also echoes other identified sources of "electrical" inspiration, for instance a poem with the same title by the occultist Eliphas Lévi, who Baudelaire knew in his youth.[12] Lévi explains many supernatural phenomena by the influence of the universal magnet. As raw electricity exists in the physical world, there is an intelligent electricity produced by the "cerebral battery", with which human beings can charge their surroundings with "magnetic influx"; "each brain is a ganglion, a station in the universal neurological telegraph, constantly connected to the central station and to all the others by thought vibrations" (Lévi 276-278). This electricity of the soul, or spiritual and universal ether, is a notion with which Nerval, the author of *Aurélia* (1855) is also familiar:

How can I have existed so long, I said to myself, outside Nature without identifying myself with her? Everything lives, everything acts, everything corresponds;

Speaking to non-experts, Chertok compares hypnosis to the intermediate state between wakefulness and sleep, through which we normally pass every night (Chertok 97).

10 "Now nobody, until well into the nineteenth century, had suspected that this little trick with amber was a sign to decipher: that it was the annunciation by enigma of a force that would change the face of the world, and that the graceful sparks shared the nature of a lightning bolt. Nevertheless all Western languages have preserved the term 'electricity', that is 'the force of amber'" (Levi 126).

11 "Comme de longs échos qui de loin se confondent / Dans une ténébreuse et profonde unité, /Vaste comme la nuit et comme la clarté,/Les parfums, les couleurs et les sons se répondent." "Correspondances" (Baudelaire I, 11).

12 Sources discovered by Claude Pichois, (Baudelaire I, 840-41).

THE ART OF DISCOVERY

the magnetic rays emanating from myself and others traverse unimpeded the infinite chain of created things; it is a transparent network which covers the world, and its fine threads communicate from one to another to the planets and the stars. I am now captive on the earth, but I converse with choiring stars, who share my joys and sorrows! (Trans. Aldington 155)

Sympathy, which is the term we currently use to designate interpersonal attraction, affinity, identification and empathy, applies not only to the effect of magnetism on things that the hermetic tradition supposed to be in accordance with one another. It also applies to the relation between magnetiser and magnetised, since this could be assimilated with thought transference, the spiritual fluid being directed through both by the will power of the hypnotist. But sympathy is also an appropriate term for the romantic or symbolist poet's "pantheistic" communion with nature. The musical metaphors in "Correspondances" suggest the attunement of the poetical I and his environment, the sympathetic *Stimmung* of the inner and the exterior world. In fact the mesmeric rapport between hypnotiser and subject could be explained even medically by the comparison of their respective nerves to the musical cords of two separate string instruments automatically vibrating in unison (Adelon, XXIX, 502). "Resounding" is the term used by Baudelaire to designate the interior movement of analogical recognition, transparency and vibrancy, accompanied by a feeling of the infinite depth of time and space, which he characterises as supernatural.[13] The classical idea of the cosmos' musical harmony may sometimes be referred to negatively by Baudelaire in more spleenful contexts: "Am I not a false note in the divine symphony?" (I, 71); but in "Correspondances", it is the musical accord or sympathy between "man" and "Nature" which makes possible the associative reverberation of scent, sound and colour, and enables him to recognise the "confused words" uttered by "forests of symbols".

Musical sympathy is also key in certain experiences of art, qualified as "surnaturaliste". Baudelaire explicitly compares the effect of Delacroix's paintings to the action of a thought-projecting mesmeriser, when living thoughts or symbolic music seem to emanate from the colours, making the

---

13 "Le surnaturel comprend la couleur générale et l'aacent, c'est-à-dire intensité, sonorité, limpidité, vibrativité, profondeur et retentissement dans l'espace et dans le temps.

Il y a des moments de l'existence où le temps et l'étendue sont plus profonds, et le sentiment de l'existence immensément augmenté." (Baudelaire I, 658)

spectator's memory resound (Baudelaire, II, 595). Even at a certain distance from a Delacroix painting, the spectator may recognise its intimate quality as something vaguely familiar. It is then as if the colours and lines establish a current of energy between the aesthetical object and the perceiving subject, combining sympathetically past and present, things and thoughts, painted with musical tones and the individual with the universal. Baudelaire relates similar experiences when reading Poe:

> The solitude of nature or the agitation of big cities, everything is described nervously and fantastically. As our Eugène Delacroix, who has raised his art to the height of great poetry, Edgar Poe likes to move his figures on purplish and greenish backgrounds revealing the phosphorescence of putrefaction and the scent of thunderstorm. The so-called inanimate nature participates in the nature of living beings, and is, like them, shivering with a supernatural and galvanic shiver. Space is deepened by opium; opium gives a magical significance to all the colours, and makes all the sounds vibrate with a more significant sonority. (Baudelaire II, 318)

The supernatural and galvanic thrill, suggestive of captured nervous tension, is enforced by the play of polarities: the confrontation of passion and melancholy, life and death, is rendered in electrical images of phosphorescent light emanating from putrefaction or lightning from dark clouds. A described object's "galvanic glow" or "supernatural varnish" is in Baudelaire's writing often the symptom of an imagination energised through sympathy. The literal understanding of sympathy reappears, not only as the unifying influence of a magnetic charge or musical harmony, but as a pantheistic fusion of subject and object – modelled on the presumed spiritual communion between mesmeriser and patient – and as a condition of true reading.

SUGGESTIONS OF HEAVEN OR HELL

To induce hypnosis one proceeds by and causes *suggestion*. The fact that this term designates both the hypnotiser's stimulation and the response to it, may again reflect the feeling of oneness of subject and object experienced in trance. The most current and attenuated use of the term apart, its semantic history is indeed revealing: *The Oxford Dictionary* defines the initial meaning of *suggestion* as a "Prompting or incitement to evil; an instance of this, a temptation of the evil one". But for Baudelaire the idea of suggestion fluctuates between theology, psychiatry and aesthetics. In *The Poem of Hashish*, the external stimuli, triggering an acceleration and intensification of associations in the intoxicated mind, are presented as "suggestions":

> All the surrounding objects are so many suggestions which stir in him a world of thought, all more coloured, more living, more subtle than ever, clothed in magic varnish. (Baudelaire I, 436)

Either as divine inspiration or as a diabolic influence, the opposite conceptions of *suggestion* seem equally relevant to Baudelaire.

The most refined level of "artificial" intoxication described in *The Poem of Hashish* is inseparable from an authentically developed "poetical spirit", and is also dangerously near the full development of "the satanic spirit" or auto divinisation (Baudelaire I, 396 and 434). In the prose poem "The Temptations", the first demon, Eros, with the intoxicating gaze, promises the narrator the gift of thought projection, or what we could call the gift of suggestion:

> I will make you the lord of souls, and you shall master living matter, even more than the sculptor can master the clay; and you shall know the never ending pleasure of going out of your self to forget yourself in other people, and to attract the other souls until they merge with yours. (Baudelaire I, 308)

The accessories of this demonic tempter allude to different means of contagious intoxication and hypnotic trance: a snake with a longing, burning gaze is coiled around the demon's waist; the knives and surgical instruments attached to it may be associated with the well known anaesthetising virtues of hypnosis; the phials of liquor, one with a red substance and an inscription: "This is my blood…", suggests a satanic parody of the Holy Communion, while the violin alludes to the musical communion evoked in poems like "Harmonie du soir" and "Correspondances". An excessive development of the poetical spirit, Baudelaire explains in *The Artificial Paradises*, leads to total identification with the environment, the marriage of subject and object (Baudelaire I, 419-420). This "going out of one's self" may be experienced as exaltation or anguish, a divine grace or a diabolic possession.

Baudelaire's poetical and aesthetical writing is haunted by oppositions, constantly joined. Preparing to describe the intoxication of his alter ego in *The Poem of Hashish*, first sublime and then satanic, Baudelaire writes: "To idealise my subject, I must concentrate all its rays into a single circle and

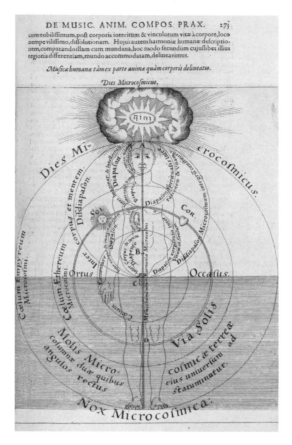

Robert Fludd, MICROCOSMI SVPERNATVRALI

polarise them." (Baudelaire I, 429) The conclusion to opposition is not an either or, but the vital tension ensured by a positive and a negative pole.

In the prose poem "The Crowds" the gift of the demon is a sacred ideal:

> The poet enjoys the incomparable privilege of being able to be himself or someone else, as he chooses, Like those wandering souls who go looking for a body, he enters as he likes into each man's personality. For him alone everything is vacant; and if certain places seem closed to him, it is only because in his eyes they are not worth visiting. The solitary and thoughtful saunterer finds a singular intoxication in this universal communion. (Baudelaire I, 291)

Like the eccentric hero of *The Painter of Modern Life* who bathes in the crowd, like in "an enormous reservoir of electricity", the solitary poet's desire in the last poem is to "espouse" the crowd, currently imagined in terms of a *fluid*, as an urban ocean. In likeness to the natural ocean, it represents the ebb and flow of some infinite and mysterious vital force within and without the mind, in which the poetic subject becomes object, "solitude" is confused with "multitude" and the individual meets the universal.[14]

SUGGESTIVE MAGIC

There are many magnetic and electrical props in Baudelaire's writing: electrifying gazes of women and demons, snake charmers (the poet is identified with a juggler) and snakes fascinating their prey, thunder and lightning, fluorescent matter, phosphoric atmospheres, cats emanating sparks. Praying is characterised as an electrical recurrence (I, 659), the actor's concentration on his role is a magnetic operation (II, 65), and the writing and painting of the genius may have the same galvanic glow. Magnetic and electrical fluids, sympathy and suggestion were well-known notions, and Baudelaire is not the only one to consider the "magnétiseur" as a model for the artist. But when he tries to determine the special quality of his favourite artist – "So what is then the mysterious something that Delacroix, to the glory of our century, conveyed better than any other? It is the invisible, the impalpable; it is the dream, the nerves, the *soul*" – the poet and critic introduces a new word into his aesthetic terminology, which again seems to be transposed from the terminology of hypnotism:

> Delacroix is the most *suggestive* of all painters, the one whose works, even the secondary, inferior ones, most incite us to think, to recall to memory the most poetic emotions and thoughts, which we already knew, but believed to be buried forever in the night of the past. (Baudelaire II, 744-745)

The word *suggestif* is italicized by Baudelaire, which indicates that it is unusual or should be understood in a special way. According to Richard de Radonvillier's *Dictionnaire de mots nouveaux* from 1845, the adjective *suggestif* at that time had only recently made its entrance into the French language. Along with other literary words like *spleen* and *dandy*, which were considered sophisticated and modern to the French elite in Baudelaire's days,

---

14 See for instance "L'Homme et la mer", "Le Vieux saltimbanque" or *Le peintre de la vie moderne*.

suggestif is imported from the English.[15] In the database *Frantext* the first occurrences in French of *suggestif* are from Baudelaire and Flaubert, in the year of the publication of *Les Fleurs du mal* and *Madame Bovary*. The next occurrences are from Baudelaire's translations of Poe. Baudelaire probably, and significantly, discovered the word *suggestive* when reading Poe, in whom he claimed to have found explicit thoughts exactly like his own. In 1852 he writes to his mother: "I have found an American author who has aroused in me an incredible sympathy".[16] The new word reappears in the introduction to an unpublished article, which Baudelaire worked on during the last years of his life, opposing the heresy of didactic or "Philosophical Art" to his own conception of "pure art":

> What is the modern conception of pure art? It is to create a suggestive magic containing at the same time the object and the subject, the world outside the artist and the artist himself. (Baudelaire II, 598)[17]

The first use of the adjective registered by *Frantext* is in Baudelaire's panegyric article on *Madame Bovary*, which he finds "essentially suggestive" – especially since he can recognise in Emma not only the specific traits of the hysterical and therefore suggestible poet, but also the novelist's masculine soul, infused into "a charming female body" (Baudelaire II, 81). In Flaubert's letter of reply, the word *suggestif* seems to echo the same topos of spiritual transmission or sympathy of souls: "You have entered into the arcana of the work, as if my brain were yours. It is deeply understood and felt. If you find my book suggestive, this equally applies to what you have written about it".[18] Far from the earnest tone of this letter, the same Flaubert uses the topos of mesmeric sympathy in a most ironical way in the novel Baudelaire found so suggestive. During the agricultural show in the second part of the novel, one may recall the progress of Rodolphe's monologue of seduction, intertwined with the official speeches on agriculture's contributions to the progress of

---

15 *The Oxford English Dictionary* quotes examples from 1828 and 1856 where *suggestive* is applied to literature: Richard Whateley's *Elements of Rhetoric* from 1828; "The suggestive kind of writing we are speaking of".

16 "J'ai trouvé un auteur americain qui a excité en moi une incroyable sympathie" (27.3.1852).

17 Cf. Cl. Pichois's note (Baudelaire, II 1377-78).

18 "Vous êtes entré dans les arcanes de l'œuvre, comme si ma cervelle était la vôtre. Cela est compris est senti à fond. Si vous trouvez mon livre suggestif, ce que vous avez écrit dessus ne l'est pas moins" (Flaubert, *Correspondance* 1857).

THE ART OF DISCOVERY

civilisation. While fragments of the grandiloquent discourses on farming, cattle and manures comment sarcastically on the seducer's strategic use of romantic clichés, Rodolphe, adopting a melancholic pose, suggests to Emma that their encounter is the result of some predestined magnetic sympathy:

> Rodolphe was talking dreams, presentiments, magnetism (…) From magnetism little by little Rodolphe had come to affinities, and while the president was citing Cincinnatus and his plough, Diocletian planting his cabbages, and the emperors of China inaugurating the year by the sowing of seed, the young man was explaining to the young woman that these irresistible attractions find their cause in some previous state of existence. "Thus we, he said, why did we come to know each other? What chance willed it? It was because across the infinite, like two streams that flow but to unite, our special bents of mind have driven us towards each other." And he seized her hand; she did not withdraw it. (Flaubert 202)

HYPNOTIC POETRY

In Flaubert's letter to Baudelaire, suggestiveness had to do with identification through reading, an ideal later claimed by the *sympathetic* criticism of George Poulet. The word *suggestif* became useful to the symbolists and later admirers of Baudelaire who apply it to works of art in the meaning "thought inspiring", "dream provoking". With his article on *Madame Bovary*, Baudelaire seems to have contributed to the launch of a literary cliché still heard, but not often considered. The question is to which extent the poet and critic, when speaking of suggestive art, implied the idea of a universal fluid communicated from the artist through the work of art and to the receiver.

The stereotypical attribution of the adjective *suggestive* to poetic writing may be a reminder of how the animal magnetism model, uniting micro- and macro-cosmos through the dynamic interplay of universal analogy, polarity, rhythm and "magnetic" force, may be applied to the poem. The transfer is obvious, at least with Baudelaire's texts, and not only due to the traditional conception of the world as divine poetry and the human poet as an imitator or a rival to God's creation. One might say that all reading is a form of trance, eliminating all external stimuli in favour of the imaginary deployment of other possible identities, communities or worlds within the mind. The conventional forms and expectations of poetry may enforce this possibility of trancelike submersions into the text. The visual, auditory and semantic concentration of a few, symmetrical lines, isolated by broad white margins, encourages dissociation. The receptiveness of the reader to the poem's suggestions may be prepared by the soothing monotony and impression of circularity, which are common effects of repetition. Isolated from its context, the poem may serve as a hypnotising pendulum in front of the eyes of the reader, producing detachment from the habitual, deepening of feeling and perception, a disposition to grasp hidden correspondences, to accept contradiction and paradox, and identify oneself with the other I through reconfiguration of personal patterns or leitmotivs. The poem's *charm* (Frye 293) gives access to a living universe governed by analogy and polarity; the rhyming of sound, syntax and meaning providing lines of communication by which the energy of the text may flow through all its elements and resound in the reader.

A poetical task for neuroscience would be to compare the alpha waves characteristic of dream, hypnosis and somnambulism with the electronic currents emitted by the brain while it is under the influence of the rotating verses – "Valse mélancolique et langoureux vertige" – of one of Baudelaire's most suggestive poems.

WORKS CITED

Adelon, Nicolas-Philibert et al. *Dictionaire des sciences médicales par une société de medécins et de chirurgiens.* 60 vols. Paris: C.L.F. Panckoucke, 1812-22.

Balzac, Honoré de Balzac. *Œuvres complètes.* 12 vols. Ed. P.-G. Castex et al. Paris: Gallimard, 1976-1981.

Base textuelle Frantext, Accessed 15 June 2009 at URL http://atilf.atilf.fr/frantext.htm.

Baudelaire, Charles. *Œuvres complètes.* 2 vols. Ed. Claude Pichois, Paris: Gallimard, 1971 and 1975.

Béguin, Albert. *L'Âme romantique et le rêve: Essai sur le romantisme allemand et la poésie française.* Paris: José Corti, 1969.

Chertok, Léon. *Hypnosis.* Oxford: Pergamon Press, 1966.

Darnton, Robert. *Mesmerism and the End of Enlightenment in France.* Cambridge: Harvard University Press, 1968.

Descartes, René. *Discours de la méthode.* Paris: Fayard, 1987.

Flaubert, Gustave. *Madame Bovary.* Paris: Gallimard, 1972.

—. *Madame Bovary.* Trans. Eleanor Marx Aveling. Accessed 10 April 2009 at URL http://www.gutenberg.org/etext/2413.

Frye, Northrop. "Rhetorical Criticism." *Anatomy of Criticism.* Princeton: Princeton University Press, 1957. 243-326.

Hansen, Uffe. *Psykoanalysens fortrængte fortid. Hypnotisøren Carl Hansen og Sigmund Freud.* København: Akademisk forlag, 1991.

Lévi, Eliphas. *La science des esprits, Révélation du dogme secret des kabalistes, Esprit occulte des Évangiles, Appréciation des doctrines et des phénomènes spirites.* Paris: Éditions de la Maisnie, 1976.

Levi, Primo. "The Force of Amber." *Other People's Trades*. Trans. R. Rosenthal, London: Simon & Schuster, 1987.

Mesmer, Franz Anton. *Mesmerism: A Translation of the Original Scientific and Medical Writings of F.A. Mesmer*. Trans. G. Bloch. California: W. Kaufmann, 1980.

Nerval, Gérard de. *Œuvres complètes*. Paris: Gallimard, 1989.

—. *Aurelia*. Trans. Richard Aldington. London: Chatto & Windus, 1932.

Orne, Martin T. "Hypnosis" in *Encyclopædia Britannica Online*. Accessed 10 June 2009 at URL http://search.ebcom/eb/article-9041814.

Poe, Edgar Allan. "Mesmeric Revelation". *The Complete Illustrated Works of E.A. Poe*. London: Octopus Publishing Group, 1981. 587-594.

"Researchers find that hypnosis can induce synesthesia", PHYSORG.COM 23 October 2008. Accessed 8 December 2009 <www.physorg.com/news43994178.html>.

Roustang, François. *Qu'est-ce que l'hypnose?* Paris: Minuit, 1994.

Starobinski, Jean. "Jalons pour une histoire du concept d'imagination." *La relation critique*. Paris: Gallimard, 1970. 173-195.

—. "Sur l'histoire des fluides imaginaires". *La relation critique*. Paris: Gallimard, 1970. 196-213.

Stengers, Isabelle. *L'Hypnose entre magie et science*. Paris: Les Empêcheurs de penser en rond, 2002.

Warner, E. and G. Hough, eds., *Strangeness and Beauty: An Anthology of Aesthetic Criticism*, 2 vols. Cambridge: Cambridge University Press, 1983.

Waterfield, Robin. *Hidden Depths. The Story of Hypnosis*. London: Routledge, 2003.

Zweig, Stefan. *Mental Healers: Franz Mesmer, Mary Baker Eddy, Sigmund Freud*. Eng. trans. Eden and Cedar Paul. New York: The Viking Press, 1932.

FROM HEREDITY OF ACQUIRED TRAITS TO ATAVISM:

THE IMPACT OF DARWIN ON SCANDINAVIAN LITERATURE

Eivind Tjønneland, University of Bergen

The impact of Darwin on Scandinavian authors, such as Ibsen, is well known. In 1878, Ibsen met the Danish translator of Darwin, J.P. Jacobsen, in Italy. Dr. Rank in the draft manuscripts to *A Doll's House* (1879) and Dr. Stockmann in *An Enemy of the People* (1882) clearly advocate Darwinian ideas. Further, the theme of heredity in *Ghosts* (1881) and in *Rosmersholm* (1886) fits well with an evolutionary perspective. In *The Lady from the Sea* (1888) Ibsen took the full step towards an adaptation of Darwin: All life began in the sea, and therefore some human beings still have a yearning towards their origin. Ibsen's use of Darwin is not scientific but highly eclectic and poetic. A fact almost totally ignored in Norwegian literary history, however, is the impact of Lamarck-Darwinism on literature in the early 1880s. Ibsen's *Ghosts* can also be understood within this paradigm, as indeed Georg Brandes suggests in his review of Ibsen's play (Tjønneland 2005a).

My general hypothesis is that different interpretations of Darwin can help us to understand the shift from naturalistic determinism to neo-romanticism and decadence in Scandinavian literature around 1890. The focus changes from the belief in heredity of acquired characteristics, i.e. Lamarckism, to a greater interest in atavism. It is not easy to decide exactly when and why this transition took place. There are many missing links in my story, and my main purpose in writing this chapter is to try to connect the pieces of the puzzle and see what they form together. The Modern Breakthrough in Scandinavian literature is connected with the belief in rapid change and development made possible by the theory of inheritance of acquired traits. When this idea of the "new human being" is discarded, the result is pessimism, which is indeed the philosophy of the decadent hero in literature of the 1890s. The evolutionary paradigm itself, however, is not rejected. When the educational optimism of the 1880s is seen to have no effect on the human race, the more unpredictable side of Darwinism – the sudden rise of atavism – becomes more acceptable to the neo-romantics. Combined with Cesare Lombroso's well known theory of the genius, the criminal and the madman as different types of degeneration, the Swedish author Ola Hansson's essay on Edgar A. Poe from 1893 clearly demonstrates this point.

The Danish author Karl Gjellerup, who won the Nobel Prize for literature with Henrik Pontoppidan in 1917, strongly advocated a kind of Lamarckism. Gjellerup defended the belief in the heredity of acquired traits in his *Arvelighed og Moral* [Heredity and Morality] (1881). Nearly twenty years later the influential Norwegian critic Carl Nærup rejected Lamarckism in his essay "Arvelighed og Arvelighedsteorier" [Heredity and Theories of Heredity] (1899). Summarising the history of the theories of heredity and evolution, Nærup described the conflict between the neo-Darwinists (Weismann, Wallace, Ray Lankester), who rejected the idea of heredity of acquired traits, and the so-called Lamarck-Darwinists (Spencer, E.D. Cope, Romanes), who supported this idea. Nærup gave a presentation of Weismann's theory of "Vererbung" and made clear that "the absolute presupposition for Weismann's theory is the rejection of hereditary acquired characteristics" (603). Convinced by Weismann, Nærup rejected the theory of acquired traits. He mentioned circumcision by Jews and the Chinese custom of deforming women's feet as strong cases against the heredity of acquired traits: If this theory was right, then one should be able to observe the effect on Jewish penises or Chinese women's feet, but in fact one cannot. Nærup also admits that the question is complicated and has great consequences. "The question of the heredity of acquired characteristics is unconditionally the most difficult that human thought today can be committed to, and its consequences are the most far reaching" (Nærup 603). The Lamarck-Darwinists encountered much resistance around the turn of the century, but works defending this position were still published, for example Eugenio Rignano's book *Upon the Inheritance of Acquired Characters*, which appeared in an American translation in 1911.

Around 1880, however, the situation was different. It was generally believed that inheriting acquired character traits was possible, a belief that is now discarded. The view on heredity also had great consequences for the belief in improving the human race by establishing good habits of conduct. When "organically" organised, habits were thought to be inheritable. The possibility of transferring one generation's acquired badness or goodness to the next became strikingly real – and human conduct came under immense pressure. Optimism and pessimism with regard to future generations were thus to a large extent made dependent upon the contemporary ethical conduct of human beings. To a large extent, Ibsen scholars have tended to explain the power of posterity on the dramatic characters and the resulting pessimism in psychoanalytic terms, by means of the compulsion to repeat in a Freudian sense. By contrast the evolutionary theories current at Ibsen's time have been neglected, such as in the research on *Ghosts* (Tjønneland 2005a).

Samuel Butler, who published the Lamarckian book *Unconscious Memory* with translations of Ewald Hering (1870) and Eduard von Hartmann, says he "was horrified to find the following passage" in Darwin's *Origin of Species* (206) where Darwin doubted the inheritance of acquired traits:

> But it would be a serious error to suppose that the greater number of instincts have been acquired by habit in one generation and then transmitted by inheritance to the succeeding generations. It can be clearly shown that the most wonderful instincts with which we are acquainted, namely, those of the hive-bee and of many ants, could not possibly have been acquired by habit. (Butler 35-36)

The first part of Gjellerup's *Arvelighed og Moral*, for which he won the gold medal from the University of Copenhagen in 1880, and which was printed as a book with a foreword dated August 1881, differentiated between physiological heredity, psychological heredity, heredity of memory, and heredity of intelligence, emotion and the will. The second part of the book discusses the consequences of heredity for morality. Antiquity already knew a kind of moral heredity in the case of alcoholism. Diogenes is said to have shouted to a young drunkard: "Young man, You were begotten by an alcoholic father!" (Gjellerup 1881,10). Gjellerup agrees with Proctor Lucas' work *Hérédité naturelle* (Paris 1847-50) in claiming that a habit that has been "organised" in the individual can be inherited almost as easily as a natural trait. When a habit is organised in this way, a corresponding nerve structure has developed (Gjellerup 59). The examples provided in support of such arguments are often curious: for instance, Gjellerup claims that branded horses can give birth to offspring with inherited branding. The state of mind at the moment of conception can also have an effect on the offspring. On this point Gjellerup is critical of Lucas. If the father is under the influence of alcohol when he begets the child, any subsequent effect on the child could still be due to the general depravity of the father, not simply his intoxication at the moment of conception. Thus the idiotism of children conceived in a state of intoxication could be due to the general degeneration of the father (Gjellerup 61).

Are freedom and liberation possible when their predecessor's patterns of conduct determine the actions of a human being? Gjellerup's main point is that the propensity for moral action is *naturalised* through hereditary development. Gjellerup is a strong advocate of both naturalism and determinism, stating that human action can be explained psychologically as being determined by character and motives (363). Acquired habits have an impact on the organisation of the nervous system, and can thus be inherited by the next generation. Freedom of the will is an illusion, and can be compared to the illusion of a werewolf (196). Freedom is to act in accordance with nature, i.e. with necessity. Influenced by Herbert Spencer, Gjellerup thought that in the long term this form of evolutionary heredity would create more happiness for humanity. The interaction between the organism and its surroundings over the generations would make the correspondence between the two more and more perfect. Humans would therefore become happier when the conflict between the individual and its environment was mediated (Gjellerup 365).

Gjellerup was of course aware of the fact that not only negative or destructive, but also positive traits can be inherited. But happiness understood as the absence of pain and the greatest possible pleasure is also the law of adaptation to the environment: Individuals who experience much pain will be less successful in reproducing themselves, and are thus headed for extinction. Moral development goes from duty to virtue. As time goes by, a disposition for good action becomes embedded in the individual as a new nature. The conflict of interest between egoistic and altruistic action will therefore eventually fade away. This is moral development, according to Gjellerup.

During the 1880s the optimism of the Modern Breakthrough faded. The evolutionary paradigm was not discarded, but attained a different focus. A mystical principle within evolutionary theory, namely atavism, came to the fore. Atavism can be defined as an unpredictable regression towards earlier evolutionary stages. Atavism could be a blessing as well as a curse. As Cesare Lombroso pointed out, both the man of genius as well as the criminal and the lunatic were results of atavism.

Lamarckism was reasonable, allowing the species to make itself better or happier. The relationship between effort and reward seemed just. When the Larmarck-Darwinian paradigm broke down, cultural optimism and the possibility of directing evolution by means of reason were discarded as well. The pessimism of the decadence movement in Scandinavia, whose representatives included the Danish author Herman Bang, the Swedish author Ola Hansson and Arne Garborg in Norway, could partly be seen as a result of the breakdown of the Lamarck-Darwinian paradigm. A positive change from one generation to the next through the effort of previous generations was no longer possible. Thus heredity became more irrational, and atavism was promoted as the new irrational principle of evolutionary theory. It seems as if atavism so to speak replaced the belief in the heredity of acquired characteristics. But there are several undiscovered "missing links" in this evolution. The inheritance of acquired traits was a principle of rationality. In his *Parias* stories Ola Hansson depicted instinct-driven maniacs like the woman who killed her own child in a somnambulistic state of mind. And in his scandalous collection of short stories, *Sensitiva Amorosa* (1887), his project was to show how whims, impulses and sudden associations could lead action on to a path which went beyond good and evil. Hansson's short stories could have been one of the impulses behind Knut Hamsun's new poetics of the unconscious (Tjønneland 2005b).

Of course, this new importance given to atavism and basic instincts made ethical responsible action difficult, even impossible. Reading Ola Hansson's short stories, we are far from the utopia of Karl Gjellerup, who dreamt of the ultimate adaptation of man to his environment. The opposite is now the case: Irrational atavism becomes the new subversive principle which attracts artists and authors. When Ola Hansson wrote a 70-page essay on Edgar Allen Poe, he located the poet's genius in atavism. Hansson followed the evolutionist Théodule Ribot's (1875, 1881) description of the pathology of will and memory. The principle is simple: The last stage in the development of a faculty is the first to disappear. This is a biological law, Hansson claimed. Those functions that are most recently acquired are the first to degenerate, both in the individual and in the species (Hansson 49).

Thus language connected with rationality will disappear first, then emotional language like interjections, and finally body language like facial expressions and gesture. Hansson found it likely that these symptoms of degeneration were expressions of atavism, so called "atavistiske Tilbagefald" (atavistic regression) (50). Atavism functioned like a joker: According to Ola Hansson, it is impossible to say anything precise about it. He spoke of it as an unknown entity, as unconquered depths in human nature, as "the misty realms of unconscious drives" (Hansson 58). Hansson had clearly read Lombroso, a fact which he also mentioned. Lombroso studied poetic language as an example of degeneration and atavism. According to Lombroso, the insane had a tendency to use alliteration and rhyme instead of logic (Lombroso 170). This was in accordance with atavism, because "among primitive peoples, all thinkers and sages were poets" (Lombroso 172). In his chapter about "insane genius in literature" Lombroso mentioned an insane person who wrote in a "mixture of letters, hieroglyphics, and figurative signs". This person experienced "so to speak a phonetic-ideographic stage through which primitive peoples passed, before the discovery of alphabetic writing".

Lombroso claimed that he was initially repelled by the idea that genius was a special morbid condition. But an analogy from the evolution of the species suddenly made him less reluctant. By losing muscles and the tail, i.e. by means of degeneration, human beings won something else, namely intellectual superiority. In the same way, the man of genius must pay for his intellectual force by degeneration and psychoses. Lombroso also tried to explain the bodily weakness of the mentally strong by the "law of the conservation of energy which rules the whole organic world" (7). One typical trait of the genius is atavism, according to Lombroso. For example, precociousness is a sign of atavism, and "it can be observed by all savages" (Lombroso 16). Another indication of atavism is the propensity of the genius to create by means of compulsion and instinct.

What role did atavism play in the earlier theories of heredity, for example that of Gjellerup in *Heredity and Morals*? Gjellerup defined atavism as a kind of heredity from grandfather to grandchildren or even further back (11). This kind of heredity made a leap over several generations (67). Gjellerup claimed the upsurge of atavism was dependent upon which ancient hereditary part was best able to adapt. Tame pigs will change into wild pigs when set free, thus the environment strengthens atavistic heredity (67-68). With crossbreeding, atavism is more likely to happen. Gjellerup refers to an observation by Livingstone, who claimed that mulattos are more inclined to cruelty than other human beings. Cruelty was of course seen as an atavistic trait associated with wildness. Unfortunate circumstances or a bad environment could hold the atavism in a latent state for generations. For Gjellerup atavism was not, however, as it was for Lombroso, a principle behind genius and poetic creation.

When atavism emerged as a new "ape energy" in the neo-romantic poetics in the 1890s as an explanation of artistic creativity, this represented a major change in the meaning of the concept. I believe that this change was made possible by the vacuum created when the theory of acquired traits was discarded. Some new principle had to fill the void in the theory of heredity. The mysterious works of atavism could – at least for a time – give the neo-romantics an explanation of their identity as creative artists.

WORKS CITED

Butler, Samuel. *Unconscious Memory: A Comparison between The Theory of Dr. Ewald Hering and The "Philosophy of the Unconscious" of Dr. Edward von Hartmann.* London: David Bogue, 1880.

Gjellerup, Karl. *Arvelighed og Moral: en Undersøgelse.* Copenhagen: Andr. Schous Forlag, 1881.

Hansson, Ola. "Edgar Allan Poe". *Tolke og Seere.* Kristiania, Aschehoug, 1893. 1-71.

Hering, Ewald. "Über das Gedächtnis als eine allgemeine Funktion der Organisierten Materie". Hering, Ewald. *Vier Reden.* Amsterdam: E.J. Bonset, 1870. 1969. 5-31.

Lombroso, Cesare. *The Man of Genius.* London: Walter Scott, 1891.

Nærup, Carl. "Arveligheds- og udviklingstheorier". *Ringeren* Vol. II, 1899: 50-51, 598-605.

Ribot, Th. *Heredity: A psychological study of its phenomena, laws, causes, and consequences.* London: Henry S. King & Co, 1875.

Ribot, Th. *Les Maladies de la Mémoire.* Paris: Libraire Germer Baillière, 1881.

Rignano, Eugenio. *Upon the Inheritance of Acquired Characters.* Chicago: The Open Court Publishing Co, 1911.

Tjønneland, Eivind. "Darwin, J.P. Jacobsen og Ibsen". *Spring: Tidsskrift for moderne dansk Litteratur,* no. 13, (1998): 178-199.

—. "Repetition, Recollection and Heredity in Ibsen's *Ghosts*: the Context of Intellectual History." *Ibsen on the Cusp of the 21st Century.* Ed. Bjørby/Dvergsdal/ Stegane. Laksevåg: Alvheim & Eide Akademisk Forlag, 2005a. 193-205.

—. "*Sult* og 'Fra det ubevidste Sjæleliv'". *Den litterære Hamsun.* Ed. Ståle Dingstad. Bergen: Fagbokforlaget, 2005b. 143-158.

THE MATERNAL BODY IN SIGRID UNDSET'S WRITINGS:

BETWEEN SCIENTIFIC OBJECT AND SOCIAL CONSTRUCTION

Christine Hamm, University of Bergen

When Sigrid Undset published her novel *Jenny* in 1911, she was attacked by conservative as well as feminist critics not because of her literary style, but because of her description of the protagonist's erotic life. *Jenny* is the tragic story of a 28-year-old successful and independent woman artist, who ends up committing suicide because she cannot live up to her own ideal of chastity, and because she cannot fulfil her dreams of being a mother and wife.

As the feminist critic Jofrid Eriksson pointed out in her 1977 article on the novel, Undset's text starts by attacking the ideal of the nuclear family and seems to proclaim a new era for women. Strangely, this attack is turned completely on its head, and the novel ends up defending the same values it criticised (Eriksson 89-90). Eriksson's reading shows that feminists of the 1970s had the same issues with the novel as the feminists at Sigrid Undset's own time: How should they relate to the belief in motherhood as women's destiny, especially when it turns out destructive? And how should they react to Undset's obvious claim that work is not enough to fulfil a woman's desires? As Jenny tells her friend Gunnar in a conversation about men and women's devotion to art, men might think that their work is what makes their life worth living, but "naturally, women have other tasks –."[1] Women have a strong desire to have a family, Jenny claims: "For a woman, having a husband and children... At any rate, sooner or later we start yearning for that." (Page 160) And she maintains that women were created like that. Does Undset, the author, share her protagonist's opinions? Does Undset believe that women will become mothers because "nature" wants them to, or is she pointing to an idea many women at that time had? Is she problematising

---

[1]   *My translation.* In this article, I have made use of the English translation by Tiina Nunnally (Page 2001). In some cases, however, I felt obliged to translate the text myself. The Norwegian runs: "kvinnen har jo naturlig andre oppgaver –." (*Jenny* 161)

the role of nature, or is she, to use a modern concept, a biological determinist, or even an essentialist, when it comes to her understanding of gender?

Just before she wrote *Jenny,* Undset had herself been an artist in Rome, and autobiographical details are certainly important elements of the literary text. Of course, one should be careful to argue that everything in the protagonist's life also was part of the author's life.[2] In my view, the important fact in the case of *Jenny* is just that author and protagonist both have a female body, and this female body becomes important to them both as a situation, and in a historical situation. Because of this focus on the body as and in a situation, I want to suggest a phenomenological approach to the text which is inspired by Maurice Merleau-Ponty.

In the last part of this article, I will reach the conclusion that it makes no sense to integrate the distinction between sex as a biologically defined essence and gender as a social construction in a reading of Undset's writings. This distinction has been much debated in gender research during the last decades, and as a consequence of this ongoing discussion, feminist readers are now expected to choose between certain theoretical perspectives when approaching literary texts. I will argue, though, that Undset, about a century ago, never wanted to make a general claim about the (maternal) body and its functioning. The female reproductive organs were just about to be known to researchers and other scientists, and the exact nature of their operation and significance was much debated. Undset's groundbreaking novel *Jenny* takes part in this debate. In her text, Undset analyses the protagonist's body as both a starting point and a background for her different projects (becoming an artist, enjoying a free lifestyle in Rome, finding a fiancé, being a single mother). When we want to understand Undset's views on female sexuality, we should look closely at how, and under what circumstances, she lets Jenny say the things she does. We should ask: What kind of project did Undset have in mind when writing her novel? Is it, indeed, a response to an important question of her time, namely the question of how to understand the implications of the female reproductive system?

In order to answer these questions, I would like to start by considering how Undset reacts to feminist responses to scientific explanations of the female reproductive system. I wish to focus on her critique of Katti Anker Møller's "Women's maternity politics" [Kvindernes fødselspolitik] (1919) and Charlotte Perkins Gilman's *The Man-Made World* (1911). I will try to show

---

2   See also Sigrun Slapgard's introductory remarks on the relation between life and literary work on p. 9 in the Undset biography *Dikterdronningen* (2006).

that these two texts can be read as interpretations of scientific discoveries about the female reproductive system and the way reproduction worked more generally, and that Undset disagreed with these interpretations. I will then return to *Jenny* and show how Undset herself presents the maternal body in her novel of 1911.

In his *Phenomenology of Perception* (1945), Merleau-Ponty approaches sexuality in much the same way as Undset does in *Jenny*. I hope to show that they both see the body in its sexual being as playing an important role in our understanding of the body's functioning more generally. The body is not something a human being has, it is what opens the person to the world and, as a consequence, what makes existence possible. Merleau-Ponty writes that erotic attraction is especially apt to let us see that our body has an intentionality; the body is not something that can be controlled, but something we have to deal with because it is our situation:

> There is an erotic 'comprehension' not of the order of understanding, since un derstanding subsumes an experience, once perceived, under some idea, while desire comprehends blindly by linking body to body. Even in the case of sexuality, which has nevertheless long been regarded as preeminently the type of bodily function, we are concerned, not with a peripheral involuntary action, but with an intentionality which follows the general flow of existence and yields to its movements. (181)

For Merleau-Ponty, as it was to be for Simone de Beauvoir, the human body is the background, and our projects are defined and/or limited by this background. More specifically, this means that men and women can have the same projects and be successful with them, but it means also that some projects are difficult for men but easy for women, and *vice versa*. In the perspective of Merleau-Ponty, we could say that Undset is interested in analysing the different ways the female body can function as a background for a woman's humanity, becoming part of her lived experience, rather than defining her. As Merleau-Ponty makes clear in the introductory pages of his study, he is interested in finding out not how our bodies differ, but how our different bodies give us different lives. In the preface, he writes:

> I am not the outcome or the meeting-point of numerous causal agencies which determine my bodily or psychological make-up. I cannot conceive myself as nothing but a bit of the world, a mere object of biological, psychological or sociological investigation. I cannot shut myself up within the realm of science.

All my knowledge of the world, even my scientific knowledge, is gained from my own particular point of view, or from some experience of the world without which the symbols of science would be meaningless. (ix)

According to Merleau-Ponty, the body is the background to our scientific understanding of the body, one might say. In order to understand the maternal body, one needs to look at the situations in which the body takes on a certain meaning for an individual. What Undset provides in her book is thus not a general theory about the female body and its meaning, as presented by her contemporary scientist and their feminist opponents. Undset wants to remind her readers of the importance of closely observing a specific situation and the many circumstances that an individual is exposed to, in order to understand the female body and its reproductive system.

UNDSET'S CRITIQUE OF THE MISUSE OF SCIENTIFIC DISCOVERIES

In 1919 the Norwegian newspaper *Tidens Tegn* published an essay by Undset called "Confusion of Concepts" [Begrepsforvirring], one of the author's most famous and also most criticised essays on the situation of women at the beginning of the 20th century. Undset attacks Katti Anker Møller's paper "Women's maternity politics", which was given as a lecture earlier that year. A well-known advocate of women's rights, Anker Møller had proposed that if mothering was not regarded as serious work, and was not paid for in the near future, women should go on strike, by which she meant that they should stop getting pregnant. She had proclaimed: "To control conception is the only weapon women have to promote our interests, and it will render the living conditions of mothers and children new and better. *A new era of motherhood will rise*"(52).[3] Anker Møller was an ardent lecturer and writer, actively spreading knowledge about contraceptive methods. She organised women's clinics, where women (especially mothers) could learn more about the organisation of their bodies.

Undset's main critique concerns Anker Møller's mixing of the realm of biology and sexuality with the realm of politics: Using economic and often explicitly Marxist terminology, Anker Møller interprets the maternal body as a production machine and the family as a modern industrial under-

---

3   All translations from Norwegian are mine, with the exception of most of the translations from Undset's novel *Jenny*.

taking. In Anker Møller's account, the father becomes the capitalistic leader exploiting his employees, Undset claims: "The lady's idea of a 'family' seems to be that it is something like an industrial undertaking, where a man pays a woman to give birth to, and to raise, his children." (*Essays* 334) Undset was against such a misuse of scientific results that had become available to the masses by way of popular papers, and she diagnosed Anker Møller's brain as "anaesthetized by the most ordinary quasi-scientific abracadabra." (*Essays* 334)

Insights into the female reproductive system were gradually gained by scientists from the beginning of the 19th century, and one could read about them in, for instance, the popular journal *Naturen*, which Sigrid Undset's father Ingvald Undset and many other bourgeois intellectuals subscribed to (Bliksrud 47). *Naturen* was published monthly by the Bergen Museum and provided the Norwegian public with knowledge of current research in the field. Readers of the journal would learn that it took more than a century for scientists to understand how the female body works and how the human egg develops.

According to Thomas Laqueur's account in *Making Sex* (1990), the German-Estonian biologist C.E. von Baer was the first "actually to see the mammalian ova", in 1828, but he thought that the production of the egg (in his dog) was due to the fact that the dog had recently been mated (Laqueur 184). In 1843 Theodor von Bischoff proved him wrong, showing that *his* bitch had ovulation without coitus, but he added that the bitch had nevertheless been interested in having contact with a male dog. At the same time, Bischoff commented that he did not think this would be the same in women; he doubted that they would ovulate without intercourse.

Such speculations indicate that scientists did not understand the production of the egg, and that they were wondering if coitus, orgasm or sexual excitement in any form were necessary in order to ovulate. Women would tell doctors how they enjoyed intercourse with their husbands, but that they still were not pregnant. Other women would get pregnant although they had not enjoyed having sex with their husbands. Quite astonishingly, the first systematic modern survey of "normal" women's sexual feelings was conducted as late as 1892 by the physician and women's health advocate Clelia Duel Mosher. The result of her study was that it was hard to say anything in general about the sexuality of women, and even less about its role in human reproduction, more specifically ovulation and conception (Laqueur 191).

It was not until 1930 that an unfertilised egg was found in a woman, and scientists concluded that sexual arousal had nothing to do with the development of the egg. Until that time, there was no precise understanding of the connection between ovulation and menstruation either: The breakthrough came around 1910 with Papanicolaou's studies of the cytology of the cervical mucosa, which gave a reliable insight into the female cycle. This was followed shortly after by an awareness of the hormonal control of ovulation (Laqueur 213).

The ongoing exploration of the female reproductive system was partly covered by *Naturen*. In 1902, for instance, readers were informed of several experiments conducted in order to see if it was possible to artificially initiate the development of a female egg cell;[4] in 1912 they could enjoy a long article on the impact of physical-chemical processes on conception.[5] While the 1902 article was careful to state that the experiments described were still "in their beginnings", the 1912 article was more optimistic, claiming that it could now be said that "the question of conception is principally solved, it can be fully accounted for by physical-chemical processes."[6]

The growing scientific insight into the independence of sexuality on the one side and the reproductive system on the other allowed women to understand that it was possible to choose whether to have children or not. Various kinds of texts were published to make the new scientific results useful for women, for instance the book *Married Love* (1918), written by the paleobotanist Mary Stopes.[7] Stopes, however, was incorrect in her description of the female cycle; being a leading scientist, she was unsure of the significance of menstruation for ovulation. She thus advises in her book: "It is generally found that the most certain date for conception is – with very few exceptions – about the last day of the monthly period, or the day or two immediately after it; so that the husband who ardently desires his wife to conceive should, with her consent, concentrate their unions so far as possible on such dates" (126). But Stopes was even more concerned

---

4   See "Kunstig 'befrugtning' af eg med kemikalier og organiske ekstraktivstoffe" by O.J.L.-P. in *Naturen, illustreret maanedsskrift for populær naturvidenskab*. Published by Bergens Museum, Bergen and Copenhagen 1902, 249-251.

5   The article is a translation from the French text by Jacques Loeb, and is called "Livet", see *Naturen, illustreret maanedsskrift for populær naturvidenskab*. Published by Bergens Museum, Bergen and Copenhagen 1912, 163-175 and 246-251.

6   "spørsmaalet om befrugtningen er løst i princippet; den kan helt tilbakeføres til fysisk-kemiske processer." (Naturen 1912, 166).

7   Mary Stopes' book was directed to women who wanted control over conception. Her text was translated into Norwegian by the Norwegian feminist Katti Anker Møller, and distributed by the maternity clinics in Oslo. See Johansen 1998, 179.

about spreading this (ironically false) information about the "fertile" days to women who would like to avoid pregnancy, without having to renounce intercourse. Her goal clearly was to enhance sexual satisfaction for married women, and to enable them to choose if and when they wanted to become mothers.

Feminists such as Anker Møller reacted to the publication of scientific results, as did Mary Stopes, by trying to make them useful for women. But it is also important to understand that the question of motherhood had become an urgent question precisely because the scientific results seemed to confirm the leading idea of the 19th century, namely that men and women were fundamentally different, since they had radically different reproductive systems. The same discoveries, which made it possible for women to control reproduction, were used by scientists to explain social theories. They claimed that women were destined by nature to take on certain roles – especially that of a mother. As Toril Moi describes it in her essay "What is a woman?", the scientific discoveries as they were described, for instance, in W.K. Brooks's book *The Law of Heredity* from 1883 and Patrick Geddes' and J. Arthur Thomson's *The Evolution of Sex* from 1889, had ended up giving a picture of sex as being all-pervasive. The sex cells determined the whole human being, since the sperm cell and the ovum were seen as protozoa, and thus the only cells in the human body that date back to the earliest stages of evolution. A woman was now a woman to her fingertips, or worse, she was a gigantic egg in herself: "For these writers, a man is essentially an enormous sperm cell, a woman a giant ovum" (Moi 20). This naturally meant that females were destined to become mothers; they were constantly producing eggs waiting to be inseminated, and they first and foremost needed to be seen as possible mothers. The very possibility a woman had of turning her body into a maternal body was thus not seen as something that implied freedom to choose motherhood, but it was used in an argument that would reduce every woman's body to a body destined for pregnancy.

From the turn of the century onwards, feminists intensified their efforts to counteract these interpretations by reinterpretations of scientific discoveries. Charlotte Perkins Gilman's reinterpretation of Darwin in *The Man-Made World* (1911), which was influenced by the botanist and sociologist Lester F. Ward's *Pure Sociology* (1898), may serve as an example. In the Darwinian theory of natural selection, the passive female animal selects as mates the most aggressive males or the most attractive – the best, in other words. According to Darwin, this is one of the reasons why males are usually more brightly coloured than females. Perkins Gilman thinks that Darwin's theory is fundamentally "androcentric", and applauds Ward's theory, which transforms Darwin's theory into a "gynaecocentric" one by claiming that the female rather than the male is the "race type" (Perkins Gilman 5). But in human beings the males choose the females, thus producing a radically unnatural system, as Perkins Gilman points out: "The man, by violence or by purchase, does the choosing – he selects the kind of woman that pleases him. Nature did not intend him to select; he is not good at it. Neither was the female intended to compete – she is not good at it" (30).

Because this selection of mates is an ongoing process, men and women will differ from one another to an increasing extent, in both body and soul. In *The Man-Made World*, Perkins Gilman did not deny the idea of the sexes being fundamentally different. But she believed women should have more influence when it comes to politics and other areas, precisely because they represent values that men lack:

> Great men, the world's teachers and leaders, are great in humanness; mere male-ness does not make for greatness unless it be in warfare – a disadvantageous glory! Great women also must be great in humanness; but their female instincts are not so subversive of human progress as are the instincts of the male. To be a teacher and leader, to love and serve, to guard and guide and help, are well in line with motherhood. (238-239)

According to Perkins Gilman, women share with female animals the interest in their children; they nurture them, protect them and raise them as best they can. To Perkins Gilman, thus, the feminist struggle for more female influence is connected to the idea that women are good mothers – and better human beings – because biology lets them be mothers.

The Man-Made World was translated into Norwegian in 1912, and in her comment on Perkins Gilman's book, Undset was critical of the famous American feminist. Perkins Gilman had tried to show that the effect that the "unprecedented dominance of the male" had on human development was "by no means an unmixed good" (6). Undset found it especially hard to accept the underlying premise in Perkins Gilman's book; the thought that Darwin's theory of evolution could help to explain why humans organise their lives in an androcentric way. Arguing in part from mere observa-tion of what was happening in society in 1912, Undset claims in her article "Some reflections on feminist issues" ["Noen kvinnesaksbetraktninger"] that Perkins Gilman is simply wrong when she states that women have not influenced the history of mankind, and when she implies that women should play a stronger role in society because the reproductive system of the female body turns the whole woman into a nice and peaceful human being. Undset concludes: "I will admit that I have always been a sceptic when it comes to the theory that the set of properties which, if they can be observed in a woman, are called 'motherly', are directly connected to the woman's physique." (*Essays* 88) Undset does not doubt the scientific data, and she does not doubt that the possibility of giving birth to children influences women's lives. But this influence is not so easily understood as it seems to be in the texts of her contemporary feminists. The fact that the female body can turn into a maternal body does not mean that women necessarily become what we understand as "motherly" (caring and passionate, for instance).

This critique of using scientific data (in this case the theory of evolution) for one's own purposes is in fact an important part of Undset's essays on the position of women. As she puts it in her critique of Katti Anker Møller's approach to the question of how one could turn motherhood into a choice, Undset wants to be more careful when dealing with her contemporaries' scientific knowledge. According to Undset, the microscope cannot give us more knowledge about the relationship between men and women than the cross could in the Middle Ages, precisely because the use of the microscope and the use of the cross are part of a much more complicated net of human relations. She sums up:

> The microscope then almost became for the 19th century what the cross had been in the 12th and the 13th centuries – it was called upon whenever it was opportune. The microscope has given us a better understanding of, for instance, the physiological processes of reproduction. But regarding the more specifically human aspects of the drive for reproduction, regarding what makes us go on, science could not tell us anything we have not known for as long as we have had history and tradition. (*Essays* 330)

UNDSET'S EFFORT TO COME TO TERMS WITH SCIENTIFIC DATA

Considering Undset's critique of the misuse of science so far, it may not come as a surprise that Sigrid Undset was quite fond of reading scientific papers. As the Norwegian Undset scholar Liv Bliksrud points out in *Natur og normer*, a very young Sigrid often had to read aloud to her sick father from the journal *Naturen* (47). During her childhood and youth she likewise collected plants and studied botanic descriptions, an interest she kept up throughout her life. It seems that Undset was especially fond of Carl von Linné. According to Bliksrud, it was mostly Linné's taxonomic system that fascinated Undset, mainly because Linné had organised plants according to their reproductive systems. Bliksrud thinks that Undset was inspired by this taxonomy and that she transferred it to her understanding of women. The individual factor in each woman gives variation to what is seen as the biologically constant essence of femininity, Bliksrud claims: "Undset's thinking works like the taxonomist's: she starts with the idea that the individual properties vary from woman to woman, in contrast to the biologically constant factor that all women are (potential) lovers, housewives and mothers". (55)

It becomes clear, then, that Undset may hardly be read as a social constructivist, as someone who claims that women just turn into mothers because they have to play certain roles. It would also be difficult to explain her image of women as the product of different discourses, among them the scientific one: For Undset, nature is something given and something to be explored, but the meaning of it for human life is very complex and needs to be studied in detail. As I have claimed earlier, she seems to end up with a position close to Merlau-Ponty's philosophy, trying to return to "that world which precedes knowledge, of which knowledge always *speaks*, and in relation to which every scientific schematization is an abstract and derivative sign-language". (Merleau-Ponty x). She is also in line with the more careful scientists of her day, who did not like to jump from the observation of animal behaviour to human relationships. For instance, in his article "On love games in animals" ["Dyrenes kjærlighedslege"], which was published in *Naturen* in 1900, Professor Karl Groos advises against a "far reaching analogy between the psychic life of animals and human beings" (56).

Although Undset's historical approach to all phenomena of daily interaction leads her to believe that one should regard specific images of femininity as the product of various discourses, she holds on to the "fact" that every woman has to deal with her body's possibility of producing a child. I thus agree with Bliksrud in her claim that while Undset is busy pointing out how women differ, she still acknowledges that they share a common set of reproductive organs and other physical characteristics. I would, though, lessen the emphasis on Carl von Linné's importance for her work. As I have tried to show, in her writings Undset responds to many different voices, and she struggles to find her response.

Undset's approach to the question of the female body in *Jenny* resembles an aesthetic experiment in the tradition of the naturalist novel. Following Zola, Undset places a character in a specific historical situation, and then traces this character's emotional and intellectual development. The 28-year-old successful and independent woman artist Jenny longs for a husband and children. Because she is unable to find the perfect man to marry, Jenny takes the next best one and gets engaged to Helge, a young student who is visiting Rome. The loveless engagement is a disappointment and they split up. Soon after she becomes involved with Helge's father Gert, but leaves him when she discovers that she is pregnant with him. She decides to live as a single mother and artist, but when her newborn son dies after just a few weeks, she is unable to take up her painting. She commits suicide having been raped by Helge.

In Undset's approach the focus is constantly on the notion of the body and its meaning for the female character's life. For instance, the beginning of the novel contains a picture of the protagonist's body, but this picture is demonstratively viewed by one of the male characters: It is Helge Gram who observes Jenny with her friend Cesca in the streets of Rome. To Helge the two women are direct opposites. While Cesca has dark eyes and hair and a round and small figure, Jenny is blond, tall and pale:

> Frøken Winge was certainly an attractive girl too, but she was no match for her friend. She was as fair as the other was dark. Her hair, which was pulled back from her high, white forehead, billowed in golden flames beneath the little gray leather beret, and her complexion was a glowing pink and white. Even her eyebrows and her lashes around her steel-gray eyes were light-colored: a golden brown. (Page 15-16)

Helge's reaction to the two women's appearances shows that he connects their bodies to their sexuality. He sees Cesca as the sensual woman and Jenny as cool and chaste. To begin with, the narrative plot confirms Helge's perception; while Cesca has had several amorous adventures, Jenny has not even kissed a man, despite her 28 years. It thus looks as if Undset wants chastity to be represented by the fair, blond woman, using the body as a symbol rather than describing it as a situation. But later on, Jenny's chastity is demonstratively undermined, with fatal consequences. While Cesca is shown as having problems with her sexuality – she lets Jenny know that she cannot enjoy intercourse with her husband (Jenny 238-240 and 201-203) – Jenny turns out to be a very sensuous, desiring woman, longing for sexual union with a man. The "taxonomic" system that Helge uses is thus seen as misleading, because it is remodelled by various disturbing factors.

In *Jenny*, Undset takes up the question of female sexuality in different characters, but for Jenny sexuality becomes the main problem. Undset makes it especially clear that desire can take over a woman's emotional life even if it is not directed towards a particular man. At one point, Jenny and Helge split up, because Helge's father has become interested in Jenny, and Helge becomes jealous of his father. But Jenny does not want to remain heartbroken after the break with Helge, neither does she want to give up the feeling of being in love. She enjoys the bodily sensations of an anticipated sexual encounter, and does not care if this spoils her concentration on painting:

> She *couldn't* die like this – so poor that she didn't have a single beloved thing to say good-bye to. She didn't dare, because she still believed that someday things would be different. So she had to try painting again. Presumably it would be an utter disaster, since she was walking around sick with love. She laughed. That's what was wrong with her. The object of her affection hadn't yet appeared, but the love was there. (Page 174)

The quotation shows how a woman can develop sexual feelings totally independent of intercourse with a man, and that a woman would not even need to be affected by a specific man in order to feel sexually aroused. It is tempting to think that Undset wants to persuade us of female sexuality as independent from male influence, when she lets her narrator describe Jenny's feelings from the protagonist's point of view. Undset seems to approve of the discoveries made by the scientists of her day, and takes the case of Jenny as confirmation that the female reproductive system functions independently of any contact with men. Simultaneously, the novel also makes it perfectly clear that sexuality is rooted in the body and that it affects the life of women, when Jenny analyses herself as someone who is "walking around sick with love". Female sexuality, which does not end up in a relationship with another human being, is felt as physical illness, Undset seems to think. The body as a situation affects the whole life of the woman: In this case, the feeling of being physically ill interacts with Jenny's production of artworks.

The narrator is quick to let Helge's father make use of Jenny's excited condition, and both Gert and Jenny try to believe that he will be able to fill the empty space left by his son. Although Jenny is convinced that he is not the right partner for her, and although she feels guilty for seducing Gert

Gram into leaving his wife, she does not manage to split up with Helge's father until she realises that she is pregnant.

The discovery that she is with child does not come as a happy one. Undset avoids all linguistic clichés when she describes Jenny's situation. There is no recourse to pictures of pride and happiness, no allusion to any literary descriptions of pregnancy that could comment on Jenny's bodily situation in any ideological way. Undset describes Jenny's discovery more as recognition of a state of affairs, something that could be seen as the growing understanding of what it means to be a woman. The discovery of her pregnancy is definitively more than the mere observation of "physical-chemical processes" – Undset here clearly distances herself from scientists such as Jacques Loeb, who had argued about the importance of such processes for life in an article in *Naturen* in 1912. Her pregnancy lets Jenny rightly discover that men and women differ on the basis of their reproductive organs, and that this difference is significant: Women would have to take care of themselves, because intercourse has consequences for them in a different way than it has for men. Jenny's discovery of her pregnancy as a situation is stressed by Undset's description of her bodily sensations:

> She lay still for a moment, trying to win control over that abominable sensation – I won't, I won't. But it didn't help; her mouth filled with water. She barely managed to reach the chamber pot before she vomited. My God, could she really be that drunk? It was getting downright embarrassing. But surely it was over now.... But after she had been lying there for a while with her eyes closed, the sea swells began again, along with the sweats and the nausea. It was puzzling, because by now she was quite clearheaded. Nevertheless, she had to get up again. The moment she was back in bed, the thought occurred to her. (Page 193-194)

The quotation has Jenny first observe the mere physical signs; the sea-swelling, the sweats and the nausea. On the background of the information available to women about the functioning of their bodies at Undset's time, it is particularly striking that it takes time for Jenny to understand that she is pregnant. Jenny clearly did not react to her missing period. Did she not know how to read this bodily sign? Obviously, she had no access to books like the one written by Marie Stopes (*Married Love* appeared seven years after *Jenny* was published). Being a young artist living in a male-dominated environment – necessarily without access to female peers – Undset's protagonist therefore would have no suspicions of her state of being. And to begin with, she misinterprets the signs of her pregnancy. She does not know what to do with them, but finally she understands their meaning.

As the story's development in the novel brings out, it is only after acknowledging that she is pregnant that Jenny starts to comprehend fully the ideological implications of her female body and the reproductive organs. It is against the background of her body as a situation that she is able to grasp the consequences her female body has for her life: Her pregnancy makes it clear to her that she needs to stop the unworthy relationship with Gert Gram as soon as possible and plan for the future of her unborn child, for which she is now responsible.

Thus, this description of a pregnant woman's bodily sensations needs to be seen as part of Undset's answer to the question of sexual difference. Jenny's situation changes when she feels sick, when she is sweating and even vomits. Her body reminds her of her condition, that she is a woman and that she cannot do what she wants without consequences.

While the female body is thus explicitly thematised in *Jenny*, it is also structurally emphasised in the text. The female protagonist has a relationship with three different men: Jenny is set against Helge Gram, Gert Gram and Gunnar Heggen. Furthermore, as Eriksson has pointed out, the situation of the woman as enclosed by the three men is stressed by the circular composition of the plot in *Jenny*. The story starts and ends in Rome, and while Jenny is seen from the perspective of Helge Gram at the outset, she is thought of by Gunnar Heggen in the conclusion. This circular composition is further stressed by the symmetrical position of the initials of the men in Undset's text: HG-GG-GH (Eriksson 74). As it becomes clear, the aesthetic pattern supports the finitude of the human body as described in Undset: Although Jenny is an independent artist who lives alone and earns her own living, her body sets limits to her life. The only time she tries to break free and gain control over her body is when she breaks up with Gert Gram and escapes to Germany, where she gives birth to her child. She even starts to paint again. But when tragedy occurs and her newborn son dies, she falls apart emotionally. Towards the end of the novel, Jenny tells her friend Gunnar Heggen what happened to her after the death of her child. She describes her mourning mostly as a physical longing, a longing for the little body of her son:

> And then there was nothing left but loss. You can't imagine what it felt like. As if my whole body ached with the loss of him. I had an infection in my breast, and it felt as if my loss erupted into pain and fever. I missed him in my arms and in my hands and against my cheek. (Page 245)

THE ART OF DISCOVERY

It is striking that Jenny describes the loss of her child as something she is experiencing with her body. Jenny does not refer to discourses of suffering motherhood; she does not appeal to the concept of suffering motherhood as it is contained in the pictures of the pietá by many painters in the churches of Rome. Instead, she keeps close to the descriptions of her bodily sensations. Jenny's tragedy of motherhood cannot be understood without an understanding of the body as something that gives us our world, as Merlau-Ponty also writes in *Phenomenology of Perception*: The body – in this case the maternal body longing for the dead child – is the situation for the protagonist. In the quotation above, it is the longing, aching body that is the background to Jenny's existence after her son's death. Undset does not want to describe what a maternal body generally looks like. She does not describe it as a scientific object, but focuses on the meaning the maternal body has for Jenny's life.

The pregnant body is certainly a specifically female situation, as is the maternal body. Undset's protagonist Jenny experiences her child as her happiness, but the quotations above also show that the dead body of the child again imposes limits on Jenny's freedom. It is precisely the focus on the female body also as a maternal body that brings the novel to a tragic ending: Jenny takes her own life after being raped by her former fiancé, Helge Gram. One of the reasons for her suicide is that she will not risk giving birth to a child conceived by the brother of her dead son. With this ending, Undset wants to show that "physical-chemical" processes are important factors in human life, but that women constantly have to choose their lives actively – against the background of their situation. If freedom to choose is denied, as it is in the case of rape, the situation and the body as such become unbearable.

As I have shown, Undset's text could be read as part of the debate about the meaning of sexual difference. Focusing on the body as a starting point for analysing the situation of women at the beginning of the 20th century, Undset shows that she takes the new discoveries about the reproductive organs seriously. Unlike many scientists and feminists of her time, however, she is careful not to give a general account of the essence of sexual difference; rather, she focuses on one particular woman, with one particular body, as a situation.

WORKS CITED

Anker Møller, Katti. *Moderskapets frigjørelse. To foredrag – fra 1915 og 1919*. Oslo: Tiden Norsk Forlag, 1974.

Bliksrud, Liv. *Natur og normer hos Sigrid Undset* (1988). Oslo: Aschehoug, 1995.

Eriksson, Jofrid. "Angrepet som forvandlet seg til et forsvar. Om kvinnelighet, kjærlighet og kjernefamilie i Sigrid Undsets Jenny." *Et annet språk. Analyser av norsk kvinnelitteratur*. Eds. Mai Bente Bonnevie, et al.. Oslo: Pax Forlag, 1977.

Groos, Karl. "Dyrenes kjærlighedslege." *Naturen*. Bergen and Copenhagen, 1900. 54-61, 79-84.

Johansen, Kristin. *Hvis kvinner ville være kvinner. Sigrid Undset, hennes samtid og kvinnespørsmålet*. Oslo: Aschehoug, 1998.

Laqueur, Thomas. *Making Sex. Body and Gender from the Greeks to Freud*. Cambridge and London: Harvard University Press, 1990.

L.-P., O.J. "Kunstig 'befrugtning' af eg med kemikalier og organiske ekstraktivstoffe." *Naturen*. Bergen and Copenhagen, 1902. 249-251.

Loeb, Jacques. "Livet." *Naturen*. Bergen og Copenhagen, 1912. 163-175 and 246-251.

Merleau-Ponty, Maurice. *Phenomenology of Perception* (1945). Trans. Colin Smith. London and NY: Routledge, 2007.

Moi, Toril. "What Is a Woman? Sex, Gender, and the Body in Feminist Theory." *What Is a Woman? And Other Essays*. Oxford: Oxford University Press, 1999.

Page, Tim (ed.). *The Unknown Sigrid Undset. Jenny and Other Works*. Transl. by Tiina Nunnally. Hanover, New Hampshire: Steerforth Press, 2001.

Perkins Gilman, Charlotte. *The Man-Made World or; Our Androcentric Culture* (1911). New York: Johnson Reprint Corporation, 1971.

Slapgard, Sigrun. *Dikterdronningen: Sigrid Undset*. Oslo: Gyldendal, 2007.

Stopes, Marie. *Married Love: A New Contribution to the Solution of Sex Difficulties* (1918). London: G.P. Putnam's Sons, 1923.

Undset, Sigrid. *Jenny* (1911). Oslo: Aschehoug, 2004.

—. *Essays og artikler 1910-1919*. Oslo: Aschehoug, 2004.

MODERNISM'S EINSTEIN:

WYNDHAM LEWIS AND THE POLITICS OF SCIENCE POPULARISATION

Randi Koppen, University of Bergen

Framed by the first and second debates on the "Two Cultures", the interwar years in Britain – the years of high modernism in British art and literature – appear in retrospect as a time when the relations between literature and science were defined by an uncharacteristic cordiality; an "entente cordiale", in the words of Michael Whitworth (Whitworth 111). From the perspective of at least one contemporary observer, however – the visual artist, novelist, and cultural critic Wyndham Lewis – the relationship ought rather to be described as corruptive; exhibiting an intimacy symptomatic of cultural pathology.

Considered in light of the charge brought against modernist literature by C.P. Snow in 1959, regarding its failure to "make something of [the] scientific revolution" (Snow 99), Lewis's view appears particularly strange. It should be noted, however, that Lewis's diagnosis describes a well-documented fashionable interest in the philosophical implications of cutting-edge scientific *theory*. The failure of engagement Snow identifies, on the other hand, pertains to applied science. Hence the cultural divide Snow so famously constructs is drawn between intellectuals and academics on the one hand (including pure scientists), and practical science, technology and industry on the other. Literary intellectuals and writers in particular are held to be ignorant of what he calls "the scientific revolution": "the application of real science to industry" (Snow 29). In Snow's historiography this occurs during the 1920s: "the time when atomic particles were first made industrial use of", indicating a rupture and a new beginning in the ongoing phase of industrialisation in which productive capacity increased through the deployment of science and technology. "I believe the industrial society of electronics, atomic energy, automation, is in cardinal respects different in kind from any that has gone before, and will change the world much more", he writes (29). In this context, the fact that highly educated members of the "non-scientific culture" cannot cope with the simplest concepts of pure science presents a dramatic challenge – though this applies even more to the fact that they understand nothing of applied science as "the material basis of our lives: or more exactly, the social plasma of which we are a part": "Industrial production is as mysterious to us as witch-doctoring; not one in ten could give the loosest analysis of the human organisation required to produce buttons – which are being made in millions every day" (Snow 30).

It is the grasp of the object world, of the everyday doing and making – in turn the precondition for a grasp of the future, of human destiny, the ethical and political decisions of whether we live or die – that constitutes Snow's ultimate concern in the Rede lecture. Against this background, literary intellectuals, "anxious to restrict both art and thought to the existential moment", warrant the question of Snow's exemplary scientist: whether it is the case that "nine out of ten" of literary modernists – W.B. Yeats, Ezra Pound and Wyndham Lewis are explicitly mentioned – were "not only politically silly, but politically wicked"; "the influence of all they represent" responsible for "bring[ing] Auschwitz that much nearer" (Snow 5; 7). "The honest answer", which Snow dutifully provides, is that "there is, in fact, a connection, which literary persons were culpably slow to see, between some kinds of early twentieth-century art and the most imbecile expressions of anti-social feeling" (8).

Among Snow's "bad modernists", as we have seen, is Wyndham Lewis – racist, homophobe, and fascist – who nonetheless (curiously and a little ironically, given Snow's claim on the moral high-ground), shares the latter's misgivings with respect to the modernists' missing grasp of science and its application in everyday life, as well as the failure of ethical engagement ensuing from it. As already indicated, however, Lewis's critique of his fellow moderns differs from what Guy Ortolano has recently described as Snow's "technocratic liberalism" (Ortolano 28) in fundamental ways, thus permitting a fuller examination of the relations between science and literary culture in the interwar years, specifically of certain economic and ideological implications of which Snow remains silent.

"The popularisation of science is a symptom of modernity; its relation to modernism is more complex", writes Michael Whitworth in his book *Einstein's Wake* (2001), a study of the interaction of modernism and the "new physics" in British literature between the wars. Science popularisation and the complexities of its relation to literary modernism is the topic of the present chapter and of Lewis's *Time and Western Man* (1927), a highly polemical, though in many ways perceptive and challenging treatise, outlining what Lewis perceives as a massive epistemic shift emanating from and validated by Einsteinian space-time, and given currency by the mis-alliance of popular science and high modernist aesthetics. Where Snow's primary concern is the intellectual's neglect of applied science, Lewis starts from literary culture's infatuation with the theory and philosophy of science, tracing its consequences for the subject's grasp of the object world. The urgency of Lewis's argument stems from his view that a collapse in the subject-object distinction is imminent, a threat which is made all the more real by the perception that Einsteinian theories of reality and matter correspond so perfectly with the structures of experience that shape the subject-object relations of modern city-dwellers: the "urbanisation of consciousness" that is at once the product and the prerequisite of commodity capitalism.[1]

Although, from a present-day perspective, Lewis's insistence on the pervasiveness of Einsteinian science in British inter-war society may seem monolithic and extreme, there can be little doubt about the resonances of "relativity" in these years among the cultural élite as well as the general public. Michael Whitworth's study details the mediation of the new physics, through newspapers, literary and generalist periodicals, broadcasts and popular science books, following the publication of Einstein's Special and General Theories in 1905 and 1916 respectively. In Britain, non-specialist accounts of the theories began to appear in 1918, in large numbers from late 1919, with scientists, philosophers and professional journalists providing non-technical expositions for the general public in various media. An unprecedented upsurge in popular science writing followed during the 1920s and 1930s, with books like James Jeans's *The Mysterious Universe* (1930) and Arthur Eddington's *The Nature of the Physical World* (1928) achieving bestseller status (Whitworth 20). Reviews and discussion of popular science books in generalist and literary journals like *The Athenaeum* (edited by the literary critic and modernist John Middleton Murray), *The Nation* (edited by Leonard Woolf), and *The Criterion* (edited by T.S. Eliot) ensured that "relativity" and other ideas and concepts in the new physics were also quickly absorbed by the literary vanguard. Indeed, "science" appeared to some extent to be the means by which the fashionable modernist élite, from Stein to Eliot, Virginia Woolf to Lawrence and Joyce, attained and maintained its edge as experimentalists always oriented towards the future. Nicola Luckhurst's

---

1   The term "urbanisation of consciousness" is David Harvey's. See his study, *Consciousness and the Urban Experience* (1985).

readings in 1920s *Vogue* show articles on modern science placed next to the latest fashions; scientists featured as society figures alongside artists and writers, in an editorial policy aiming at images of *au courant* modernity, where familiarity with the latest science was as important as the latest art and literature (Luckhurst 27-31).

To the extent that modernist writers defined themselves in opposition to the masses, their interest in popularised, and potentially vulgarised, science may seem a contradiction in terms. As Michael Whitworth convincingly argues, however, and as Wyndham Lewis's critique in *Time and Western Man* confirms, it was the framing of the "new physics" in philosophical and aesthetic terms that made it so attractive to the modernists. Science popularisers of the 1920s promoted a conception of the new developments in physics as a definitive and dramatic shift, setting Einsteinian "pure" science, the non-mechanical nature of the theory of gravitation and the non-mechanical aspects of quantum mechanics against the mechanistic materialism ascribed to Victorian science (Whitworth 112). Scientific developments in the period 1890 to 1930 seemed to carry the implication that not only the laws of science, but also its fundamental concepts such as "matter" were human constructs, rendering science a rich source of metaphor for writers pondering the instability of subjectivity, the porousness of matter, the relativity of truth and knowledge. Many commentators, as Whitworth also points out, drew attention to similarities between Henri Bergson's philosophy and the philosophy implied by Einstein's special theory, effectively conflating Einsteinian simultaneity, the simultaneous existence of distinct moments, with the blurring of time entailed by Bergson's *durée*, in which every moment is simultaneous with every other (Whitworth 160; 190-91). The formal abstraction of relativity, and the suggestion that Einstein was led by aesthetic considerations, further contributed to the theory's aesthetic appeal. Whitworth cites Eddington to the effect that, "regardless of whether it was right or wrong, Einstein's theory was 'beautiful'", with Bertrand Russell echoing Eddington's view of the theory's aesthetic merit, declaring that "'every lover of the beautiful must wish it to be true'" (Whitworth 130).

It is precisely the displacements and conflations marking contemporary science mediation, reception and appropriation that constitute the core of Lewis's discussion in *Time and Western Man*. Rather than attempting to correct the confusion of Einstein with Bergson that informs the popularisation of relativity, Lewis's objective, as stated in his introduction, is to show "how the 'timelessness' of einsteinian physics, and the time-obsessed flux of Bergson, merge in each other; and how they have conspired to produce, upon the innocent plane of popularization, a sort of mystical time-cult" (Lewis 1993 xviii).[2] More than ever before, it seems, everyday life is affected by "the speculative activities that are renewing and transvaluing our world". Confronted by this epistemic shift, the choice of the individual is to sink to the level of "slavery", or "get hold as best he can of the abstract principles involved in the very 'intellectual' machinery set up to control and change him" (TWM xi). To this end, complicated by the tangled paths leading from the abstract principle to the everyday occurrence, Lewis starts from the concrete manifestations of the "Time-mind" – the "representative ferment" it produces in art and literature – working his way towards "the will behind" the Time-philosophy (TWM xix).

The root of Lewis's objection to Einstein's philosophy is its emphasis on sense data as the fundamental elements of science. The "object" as conceived by post-Einsteinian science is a multitude of colourless particles, moving about at extreme velocities. Distinct from the scientific object is the "optical object" or "sensum", and distinct from both of them is the perceptual object of common sense – each a separate and often contradictory reality. Where commonsense perception involves experience, memory and contemplation, the sensa-world is a world of unconscious, automatic sensing. Temporally and ideationally affiliated with Bergson's plunge into the sensational flux, according to Lewis, the "Theory of Sensa"

> gives you the "objects" of life only as strictly experienced in Time; evanescent, flashing and momentary... ideally having no prolongation in memory, confined to the "continuous present" of their temporal appearance: consumed (and im- mediately evacuated) as "events": one with action, incompatible with reflection, impossible of contemplation (TWM 389).

What ensues from a theory that assumes that sense data are private to each separate person, is a world of apparitions, a mental world, in which the so- lidity and stability of a table, a chair or a handkerchief becomes as suspect as that of a "soul" or "psyche" (TWM 408). At first sight, Lewis writes, it would be hard to see how any politics could enter into the destruction of a table or a chair:

---

2 *Time and Western Man* hereafter abbrev. TWM in parenthetical references.

It may still be objected that this is only a mathematician's technical device, necessitated by the present march of knowledge: as a technical device it interferes with nobody, it is the business only of the physicist or mathematician... This would be ignoring, however, the fact that these conceptions of the external world are intended to supersede those of the classical intelligence and of the picture of the plain-man: that it is proposed to teach Relativity-physics and the relativist world-view everywhere in our schools: and that vast propaganda is carried on by popular treatises and articles to impose this picture upon the plain-man and the simple common-sense intelligence. In other words, the common sense of tomorrow, it is proposed – the one general sense of things that we all hold in common – is to be transformed into the terms of this highly-complex disintegrated world, of private "times" and specific amputated "spaces," of serial-groups and "events" in place of "things". (TWM 432)

What Lewis is concerned with here is the performative force of popularisation, specifically the implementation of the practical training to see discontinuity that philosophers like Bertrand Russell, certain educators, representatives of the mass media, and other public voices were advocating. Lewis thus imputes to (pure, formalist, disinterested) science the possibility of radically altering everyday life by altering perception and thus seriously imperilling the subject's grasp of the object, as well as the subject's hold on itself. With a theory that makes each impression (unassisted by thought) more real than the "ideal rounded perceptual object"; that suspends the distinction between sensation and sense-datum, the statement "I am the same person I was yesterday", becomes as illusive as "This pen is the same pen that it was yesterday" (TWM 385; 338-39). The fundamental point, for Lewis, is that the subjectivities enabled by the new experience of space and time do not constitute a politically neutral fact. To adopt "relativity" is to abandon the adult capacity for abstract thought and judgement, and to fall into the primitivism Lewis termed the "child-cult", a fact confirmed by the recurring trope of the "innocent eye" or the "child's perspective" in much popular science (Whitworth 193), or as Lewis sarcastically puts it: "What the Relativity-handbook is saying all the time is: Now try and feel about all these things just like a little child. Look at all these things primitively... as though you saw [them] for the first time" (TWM 404-5).

It is as children, then, that the mass of the people is interpellated by science, and as children they receive its products: "All the great inventions reach the crowd in the form of toys (crystal sets, motor cars)", writes Lewis; "it is as helpless children that, for the most part, [the crowd] participates in these stirring events" (TWM 119). In the course of "democratic vulgariza-tion", the revolutionary energy of science's discoveries is diluted and adapted to "herd-consumption" (TWM 120). Beyond such infantilisation, however, the politico-economic implications of the Theory of Sensa proceed from the fact that its object (the sensum as opposed to the percept) corresponds so perfectly to the fetishised objects of the commodity spectacle and its technology of advertisement.

"Time for the Bergsonian or relativist is fundamentally sensation", insists Lewis: "It is the glorification of the life-of-the-moment, with no reference beyond itself and no absolute or universal value". Correspondingly, "the spirit of advertisement and boost has its feverish being in a world of hyperbolic suggestion", a world in which only a single temporality exists (TWM 27-28). The influence of this state of affairs on the structure of human life and on human psychology occurs as the "average man is invited to slice his life into a series of one-day lives, regulated by the clock of fashion" (TWM 28). Predictably, a reflective, historicising approach is not at all in the interest of Advertisement; on the contrary, the perfect response to the here-and-now of the Fashion-day and its "giant hyperbolic close-up of a moment" requires "the perfect sensationalist – what people picture to themselves, for instance, as the perfect American" (TWM 28-29).

For Lewis, then, what the "pretentious metaphysic" of Bergsonian time-philosophy boils down to is no more than the metaphysic of the Money-Age, of advertisement and fashion – a metaphysic which mathematical physics has given its empirical sanction. The result of this coincidence of modern science and modern mass-market advertising strategies is the restless will of the modern consumer:

> The Will that "objectifies" itself... is a will to what? To nothing... it produces Charlie Chaplin, the League of Nations, wireless, feminism, Rockefeller; it causes, daily, millions of women to drift in front of, and swarm inside, gigantic clothes-shops in every great capital, buying silk underclothing, cloche-hats, perfume, vanishing cream, vanity-bags and furs... It is a quite aimless and, from our limited point of view, nonsensical, Will. (TWM 312)

It is hardly surprising that this aimless and restless will is figured in terms of the female shopper, not least given the habitual gendering of the masses and mass culture as feminine in contemporary discourse. Lewis's allegiance is to the integrity of the object and to a forceful subjectivity, both of which are under threat by the twofold attack of science and commodity culture.

The stakes for Lewis in maintaining, as he puts it, "the Subject as King of the Psychological World" and "the Object as King of the Physical World", are the possibilities of an ethical relation to the world: a life fully embedded in political conflicts, as opposed to the sham independence offered the individual by modern mass democracy, or the "childlike condition of tutelage and dependence" produced by urban mass-life and the prevalence of technology (TWM 297).

What, then, is the place of modernist art and literature in this argument? The epigraph to Book One of *Time and Western Man*, taken from A.N. Whitehead's *Science and the Modern World*, indicates the drift of Lewis's argument: "It is in literature that the concrete outlook of humanity receives its expression" (TWM 1). Where the majority of the people, as Lewis has it, "humbly and reverently" pick up the current findings in science or the dominant theories in philosophy, in an "abridged, and usually meaningless form", the pseudo-creative artist, equally passively and blindly, proceeds to embody them in his work, all the while failing to make clear, either to himself or others, the steps by which that theory has entered his mind – whether, in Lewis's words, as "conqueror", "seducer", "business partner", or any other of "the hundred ways and degrees in which assent is arrived at" (TWM 86-87). The problem is not simply that the artist as receptacle and mediator channels the force of popularisation, but that art and literature in this way serve to naturalise an epistemic shift while covering over the conditions and consequences of its ascendancy.

Lewis's main case in this regard is against a fashionable modernism whose infatuation with "Relativity" prevents it from grasping its own implication in either the politics of science or the culture of the commodity. The turn to "internalism" in modern art and writing – the preoccupation with the stream or flux of internal experience whether in sculpture or literature – provides Lewis with a perfect example of the workings of the Time-mind, as well as of the coincidence between the Time-mind and the advertising principle of competitive industry: what he calls "the giant, hyperbolic close-up" on the moment. Where the philosophers and scientists provide this principle with its intellectual super-structure, artists and writers like Rodin, Stein, Joyce, Woolf and Lawrence translate it into an aesthetic. The sculpture of Auguste Rodin – "those flowing, structureless, lissom, wave-lined pieces of commercial marble" which, incidentally, "infest the tables and mantelpieces of Kensington and Mayfair, and are to be encountered in great profusion in the shop windows of Bond Street" – are "Bergson's élan vital translated into marble", writes Lewis in *Men Without Art* (96).[3] Their equivalents in literature would be the equally decadent internalist methods employed by Woolf, Joyce and Lawrence: "the romantic snapshotting of the wandering stream of the Unconscious" and its private sensations (MWA 104). The repetitive, rhythmic, narrative prose of Gertrude Stein, with its naïve child's eye view on the world, offers the reader reality in the form of "a never-ending prose-song"; a continuous present forever infected by the malady of childhood; a world replete with the phenomenological "mysteries" of inconsequential objects: buttons, pieces of glass, bric-a-brac (TWM 53-60).

It is Joyce's *Ulysses*, however, which emerges as the primary example of the self-conscious time-sense of the "Space-timeist"; equally of the elevation of the trivial object that accompanies the turn to interiority, as artists and writers from Picasso to Woolf appear to be collectively losing themselves in contemplation of the fuzziness of objects, the porousness of matter, the instability of truth. To Lewis's mind, the naturalism employed in *Ulysses*, the "telling from the inside", transforms the solidity of the object world into "a suffocating expanse of objects, a stupendous outpouring of matter," corresponding to the "einsteinian flux" or, equally well, "the duration-flux of Bergson" (TWM 100). Moreover, this "Aladdin's cave" of vague, fuzzy objects exactly replicates the sensationalism and fetishism that defines the commodity spectacle: in both cases the subject is rendered passive in the face of the world, incapable of distinguishing the subjective from the objective, the inconsequential from the important (TWM 89).

It should be noted that Lewis's concern with the predicament of the object, in *Time and Western Man* as elsewhere in his writing, differs from that usually ascribed to modernists as regards both the notion of science and the notion of the object involved. Theodor W. Adorno, among other writers on modernism, typically posits an opposition between the particular, concrete, auratic object and the objectifying, quantifying methods of modern science (Adorno 43). Similarly, as Douglas Mao shows in his study of Anglo-American modernism, *Solid Objects* (1998), it is a commonplace among these writers (the Imagists *par excellence*) to think of the work as preserving the qualities of the particular from the generalisations and abstractions of science as system. Further, for modernists like Woolf and Joyce, the fascination of "internal life" includes its interchanges with the concrete object as representative of the mystery and alterity of "non-human Being" (Mao 6-7;

---

3   *Men Without Art* hereafter abbrev. MWA in parenthetical references.

16-17). Lewis, by contrast, laments the passage from a conception of science as "hard and visible truth" to one that is "fluid and infinitely malleable", informed by the assumption that truth can be reached only "symbolically and indirectly" (TWM 295). He rages at a science by which dead, physical nature comes to life; where chairs and tables are animated into a magnetic restlessness and sensitiveness to exist on the same vital terms as men, while, at the same time, in industrial colonies men become mechanised by technology and behaviourist psychology into specialised insects (TWM 421; 326-27). The threat, for Lewis, is directed not against the auratic object but against the object of common sense; not by the triumphant positivist science of modernity, but by a science that paradoxically extends its dominance by reducing its claims to truth; science, moreover, as mass discourse that serves the interests of commodity capitalism and the industrialised world.

It may be instructive at this point to return to the Snow-Leavis debate in order to bring forth more clearly the specificity of Lewis's perspective and what it means for an understanding of the contested relations between science, modernity and modernism. To begin with it may be recalled that Snow and F.R. Leavis were radically opposed in their assessment of modern civilisation and the role of science in the civilising process. Where Snow eulogised scientific modernisation and material prosperity, Leavis saw the standardisation and levelling-down of mass-civilisation. Snow depicted science as a progressive, democratic, humanising force; Leavis depicted a technocracy headed towards dehumanisation. For Snow literary modernism is by definition "against" modernity, hence against science. For Leavis modernism implies critique of modernity but not rejection: (modernist) literature, rooted as it is in that "supremely human" instinct of "creative response" to the challenges of time is what keeps us human and so makes it possible for us to live humanely within modernity (F.R. Leavis 27). His ideal literature is that of D.H. Lawrence, the exponent of a vitalism that implies that "only in living individuals is life there, and individual lives cannot be aggregated or equated or dealt with quantitatively in any way" (F.R. Leavis 20). Life in its essence goes on beyond the social domain, and so, being in possession of one's humanity, for Leavis and Lawrence, "means, not confident ownership, but a basic living deference towards that to which, opening as it does into the unknown and itself unmeasurable, we know we belong" (F.R. Leavis 26).

Wyndham Lewis shares F.R. Leavis's assessment of modernity but not of modernism, the point of Lewis's critique being precisely that the fashionable modernism he attacks fails to posit itself "against" either modernity or its alignment with science. Where Snow speaks of the need for science to be assimilated and naturalised in art, rather than being treated at best as a source of fanciful conceits, Lewis rails against the destructive consequences of a literary culture which has given itself over to "Science as religion" and the "new sacred books"; the "Popular Science Series" and its "semi-magical prescriptions" (TWM 294; 296).

One of the questions opened up by Lewis's critique of the alliance between modernism and science concerned the nature of the modernist's grasp of the "Money Age" and its structures of experience. As a means of examining this assertion more fully, it may be useful to place the Time-cult Lewis objects to in the context of the concepts of time the "cult" claimed to evade: Evolutionary time, with its long view of patterns of change and destruction; and, more pressingly, Clock-time, the standardisation of time that is a consequence of market capitalism. As David Harvey elaborates in *Consciousness and the Urban Experience* (1985), drawing on Georg Simmel's writings on the connections between time, space and money in *The Philosophy of Money* (1920) and elsewhere, the modern concept of time as a value determined by its usefulness and scarcity (literally: time as money) became widely accepted only to the degree that market capitalism flourished. The cultivation of urban labour, along with the organisation of commercial networks over space, forced a change in the measurement and concept of time itself. Symbolised by clocks and bells, the "chronological net" in which urban life was caught came together finally at the end of the nineteenth century. Commodity exchange and monetisation equally challenged the qualities of space, however, making it impossible, as Harvey shows, to consider either time or space independently of money (Harvey 170-71; 174). Nonetheless, the "internalist" techniques of literary moderns from Baudelaire to Conrad, Stein and Joyce asserted the power of literature to evade the realities of the Money Age through subjective appropriations of time as well as space, supported in their claims, it seemed, by the time-philosophies of Bergson and Einstein. Taking seriously the cliché that "Time is Money", and so tracing the connections between mental structures and their material expression, Lewis's point, by contrast, is to bring back the realities of the Money Age: to show that the *durée* with its "hyperbolic close-up on the moment"; and popular space-time with its "disintegrated world of private 'times' and specific, amputated 'spaces'", constitute indeed the perfect match for the culture of the commodity (TWM 28; 432).

F.R. Leavis's idealist vision for modernist literature was that it would provide a grasp on the condition of scientific modernity by humanising it. For Wyndham Lewis literature has nothing to do with "reminding us of what makes us human" or keeping us attuned to the vitalist principle: the Life Force of which we are a part. Our humanness, for Lewis, resides in a forceful subjectivity, a Will-to-Self. The literature he advocates is that of a satiric externalism focused on "the outside of people... their shells or pelts" (MWA 97), "our Wild Body" (as he titled an essay published in *The New Age* in 1910): the body as a surface, a physical structure explored through relentlessly physical depictions of facial and gestural mechanics; characters reduced to mindless things, lacking both intelligence and feelings (Lewis 1982). The externalist approach is not merely a prescription for objectivity, but a reminder of the subject's inextricable grounding in a body which is that of an animal or a machine – not the Futurist machine-body but the "something mechanical in something living" of Bergson's theory of laughter. It is a reminder of the comedy, yet urgency and necessity, of the repeated human attempt at separation and distinction from the non-human.

For Lewis there is nothing romantic about primitivism, nor about the merging of human with non-human, subject with object, individual consciousness with that of the mass – all of which he finds in modernism. His insistence on discontinuities rather than continuities, however, should not be ascribed to the fears of regression and atavism so familiar to older generations; rather, it needs to be understood in connection to the strong subjectivity Lewis promotes. The corporeality depicted in his novels involves struggle and contradictions rather than the organic, embodied seamlessness (of mind and body) suggested by the internalists; the literature he advocates satirically exposes and re-enacts the struggle towards separation and human subjectivity. That, he implies, is the best way for literature to retain a grasp of the world and its things, to distinguish subject from object, human from non-human, individual from mass in the Age of Money and the Cult(ure) of Time.

In his depiction of modernist literature, Snow's engagement (as distinct from F.R. Leavis's metaphysics) was with the literary responsibility to represent "the material basis of our lives", "the social plasma of which we are a part", both of which he saw as inextricably connected with science. With modernism, as he argued, this representative function had been taken over by what was effectively becoming the "third culture": the new class of expert, the sociologists (Snow 70). Snow welcomed the experts while lamenting the decline in classical realism; Lewis, for his part, repudiated both. Through a massive act of refusal, the argument of *Time and Western Man* dismisses the work of the passive, receptive artist (whether realist or modernist) that does not actively shape the world through the imprint of a forceful subjectivity, or serve to empower the subjectivity, the individual Will-to-Self of its audience. Further, Lewis's argument renounces the narratives and plots of science to the extent that they "rob the individual of their will and reason": whether the evolutionary plot of "ruthless struggles for existence" or the new narratives of "'progress', the gift of the good God, Science" (TWM 294).

If C.P. Snow was right to raise the question of the two cultures, he was clearly wrong in his assessment of modernism with regard to both its grasp of the everyday world and its relations to science. So, for that matter, was Lewis. As thoroughly documented in more recent research on modernism, the topography of British inter-war literature bears only an intermittent resemblance to the maps drawn – concurrently by Lewis, retrospectively by Snow. It is striking that both exaggerated the influence and importance of literary culture: for Snow the literary academic would continue to influence the government official, the administrator or the member of parliament "against" science; for Lewis the literary élite would pave the way for science as epistemic shift.

Granted that both contenders were wrong in their different ways, some final consideration still remains as to what is achieved by introducing "the brutal and boring Wyndham Lewis" (in F.R. Leavis's words) in a debate on the relations between literature and science (F.R. Leavis 20). Most obviously, of course, such juxtaposition serves to bring out the differences in position – the shifting accentuations in terms like "modernism", "modernity" and "science" – and the consequences for the maps being drawn. More importantly, I think, Lewis's perspective removes the "cultures" debate from the terrain of (an idealised) education into the arena of popular mediation. Looking with scepticism at science popularisation as a process of deferral and displacement; framed in highly particular terms; inscribed in ideology and relations of power, as Lewis does, may allow one to trace more completely both the history of discursive shifts and their consequences for everyday experience. The strength of Lewis's approach to science is to remove the question of influence first, from the level of abstraction and speculative philosophy to the level of metaphor and literary technique; further, to the domains of everyday life, politics and economy. Lastly, I would argue, Lewis's sceptical view on popularisation is worth recalling, if not retaining, because it reminds us of the question that haunts all inter-disciplinary work as much as it does the work of the literary writer: the responsibility, as Lewis defines it, for the artist to "know enough of the sources of his ideas" so that, "when the idea-monger comes to his door he should be able to tell what kind of notion he is buying, and know something of the process and rationale of its manufacture and distribution" (TMW 10). Ironically, as demonstrated in some of the massive conflations marring *Time and Western Man*, this was an ideal Lewis himself did not entirely live up to.

WORKS CITED

Adorno, Theodor W. *Negative Dialectics*. Trans. E.B. Ashton. New York: Continuum, 1990.

Bergson, Henri. *Laughter: An Essay on the Meaning of the Comic*. Whitefish, Montana: Kessinger Publishing, 2004.

Eddington, Arthur. *The Nature of the Physical World*. Cambridge: Cambridge University Press, 1928.

Harvey, David. *Consciousness and the Urban Experience*. Oxford: Basil Blackwell, 1985.

Jeans, James. *The Mysterious Universe*. Cambridge: Cambridge University Press, 1930.

Leavis, F.R. *Two Cultures? The Significance of C.P. Snow*. London: Chatto & Windus, 1962.

Lewis, Wyndham. *Men Without Art*. Ed. Seamus Cooney. Santa Rosa, CA: Black Sparrow Press, 1987.

—. *Time and Western Man*. Ed. Paul Edwards. Santa Rosa, CA: Black Sparrow Press, 1993.

—.*The Complete Wild Body*. Santa Rosa, CA: Black Sparrow Press, 1982.

Luckhurst, Nicola. *Bloomsbury in Vogue*. London: Cecil Woolf, 1998.

Mao, Douglas. *Solid Objects: Modernism and the Test of Production*. Ewing, N.J.: Princeton University Press, 1998.

Ortolano, Guy. *The Two Cultures Controversy: Science, Literature and Cultural Politics in Postwar Britain*. Cambridge: Cambridge University Press, 2009.

Snow, C.P. *The Two Cultures and A Second Look*. Cambridge: Cambridge University Press, 1964.

Whitworth, Michael. *Einstein's Wake: Relativity, Metaphor, and Modernist Literature*. Oxford: Oxford University Press, 2001.

THE RIDDLE OF THE ROBOTS[1]

Jon Bing, University of Oslo

In 1993 I made a journey to Chicago, an excursion with some colleagues and graduate students to visit the Chicago-Kent School of Law and other institutions related with my own research area, computers and law. During the stay, we visited the Art Institute of Chicago. And there I made a remarkable discovery. In its collection I found a small, three-dimensional figure made of cardboard. The head is reminiscent of a cathode ray tube; the body is made up of boxes decorated with numbers, the feet are two tubes. Anybody would interpret this figure as a robot, and this is indeed the name of the artwork. The artist is Alexandra Alexandrovna Exter, and she made this small figure in 1925.

It was the date that puzzled me because "robot" is a rather recent word. It was used for the first time by the Czech author Karel Čapek (1890-1938). Čapek was an important and prolific author, famous for his many novels and plays. Many people have read *War with the Newts* (1936), which is a very funny and very serious science-fiction novel ridiculing the emergence of the Nazi movement, and indicating Čapek's strong political involvement. His play *R.U.R.*, which is an abbreviation for "Rossum's Universal Robots", is also political in nature. In this play, the main character is Rossum, an industrialist who creates artificial beings from biological material in order to have slaves in his production plants. There is a description of the process of building these beings:

---

1   This is a rewritten version of a guest lecture at "IRIS – Internationales Rechtsin-
    formatik Symposium" at the Universität Salzburg, introducing the parallel session
    "Science Fiction and AI". Other versions of this paper have been published in Nor-
    wegian, for instance "Dobbeltgjengere: Om maskinmennesker og menneskemaskiner
    i fantastisk litteratur", Jon Bing *Landskap med tegn*, Oslo Pax, 1998: 89-106. I want
    to thank Associate Professor Dr Erich Schweighofer, University of Vienna, Faculty
    of Law, Research Center for Computers and Law for giving me the opportunity to
    develop this English version.

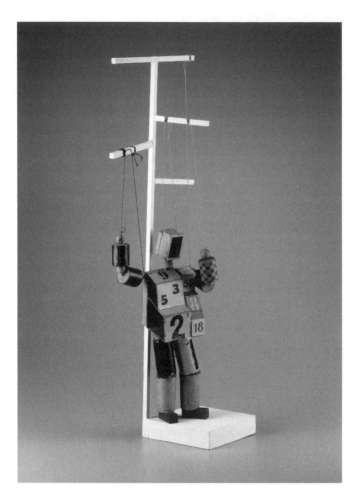

Spinning mills for weaving nerves and veins. Miles and miles of digestive tubes. … in the fitting-shed, all the parts are put together like motorcars. They learn to speak, write and count. They have astonishing memories. But they never think of anything new. Then they are sorted out and distributed. Fifteen thousand daily, not counting a regular percentage of defective specimens which are thrown into the stamping-mill …

It is maintained that the idea of such a play came to Čapek rather suddenly, and that he immediately discussed his idea with his brother Josef, who was a cubist painter: "But," the author said, "I don't know what to call these artificial workers. I could call them Labori, but that strikes me as a bit bookish." "Then call them Robots," the painter muttered, brush in mouth, and went on painting. And that's how it was. Thus was the word Robot born; let this acknowledge its true creator."[2]

The word 'robot' is derived from the Czech word 'robota', which means drudgery or 'servitude', and 'robotnik', meaning a 'servant' or a 'serf'. The play R.U.R. opened in Prague early in 1921 and was extremely successful. It was produced in New York in 1922, and the English translation of the play was published in 1923.

Perhaps this is sufficient to explain what puzzled me about the figure made by Alexandra Exter. For in Čapek's play, the robots are artificial human beings – they look exactly like humans, and in modern science-fiction jargon they would be known as an 'android' or a 'biomat', a machinelike man. But 'robot' is reserved for something different, for a mechanical man or a man-like machine, an artificial being built of hardware. The word was created in 1921. Today it has a different meaning from what was originally intended. Somewhere along the line the meaning changed from 'machinelike man' to 'manlike machine'. And that point in time would seem to be located between 1921 and 1925 – because Exter's figure is obviously that of a 'manlike machine', a robot in the modern sense of the word.

I admit it is a small mystery, but my own preoccupation with science fiction,[3] artificial intelligence and robots made it an intriguing one. In search of an explanation of the mystery, this essay traces some intertwining threads, taking us from the 16th century to the 21st; from ancient legend to contemporary popular culture; from the Golem to the cyborg. The question consistently before us in this quest has already been anticipated: the shifting lines of distinction between a machinelike man and a manlike machine.

PRAGUE, ČAPEK AND THE GOLEM

It cannot be a coincidence that Čapek wrote his play about the artificial slave workers in the city of Prague. The famous Jewish ghetto of Prague is symbolised by the Golem. A Golem is an artificial being, created by Man from earth and clay. It is said to be mentioned in *Psalms* 139:15-16:

My bones were not hidden from you,
When I was being made in secret,

---

2   http://capek.misto.cz/english/robot.html.
3   Along with Tor Åge Bringsværd, I have edited a science-fiction anthology with stories about robots, *Jeg – en maskin*, Oslo: Gyldendal, 1973.

Fashioned as in the depths of the earth;
Your eyes foresaw my actions;
In your book all are written down;
My days were shaped, before one came to be.

The "depths of the earth" is a metaphor for the womb, emphasising the mysterious operations occurring there. And legend has it that at the end of the 16th century, Rabbi Judah Löw followed the formula and fashioned in secret an artificial being from clay dug out of the banks of the river, and gave him life by placing a *Schem* – a capsule containing a piece of paper with a cabbalistic word – in the mouth of the giant.

Rabbi Judah Löw, called The High Rabbi Löw because he was unusually tall, was a real person (1520-1609), his full name being Jehuda Liva ben Becalel. He was an acknowledged theological scholar, sharing his time between Prague and Krakow in Poland. In Prague, he founded the Talmud school Klause, part of the ghetto. His grave can be seen in the cemetery, and even today one may find leaves weighted down by pebbles on his gravestone. He is believed to be a powerful rabbi whose spirit can be called upon for intercession.

In the Jewish ghetto living space was cramped, the lodgings small and often crowded. But the ghetto was generally believed to be very rich, as the Jews were often successful business people. Furthermore, there was considerable tension between the Jews and the rest of the population of the city – it was rumoured, for instance, that Jews ate babies in their un-Christian rituals, especially at Easter. The Golem was created by Rabbi Löw as a defender of the ghetto, and over time the Golem became the symbol of the spirit of the Ghetto, as it appears in the well-known novel *The Golem* by Gustav Meyrink (1868-1932). Meyrink was also a Czech author living in Prague, and his novel was published in 1915, predating Čapek's *R.U.R.* by a few years. Even today, clay figurines and other trinkets representing the Golem are popular souvenirs sold in the Ghetto. And the tale of the Golem continues to fascinate writers, one of the more recent illustrations being Marge Piercy's *He, She, and It* (1991).[4] In the original legend of the Golem, the artificial giant was somewhat simpleminded, taking all orders literally. In one episode, he behaves like the sorcerer's apprentice: when asked to fetch water he continues to do so even when the bowl overflows

---

4 Published in Europe as *Body of Glass*.

and the house is flooded, the housekeeper having forgotten to ask him to stop.

Rumours of the giant reached Emperor Rudolph II of the Habsburgs. His court must at this time have been a remarkable place. The Emperor collected scholars and artists around him, and among them was another fascinating figure of that time, the astronomer Johannes Kepler. One may speculate on what form a dialogue between him and Rabbi Löw would have taken, but whether they actually met is not known. It is said, however, that the court protocols of 22 February 1592 indicate that Rabbi Löw was called to an audience before the Emperor, with Prince Bertier also present. The protocols tell us nothing of what was said at this meeting; but on leaving, Rabbi Löw is reported to have said: "We do not need Jossele Golem anymore". Accompanied by two friends and relatives, Jakob Katz and Jakob Sosson, Rabbi Löw takes the Golem to the chamber in the tower of the Altneu Synagogue, which, to this day, stands at the edge of the ghetto. Here he reads a secret cabbalist formula over the Golem, reducing him once again to clay and dust.

It has been argued, even proved, that the tale of the Golem is much older than Rabbi Löw, and that there are better candidates for his part in the story. "Golem" is also said to have been used in Yiddish for a simpleminded person, almost synonymous with a village idiot. This is of little concern in our context – the living tradition attributed the creation of the man of clay to Rabbi Löw, and he became an obedient slave labourer.

As Meyrink's novel shows, the legend was very much alive at the time of Čapek. One of Čapek's acquaintances was the journalist Egon Erwin Kisch (1885-1948), who at that time worked at the German language newspaper *Bohemia* in Prague, writing local stories. Kisch would go on to become a famous reporter, earning himself the nick-name "*Der rasende Reporter*" or "The furious reporter", especially due to his reports from the Spanish Civil War and other war theatres. His interest in the alleys and tales of Prague led him to write *Dem Golem auf der Spur*,[5] in which he traced the legend of Rabbi Löw and his Golem. He even entered the tower chamber of the Altneu Synagogue and looked for the clay or dust remnants from the Golem, but without success. Thus, when Čapek conceived his idea of the industrialist Rossum and his artificial slave labourers, the Golem provided an obvious reference for his robots. But rather than creating them from

---

5 Egon Erwin Kisch, *Der rasende Reporter* (2001) (3rd edition). The collected essays were first published in 1925.

clay and mystic rituals, Čapek let them be manufactured in vessels similar to the chemicals apparatus provided for the factories of his own and the modern age.

FRANKENSTEIN, HIS MONSTER AND THE SUMMER OF 1816

It was not the first time that the tale of the Golem inspired the creation of an artificial being which has ever since haunted our literature. In 1816, the British poet Lord Byron (1788-1824) fled England due to rumours of his less than appropriate behaviour involving his half-sister. He fled in style, in a large horse-drawn carriage containing a library and a sleeping room, taking with him a social companion, a young man by the name of John Polidori (1795-1821), a brilliant graduate from Edinburgh medical school, and the son of an Italian who translated Gothic horror novels. This background may not be completely irrelevant, because the medical school of Edinburgh was famous for its expertise in human anatomy, an expertise gained by dissecting corpses. In the 18th century, the trade in corpses was brisk, with graves in the city being robbed and their content sold to the university. This practice was sufficiently common for iron cages to be put on the graves to keep out the grave robbers.

In the summer, Lord Byron's travels took him Lac Lehman, where he rented a house, Villa Deodati (9 Chemin de Ruth, the house is still there) just outside the city of Geneva. At the same time, another famous British poet also travelled to the Continent: Percy Bysshe Shelley (1792-1827) and his wife Mary Godwin (1797-1851), the daughter of the philosopher William Godwin and the suffragette Mary Wollstonecraft. Neither of the two spoke much French, but they brought with them Mary's stepsister, Claire Clairmont (1798-1879). She was an actress, and it is believed she had an affair with Lord Byron while she was performing at Drury Lane Theatre. She was still infatuated with him, and it was therefore probably not by chance that they came to rent Maison Chapuis, very close to Villa Deodati.

It is reported that it was a wet summer, robbing the two groups of the most obvious way of passing the time: making excursions into the splendid landscape. They had visitors, one of whom was Matthew Lewis (1775-1818), one of the best known Gothic authors, his most famous book being *The Monk* (1796). He read aloud to them from the first volume of Goethe's *Faust* (1808) and translated the text from German as he read. The group also read aloud from other books, among them *Phantasmagoria*, a collection of Jewish folk tales which also included the legend of the Golem.

When reading about this summer and the persons staying on the shore of Lac Lehman, one gets the impression of a company of rather bored people willing to experiment with intoxicating substances like belladonna in order to pass the time. Lord Byron suggested that they should have a literary contest requiring each of them to write a Gothic tale. His own attempt was a less than successful story about a vampire. It was just a fragment, though nonetheless recognised as the first literary vampire tale. Polidori came to publish his story "The Vampyre" (1819) in such a way that it was attributed to Lord Byron, and it is still disputed whether this was by design or accident.

The winner of the contest was, of course, Mary Wollstonecraft Shelley, who published her story as *Frankenstein – A Modern Prometheus* (1818). The story has become part of our shared literary mythology, repeated and retold in numerous movies; indeed, the many trivial versions may overshadow the importance of the novel. One of the major themes of the novel is the moral responsibility of man – just as God has moral responsibility for his creation, man has a moral responsibility for his own creation (in Frankenstein's case, the monster). The moral relations between a creator and the created is a theme that is still relevant, biotechnology making it perhaps more acute than in the time of Mary Shelley.

In the novel, the natural scientist Victor Frankenstein creates an artificial being by stitching together parts of corpses, and bringing them to life by sending the electrical power of a bolt of lightning into their nervous system. Mary Shelley was clearly using methods of current science when writing this. The Italian anatomist and physician Luigi Galvani (1737-1798) was one of the first to experimentally investigate the phenomenon of what came to be named 'bioelectrogenesis'. In a series of experiments started around 1780, Galvani, working at the University of Bologna, found that the electric current delivered by a Leyden jar or a rotating static electricity generator would cause contractions of the muscle in the leg of a small animal by applying the charge either to the muscle or to the nerve.

While Frankenstein's monster is created using electricity, in Čapek's play the robots are created on some sort of assembly line in a chemical and industrial facility. The major difference is, perhaps, not the method of creation, but the fact that Frankenstein's monster is unique, while Rossum's robots are numerous, indicating a change of perspective from the moral responsibility of the individual to the political responsibility for a social order allowing the exploitation of the masses. In both cases, the artificial being is of flesh and blood. We still have to find the solution to the riddle of the robot.

EXCURSION: LADY LOVELACE AND THE
ANALYTICAL MACHINE OF CHARLES BABBAGE

A note should be permitted on another curious connection between the summer of 1816 and modern information technology. While staying in Villa Deodati, Byron worked on the third canto of "Childe Harold's Pilgrimage", which the Shelleys and Clare Clairmont brought back with them to England while Byron continued his fateful journey. This canto was dedicated to his infant daughter, Ada Augusta (1815-1852), later Lady Lovelace. Ada Augusta had a talent for mathematics, and would become the collaborator of the grumpy genius Charles Babbage (1791-1871), holder of the Lucasian Chair of Mathematics at Cambridge University (and famous for never giving a lecture to the students). He designed the Difference Engine, an advanced calculator, and the Analytical Engine – the latter in principle a general, mechanical computer using stacks of cogged wheels as a short-term memory and programmed by the same punched cards as those used for Jaquard's looms. The best description of this machine can be found in Lady Lovelace's notes on a translation of an essay published by the Italian engineer and mathematician Luigi Menabrea (1809-1896) in 1842. Menabrea himself was not a minor figure, becoming Italian Premier and Foreign Minister in 1867. Today Lady Lovelace's notes provide the best account of the Analytical Machine, its construction, and the vision of how it could be programmed to solve any problem. Her insights have earned her the title of the world's first programmer. In this curious way one may trace a thin thread of relationship between the modern computer and the origin of Frankenstein's monster.

Perhaps of more importance in our context is one of the questions addressed by Lady Lovelace: Would the Analytical Machine be able to "think" in the sense that it would be able to create something novel? The question is disturbingly modern, still recurring in the field of artificial intelligence research. Her answer, known as Lady Lovelace's response, is that as the machine could only carry out the processes it had been programmed to perform, it would not be able to do anything novel. This has subsequently been challenged, perhaps most notably by Alan Turing (1912-1954) a century later, when he emphasised that the machine could be programmed to learn from experience through feedback, and that it, in this way, could possibly improve its own programs beyond the foresight of the programmer, consequently arriving at surprising results or behaving in unexpected ways.

We may wish to compare Lady Lovelace's response to the description of Rossum's robots, which are said to be incapable of "thinking of anything new". I have no reason to believe that Čapek was familiar with Lady Lovelace's notes. In his day, the work of Charles Babbage was regarded as a curiosity of no practical importance; Babbage's restoration only came after the construction of the first electronic computer, which in principle paralleled his Analytical Machine, and this realisation also brought fame to Lady Lovelace.

ALEXANDRA ALEXANDROVNA EXTER AND *AELITA*

Alexandra Alexandrovna Exter (originally Grigorovich, 1882-1949) was born in Bielostock and attended art school in Kiev. In 1916, at a time when non-figurative art was still relatively unknown, Exter created her first entirely abstract paintings. In the same year she began designing sets and costumes for a Moscow play. Her revolutionary designs won critical acclaim, and her theatrical career was launched. In 1921 she joined the Soviet constructionists, artists who put their talents to use for the new communist state. Most of them abandoned painting, even in its most radical forms, as overly bourgeois, and turned instead to design. The general slogan of the constructivists was "Art into Life", and their goal was "to unite purely artistic forms with utilitarian intentions". In their most extreme formulations, the constructivist Alexei Gan announced: "Art is finished! It has no place in the human labour apparatus. Labour, technology, organisation … that is the ideology of our time" (Bowlt 584).

For the next several years Exter produced innovative and influential stage designs for plays, ballets and experimental films. However, like many radical artists whose work did not fit in with Soviet ideology, Exter eventually left the country, settling permanently in Paris in 1924. There she remained an important influence through her exhibitions, her stage work, and her teaching. Exter continued experimenting and sometimes incorporated modern industrial materials such as celluloid and sheet metal into her futuristic designs.

Just before Exter emigrated to France, she worked with the Soviet film director Yakov Protazanov (1881-1945) on the production of *Aelita, Queen of Mars*. Protazanov was called "the old man" of Soviet film because he had started his career before the revolution, and he commanded considerable respect. The film was – for its day – a major production which started in February 1923 and took over a year to complete.[6]

---

6   Around 22,000 metres of film were shot, which resulted in the 2,841 of the final product. The film opened on 30 September 1924 at the Arts Cinema in Moscow, and

The story is based on a novel by Alexei Tolstoi, a distant relative of the famous author Leo Tolstoi. Alexei Tolstoi had actually gone into exile, but had voluntarily returned to the Soviet Union to join the team making this film. However, very little of his novel was used for the film, and Tolstoi was deeply disappointed. The film plot was rather simple. The story starts in December 1921 in the chaos of Civil War in the Soviet Union, and the start of the New Economic Policy. An engineer working among the starving masses of Moscow designs a spacecraft with a friend, who is a solider. Together they go to Mars, and there find a society divided into a ruling class and a working class. The engineer falls madly in love with the Queen of Mars, Aelita, and like a good Bolshevik he starts an uprising among the slave workers of the planet.

Alexandra Exter's designs for the film were cubistic and quite remarkable. One sketch shows the costume for one of the oppressed workers. It is angular, with obvious associations to a machine.[7] *Aelita* became an international success and was also exported to the United States. In English it bore the subtitle "Revolt of the Robots". The play by Čapek was in circulation at the time *Aeltia* was released, and the theme of *R.U.R.* was similar to that of the film: the oppression of workers by the upper classes. In the subtitle, "robots" retained the original meaning of "machine-like men", or slave workers, used without respect for their individual rights as human beings, but rather as tools in an industrial process.

Alexandra Exter's little figure at the Art Institute of Chicago was made in 1925, a year or so after the design of the costumes for the slave workers on Mars. My interpretation of the figure and its title was not correct. It does not render a man-like machine, a "robot" in modern terminology, but rather a machine-like man, a "robot" in the sense of Čapek and *Aelita*. Its association with a machine is a political comment on the exploitation of workers as if they were parts in a huge, industrial process.

We therefore still have to determine how the word changed its meaning.

a special musical score (by Valentin Kruchinin) had been composed to accompany the silent scenes.

7   I am grateful to the Arts Institute of Chicago for providing material on Alexandra Exter and her designs for the film.

THE ART OF DISCOVERY

One of the finest films ever made is Fritz Lang's *Metropolis,* and it is in fact included in the UNESCO list of the Memory of the World. It was produced in Germany in 1925-26 by the Austrian film director Fritz Lang (1890-1976). The film is based on the screenplay *Metropolis* written by Lang's wife, Thea von Harbou (1888-1954) and published as a novel in 1926. The production of the film was itself a major undertaking: new cinematographic techniques were developed, and in some of the scenes as many as 36,000 extras participated. It was produced by Universum Film AG (Ufa) in Berlin, and nearly brought the company to bankruptcy.

To some extent the film is inspired by *Aelita,* and the story has many parallels with both *Aelita* and *R.U.R.* It is set 100 years in the future (2026), in a city much like a Gothic version of New York. Again we have the privileged few and the oppressed workers. The Master of Metropolis is John Masterman. His son, Freder, happens to meet a girl, Maria, in the subterranean city of the workers, where they struggle among the machines, ruthlessly exploited by the privileged ones. Maria encourages the workers to rise against the tyrants. The Master of Metropolis becomes concerned both with his son's infatuation with Maria and with Maria's radical agitation. So far in the plot, the parallels with the former versions of the uprising of the workers are clear enough. But a new element is now brought into the story: the evil scientist Rotwang – a figure which still haunts science fiction. He is a genius, his right hand is replaced by prosthesis and covered in a black glove.[8] Rotwang is asked to make an artificial copy of Maria to take her place in front of the workers and render them harmless, and at the same time provide a solution for the lovesick son.

The plan fails. But in our context, the creation of the artificial Maria, played by the magnificent Birgitte Helm (1906-1996), is important. In Rotwang's laboratory the real Maria is placed in a device, and by her side is placed a replica of her in metal. Using electricity, the life force of the human is transferred to the machine. The laboratory echoes the operating theatre of Dr Frankenstein, where he harnesses the electrical power of lightning to bring his monster to life. The artificial Maria cannot be mistaken for an android; she is built of metal and circuitry. In her, then, we encounter a "robot" in the modern meaning of the word. But the word "robot" is not used to describe the artificial Maria, either in the film or in the novel.

---

8   Stanley Kubrick's *Dr Strangelove* (1964) also wears a glove like this over his artificial
    hand as a tribute to Lang.

Though *Aelita* was made a couple of years prior to *Metropolis,* they were distributed to the American market at about the same time. As shown above, the themes of the two science-fiction films were fairly similar, and both were spectacular by the standards of the time – even if *Aelita* could not rival *Metropolis* in the force of the allegory told. *Aelita*'s subtitle was "Revolt of the Robots", and the workers were dressed in cubistic costumes associating them with mechanical beings. In the other film, a humanoid, clearly built of metal, leads the uprising of the workers. It seems to me that this is the explanation of how the word "robot" subtly changed its meaning, from "machinelike man" to "manlike machine". In the wake of the popularity of the two movies, the riddle of the robots is explained.

ROBOTS ENTERING POPULAR CULTURE: BUCK ROGERS IN THE 25TH CENTURY

In 1928, the science-fiction magazine *Amazing Stories* published the short story entitled "Armageddon 2418 A.D." by Philip Francis Nowlan (1888-1940). The story caught the interest of John Dille Company, who contracted the author to develop a comic strip based on the same basic idea. The result was *Buck Rogers in the 25th Century,* one of the first true space operas to be created, and a forerunner of other well-known adventure comic strips like that of Flash Gordon (and his companion, the scientist Dr Zarkow). The first episode, "Meeting the Mongols", was drawn by Dick Calkins and published in 1929. Here, we find a detailed drawing of something called an "iron man". It has video cameras for eyes, speaks through a loudspeaker, the arms end in pliers, and it moves on rolling belts like a tank. It is not autonomous, but is operated at a distance – and might therefore not qualify as a "robot" according to the modern usage of the word. Robot, however, is the exact term used by Nowlan, the iron man bearing the title "Robot #792". This is the earliest example I have found of the word definitely having changed its meaning.[9]

The earliest short story I have found that uses the term "robot" is Harl Vincent's "Rex" (*Amazing Stories* 1934); but intelligent or man-like machines were very popular at this time, and one can find several examples. Robots in fact became a theme in science fiction, the stories typically recalling the

---

9   *Buck Rogers* became very popular as the first comic strip intended for an adult audi-
     ence. The strip ran in US newspapers 1929-1967, the last feature film being made as
     late as 1979, and a television series ran for several seasons, ending in 1981.

original Frankenstein motif, the intelligent machine that turns against its creator.[10]

THE MODERN ROBOT: ISAAC ASIMOV AND
THE THREE LAWS OF ROBOTICS

The image of the modern robot was forged by the extremely prolific and diverse Isaac Asimov (1920-1993), an American science-fiction writer with a Russian background. His first short story about robots was 'Robbie' (*Super Science Stories* 1940). The same year, Asimov submitted a proposal for another story to one of the most influential science-fiction editors ever, John W Campbell of the legendary science-fiction magazine *Astounding Stories*.

> My notion was to have a robot refuse to believe he had been created mechanically in a factory, but insist that men were only his servants and that robots were the peak of creation, having been created by some godlike entity. What's more, he would prove his case by reason, and "Reason" was the title of the story. (Asimov 281)

The story was published in *Astounding Stories* (1941). In our context, it is important to emphasise that this story too revolves around the Frankenstein motif, the relation between a creator and the product of the creative process. The robot and its two constructors are in an artificial satellite orbiting the Earth, with no direct evidence that human society had produced the autonomous robot, since it was brought to consciousness for the first time aboard the satellite. With considerable force the robot argues that the two men could not have created it:

> Look at you. I say this in no spirit of contempt, but look at you! The material you are made of is soft and flabby, lacking endurance and strength, depending for energy on the inefficient oxidation of organic material. Periodically you pass into a coma and the least variation in temperature, air pressure, humidity, or radiation intensity impairs your efficiency. You are *makeshift*.
>
> I, on the other hand, am a finished product. I absorb electrical energy directly and utilize it with an almost one hundred percent efficiency. I am composed of

---

10 There are a few anthologies that give broad samples of the contemporary stories. See for instance Isaac Asimov, Patricia S. Warrick and Martin H. Greenberg (eds) (1983) and Sam Moskowitz (ed) (1963).

strong metal, am continuously conscious, and can stand extremes of environment easily. These are facts which, with the self-evident proposition that no being can create another being superior to itself, smash your silly hypothesis to nothing.

The final addition to the modern robot was the Three Laws of Robotics that made Asimov famous. This set of rules first appeared in his 1942 short story "Runaround", but he himself attributes them to Campbell, from a conversation on 23 December 1940:

1. A robot may not injure a human being, or, through inaction, allow a human being to come to harm.
2. A robot must obey the orders given it by human beings except when such orders would conflict with the First Law.
3. A robot must protect its own existence as long as such protection does not conflict with the First or Second Laws.

Asimov created a series of stories on the basis of these laws. The short stories are collected in *I, Robot* (1950) and *The Rest of the Robots* (1964). The novels include *Caves of Steel* (1954) and *The Naked Sun* (1957). Towards the end of his career, Asimov started a project of intertwining his robot tales into the original *Foundation* trilogy, and it is difficult to sort out their relations. Recently the film *I, Robot* (2004) directed by Alex Proyas (1963-) has been based on the characters and plots from the robot stories.

ARTIFICIAL INTELLIGENCE, REPLICANTS, CYBORGS AND OTHER FAMILY MEMBERS

It would be futile trying to follow in detail the image of the intelligent machine in fiction after Asimov introduced the modern robot. We simply have too many examples. In science fiction we find that robots lived strangely apart from proper computers. When computers were introduced, the image was of a very large machine, typically a computer that governed society. The miniaturisation and distribution of computers that took place throughout the late 1970s had not been foreseen in science-fiction literature.

A typical image of the intelligent computer is presented in the legendary movie by Stanley Kubrick (1928-1999) entitled *2001: A Space Odyssey* (1968), which was based on a script by Arthur C. Clarke (1917-), a British science-fiction author with a crisp, nearly academic, matter-of-fact style. In the film, the computer is governing a space vessel journeying to Jupiter and is called

HAL (Heuristically programmed ALgoritmic computer).[11] The force of the image of this computer is partly its soft and emotional voice, and partly the way it develops some sort of paranoia, a mental disorder making it even more human. It may be maintained that in this respect the Frankenstein motif again emerges – at least, the dialogue between man and machine is part of a discussion of what essentially makes a human being different from an intelligent machine.

This becomes one of the major themes in the work of the American science-fiction author Philip K. Dick (1928-1982). In his many books and stories, one major question is: "What is reality?" His own tongue-in-cheek answer is: "Reality is what refuses to go away when I stop believing in it." In all his books he finds new ways of discussing the relationship between reality and perceived reality. An important version of his basic question is how to see the difference between a human and an imitation of a human. The novel in which this question is perhaps most clearly in focus is *Do Androids Dream of Electric Sheep?* (1968). "Androids" are, of course, the name given to artificial beings constructed not from metal but rather from organic material. In the novel, androids are prohibited from visiting Earth, and have a very limited life-span. Rogue androids frequently trespass, and a corps of law enforcement officers hunt them down, administer tests to make sure they have caught an android and not a human being, and then "retire" them. The protagonist is an officer who becomes deeply troubled when he finds it difficult to identify androids, falls in love with one of them, and finally starts to believe he himself may be an android. This novel was turned into the widely known film *Blade Runner* (1982), directed by Ridley Scott, with Harrison Ford in the role of the protagonist. In the film, the androids are called "replicants", emphasising the central issue of similarity between the hunter and the hunted.

In a way, this closes the circle. We started out with Čapek's robots, produced from organic material in chemical vats, and end up with the replicants, sophisticated and smart human look-alikes. But we still have one more step to go – the fusion, even union between man and machine, the cybernetic organism, the cyborg.

In the 1980s a strain of science fiction usually called "cyberpunk" appeared. Several prominent authors could be regarded as belonging to this school, but the leading exponent is no doubt William Gibson (1948-), who,

11 The acronym is an obvious pun: transpose the letters one place to the right, and you get IBM.

in his first and vibrant novel *Neuromancer* (1984), coins the word "cyber-space", which has been absorbed by everyday language as a reference to the virtual reality of computerised networks and machines. In the work of Gibson and many other cyber-punkers, the computer is directly interfaced with the neural network of man. An extra memory chip can be slotted into a socket behind the ear for easy access to a foreign language; a readout from your personal agenda is available in your field of vision, including a face recognition module to prompt you for the name of people you met at cocktail parties, outlining the personal information they gave you on that occasion – supplemented with what is available on the Net. And for a "high", the pleasure centre of the brain is directly stimulated by an inserted probe.

In this fiction, the distinction which has followed us through this essay – between "machine-like man" and "man-like machine" – is absorbed in a new synthesis, which may be an apt symbol for the post-industrial society. Frankenstein's monster was born from the emerging understanding of the power inherent in natural sciences. The robots were an allegory of the social and political forces in industrial society. The cyborg may be the symbol that makes explicit the new and ethical challenges arising as biotechnology, nanotechnology and information technology converge to create new possibilities for both the individual and society.

POSTSCRIPT: THE PIN AND ZAMYATIN

In this essay, the robot has been regarded as a powerful literary symbol, high-lighting the way humans may be used without respecting their individual dignity, as machines in an industrial production system. In our modern society there is at least one other such symbol: the concept of numbers, often used in phrases such as "Individuals are reduced to numbers in the machinery of bureaucracy".

The reason why numeric signs have this symbolic effect has not been quite clear to me. One might think it was related to the introduction of early computerised systems, in which storage capacity was scarce and numbers were somewhat more easily handled than letters. Some countries have introduced general personal identification numbers, a unique number used typically in communication with government systems to avoid mistakes of identity. Obviously, numbers are also used for similar purposes by countries which do not have a unique PIN, like the social security number in the United States, or the tax administrative number in Canada. But clearly the symbolic value assigned to numbers predates government computer systems. Perhaps some of the negative associations are related to the use of numbers tattooed onto the skin of prisoners in German concentration camps during the Second World War. But this must only have augmented a quality already present in "the reduction to a number". Perhaps this, too, has a literary explanation – there is certainly an important Utopian novel from the time of the Soviet revolution which, to the best of my knowledge, introduces numbers as a symbol of the lack of respect for human individuality for the first time.

Yevgeny Ivanovich Zamyatin (1884-1937) was a powerful literary figure in the early Soviet state. He welcomed the revolution, but he criticised its repression of freedom. He was close to the leaders of the revolution, but was arrested several times, and came to be regarded as a heretic, constantly attacked in the late 1920s by Communist Party-line critics. He had to give up the leadership of the All-Russian Writers' Union. His works were banned and removed from libraries, and he was unable to publish. After writing a letter to Stalin, Zamyatin was allowed to go with his wife into exile in 1931. He settled in Paris in 1932, where he died in poverty. He completed his only novel, *We*, in 1921. Extracts from the original text were published in an émigré journal in Prague in 1927. In Russia *We* circulated in manuscript form, and was finally published in Paris. Zamyatin's *We* (original title *My*, 1921) takes place in the One State, where all buildings, tools and machines are made of glass. People are called "numbers" and all live, work and act precisely in unison, to the point that they chew their food together. Their actions are dictated by the "Table of Hours", a clock system which synchronises precisely what everyone is to do and when. The people are ruled by the Benefactor and policed by the Guardians. The protagonist is D-503, a mathematician and builder of the Integral, a gigantic glass spaceship which is being constructed to go to other planets and spread the joy of the One State – here one may see the parallel with *Aelita*.

One will recognise the theme of the novel as common to that of the two most influential utopian novels of the last century, *Brave New World* (1932) by Aldous Huxley (1894-1963) and *1984* (1949) by George Orwell (1903-1950). The theme is also closely related to that of the revolt of the robots in *R.U.R*, *Aelita* and *Metropolis*, indicating that the web of literary symbols and allegories is much more tangled than we have been allowed to glimpse through the small aperture opened by Alexandra Exter's cardboard figure in the Art Institute of Chicago. We will not pursue these tantalising threads to find new and intertwining patterns. They remain reminders not only of the richness of the literary imagination, but also of the importance that these symbols and allegories have with regard to our understanding of ourselves and our relation to society.

I am pleased to have solved, at least to my own satisfaction, the riddle of the word "robot".

WORKS CITED

http://capek.misto.cz/english/robot.html

Asimov, Isaac. *In Memory Yet Green: The Autobiography of Isaac Asimov.* New York: Doubleday, 1979.

Asimov, Isaac, Patricia S. Warrick and Martin H. Greenberg, eds. *Machines that Think.* NewYork: Holt, Rinehart & Winston, 1983.

Bing, Jon and Tor Åge Bringsværd. *Jeg – en maskin.* Oslo: Gyldendal, 1973.

Bowlt, John E. "Russian Art in the Nineteen Twenties". *Soviet Studies.* Vol. 22, No. 4, University of Glasgow, Vol. 22, No 4, (1971): 575-594.

Kisch, Egon Erwin. *Der rasende Reporter.* (1925) Berlin: Aufbau Taschenbuch Verlag, 2001.

Meyrink, Gustav. Der Golem, Stuttgart: Reclam, 2008.

Moskowitz, Sam, ed. *The Coming of the Robots.* New York: Collier, 1963.

Piercy, Marge. *He, She, and It.* New York: Fawcett Crest, 1993.

Shelley, Mary Wollstonecraft. *Frankenstein, or The Modern Prometheus.* Oxford, Bodleian Library, 2008.

Zamjatin, Evgenij. *We.* New York: Penguin Books, 1993.

LEO SZILARD: IMMORAL SCIENCE – MORAL FICTION?[1]

Roger Strand, University of Bergen

Several nuclear physicists who took part in the development of the atomic bombs over Hiroshima and Nagasaki later expressed deep concerns about the post-war historical developments. This chapter presents a reading of two short stories by the atomic physicist Leo Szilard (1898-1964), discoverer of the idea of the nuclear chain reaction and instrumental in developing the Manhattan Project. In 1939, Szilard and Enrico Fermi conducted the first experiment with neutron multiplication in uranium: "All we had to do," Szilard later wrote, "was lean back, turn a switch... We saw the flashes, we watched them for about ten minutes – and then we... went home. That night I knew that the world was headed for sorrow" (Szilard et al., xxix). In the short stories "The Voice of the Dolphins" (1961) and "My Trial as a War Criminal" (1947), Szilard struggles with his moral dilemmas, showing a level of imagination and wit perhaps not often attributed to natural scientists. The question under debate is this: Can fiction set straight the sins of science?[2]

---

1 This paper was presented at the *Literature and Science* workshop in Bergen, December 2008, and the many useful comments from the participants, organisers and an anonymous reviewer are gratefully acknowledged. Special thanks to my colleagues in and around the Centre for the Study of the Sciences and the Humanities, where we have discussed *Frankenstein,* the social responsibility of science and related matters for years.

2 Extensive biographies have been written on Leo Szilard (Esterer and Esterer; Lanouette and Silard). In this brief note there is space to mention only a few of the many fascinating features of his life as a scientist, intellectual and world citizen. An emigré to the USA, exiled from his native Hungary and forced to escape from Nazi Germany, Szilard held a secret patent on the nuclear chain reaction before he convinced Albert Einstein to address President Roosevelt on the possibility that the Germans might develop nuclear weapons. If direct historical lines between individuals and the entry into our nuclear age were to be drawn, the line of Szilard, together with those of Einstein and Oppenheimer, would emerge as the most conspicuous. Perhaps even more vigorous than his nuclear initiatives prior to the Manhattan Project, were Szilard's efforts to stop the attacks on Japanese cities. Through petitions and attempts at direct contact with the US president, Szilard warned against the attacks, though

The modern European states, built on the ideals of enlightenment, science, rationality and at times democracy, took it for granted that knowledge is better than ignorance, that the search for truth is an inherently virtuous activity, and that science in this sense is among the finest expressions of progress, rationality, human grandeur – indeed, of the Good. In one respect, this belief has been part of the European tradition since Plato and Aristotle, with their view of knowledge as essential to human fulfilment. In the modern sense, however, we may turn to how the philosopher, politician and (amateur) scientist Francis Bacon and his contemporaries celebrated science as the new human organ: "Human knowledge and human power come to the same thing, for where the cause is not known, the effect cannot be produced" (Bacon, Book I, Aphorism 3).

At least since Mary Shelley's novel *Frankenstein; or, the Modern Prometheus*, however, the unsettling question has been asked: What if Science produces Evil? Often, the question has been reduced to that of scientists' improper, corrupt or cruel behaviour, or to instances of the irrational or perverse application of inherently good knowledge. Alternatively, the question might be dismissed as uninformed, irrational and unworthy. Indeed, the narrative of *Frankenstein* itself lends itself to the reduction of the moral point to a trivial one of misuse and abuse. Victor Frankenstein is a charlatan, perhaps; surely he is a coward, overtaken by fear, disgust and self-pity at the critical moments when he had the opportunity to right the wrongs – by catching his creation, or warning his surroundings, or at least preventing the miscarriage of justice that occurs when Justine is executed for a murder she never committed. In this obvious sense, there can be no doubt that Victor Frankenstein acted irresponsibly and had blood on his hands.

Since the 1970s, the idea of unworthy and unholy objectives of research has also become a political issue as the possibility of creating and designing life moved from B-movie sets to scientific laboratories. With molecular biology and the cloning of *Dolly*, famously the first cloned mammal, the fiction of Frankenstein's creature met its ovine equivalent of actual flesh and

---

to little avail. After the war, he changed scientific field – from physics to biology – and spent a considerable part of his time and energy on public and private letters to political leaders, warning against the hydrogen bomb and proposing political measures to avoid nuclear war. Perhaps the only political leader to be impressed by Szilard was Nikita Khruschev, with whom he corresponded and who he also briefly met in 1960.

blood. Disputes over cloned and genetically modified animals and plants apart, the creation of *Dolly* became a milestone in the development of the ethics of science. After *Dolly*, the possibility of cloning humans could no longer be dismissed as science fiction, and most countries actually outlawed it. Frankenstein-like research, then, has come to denote a rare exception in the family of science: research that, by nature of its unworthy objective, itself constitutes abuse.

The question remains, of course, how to draw the line between normal, dignified science and its unethical deviations; between, as it were, the flock of white sheep and the exceptional black ones cloning themselves, others or *Dolly*. Even in the world of fiction, film makers had to invent *Igor* (or indeed *Fritz*), the hideous, deranged assistant who by his sheer ugliness conveyed the signs of immorality to the audience. The conflation of ethics with aesthetics is of course a dangerous game; still, the ethics of science appears to assume that abuse somehow *shows* by its bizarreness and monstrosity violating human dignity.

Nevertheless, it is not difficult to read *Frankenstein* as presenting a more fundamental critique of modern man and modern societies; or, as some commentators argue, an attack on the unrestrained beliefs in progress personified by the author's own father. Shelley's own life aside, Victor Frankenstein's voice in the novel appears unequivocal. He does not distinguish between normal and bizarre science, but invokes the virtue of restraint, moderation, *temperance* as a general first principle: "never to allow passion or a transitory desire to disturb his tranquillity. I do not think that the pursuit of knowledge is an exception to this rule" (Shelley, Vol. I, Chapter 4).

Temperance is a recognised virtue in many aspects of modern life, including political life. In the world of science and knowledge-based capitalist economies, however, temperance is obsolete and unbearable: it is inefficiency. Since the Second World War, and especially since the famous 1945 report to President Roosevelt on the future of science by the presidential science advisor Vannevar Bush, entitled *Science: The Endless Frontier*, science policies have recommended full speed ahead in science and innovation for the production of new facts, new technologies and new goods. Accusing scientists of a lack of temperance would be like accusing modern consumers of greed and gluttony: if they were to take the accusation seriously, the market economy as well as the models that explain it would collapse.

While Mary Shelley's novel about science could be interpreted in terms of the ethics and perhaps the politics of science, Leo Szilard[3] wrote short stories about politics and perhaps ethics in the aftermath of Hiroshima and Nagasaki. "The Voice of the Dolphins" (1961) is the piece in his literary production that has received most attention. Indeed, it is the most elaborate of his short stories. Its opening is characteristic of Szilard's dry but witty style:

> ON SEVERAL OCCASIONS between 1960 and 1985, the world narrowly escaped an all-out atomic war. In each case, the escape was due more to fortuitous circumstances than to the wisdom of the policies pursued by statesmen. That the bomb would pose a novel problem to the world was clear as early as 1946. It was not clearly recognized, however, that the solution of this problem would involve political and technical considerations in an inseparable fashion. In America, few statesmen were aware of the technical considerations, and, prior to Sputnik, only few scientists were aware of the political considerations. After Sputnik, Dr. James R. Killian was appointed by President Eisenhower, on a full-time basis, as chairman of the President's Science Advisory Committee, and, thereafter, a number of distinguished scientists were drawn into the work of the Committee and became aware of all aspects of the problem posed by the bomb. (Szilard 47-48)

The story describes how, during the Cold War period, the superpowers with the aid of scientists manage to devise institutions for collaboration and for avoiding nuclear conflict. The main element of the story is the (fictitious) Vienna Institute, an elite research institute for scientists from both sides of the Iron Curtain, specialising in research on dolphins. In the course of the story, dolphins and humans develop a common language, allowing the dolphins to become man's saviours by providing neutral, creative and highly intelligent advice on difficult political issues. By the mid-1980s, when political stability and nuclear disarmament have been achieved, the dolphins allegedly die in a viral epidemic, and the Vienna Institute and its archives are destroyed in a fire.

The fact that "The Voice of the Dolphins" has received acclaim is not due to its poetic quality (Rosenheim). Indeed, its prose style is closer to that of a historical report or chronicle. This is fiction in the bare sense of describing

---

3   Sources vary as to spelling his name with or without accents (Leó Szilárd or Leo Szilard). For convenience I will use the spelling that is associated with his fictional writings, i.e., without accents.

fictitious future events. Also, although one might defend labelling the story as science fiction, a more suitable category would be "political fiction". Science and scientists prevail in the narrative owing to their key role in Szilard's ideal political universe. The satire penetrates the story in its many details, but above all in the conception of the talking dolphins. If people and especially politicians were rational, they would have listened to the scientists. People being irrational, the scientists had to find – perhaps invent – a solution in the form of the voice of the dolphins. Whether the dolphins "really" existed within the story's fictional universe is unimportant. The main point is the rationality of the mechanisms proposed for international politics, including disarmament and conflict resolution. Szilard's short stories are all moral allegories, offering solutions to political, ethical and moral problems in a world with nuclear weapons. Most often, as in "The Voice of the Dolphins", the solutions are discovered by scientists and involve the agency of scientists. The scientists, in short, are the heroes.

SZILARD'S TRIAL AS A WAR CRIMINAL

On the day after the Hiroshima bombing, Szilard wrote in a letter to his wife-to be: "Using atomic bombs against Japan is one of the greatest blunders of history... both from a practical point of view and from the point of view of our moral position" (quoted in Bernstein 14). It is sometimes said that the nuclear physicists "wrestled" with ethical issues and doubts after WWII, and Szilard's writings can be read in such a frame of understanding. Another reading, however, would emphasise the lack of doubt in Szilard's writings. There is an awareness of the graveness and urgency of the problems, but also clear and unequivocal advice on what to do. And his solution, implicitly and explicitly, is always to assign more power to the scientists and allow them to educate the people. The *tragedy* is not there. Rather, Szilard writes comedy, with politicians and the mass media as clowns, and with a happy ending at the point when the scientists convince or trick the politicians and the people into accepting the rational answer to every question. The question that is never asked is how the state of destruction was reached in the first place. How was it that the world entered the nuclear age? Who are to be held responsible? Why should people trust the advice of the scientists who created the bombs? What about the scientists' responsibility for the development?

Writing "The Voice of the Dolphins" in 1961, it seems that Szilard has no time for such questions, fighting cold warriors but also the finitude of his own lifetime (he recovered from cancer but then died of a heart attack in

1964). To find him in a less self-assured moment, we have to turn to Szilard's first short story "My Trial as a War Criminal" (1947), a 10-page, darker piece written little more than a year after Hiroshima and Nagasaki. Let us remind ourselves that the story is fictional. The real Szilard was not accused of war crimes. As in the later "Voice of the Dolphins", the story consists of a description of imagined future events. The scenario is a post-World War II world in which the US has surrendered to the Soviet Union. The narrator, called Szilard and bearing a number of biographical similarities to the real Leo Szilard, is placed on trial with other US scientists and politicians, accused of war crimes on the grounds of the Hiroshima and Nagasaki bombings. The main part of the story takes place in the court room. Szilard presents his own defence, in particular his petitions and attempts to stop the bombings. Whether the defence is meant to be convincing to the reader remains unclear at best. As for the US politicians, their defence is even less convincing. Towards the end, however, the story takes a different turn. In the midst of an uncontrolled Soviet health emergency the US scientists are called in to help, and the trial is closed before a verdict can be reached. "Naturally, all of us who had been on trial for our lives were greatly relieved," the narrator concludes (Szilard 114). A humanitarian disaster (created by the Soviets themselves) saves the scientists from their judgement, perhaps reminding the readers of how German scientists were absolved in post-World War II USA.

Were they guilty? Szilard – the narrator of the short story – defends himself by claiming that he tried to stop the bombings. In the fictional trial, the claims are refuted on the grounds of lack of evidence. Also, the prosecutor accuses him of gullibility in not presenting his protest against using the bomb to the president in person: "The prosecutor said that I, Szilard, should have known better than to agree to such a method of transmittal" (Szilard 108-109). At this critical point the story appears to slip away from the issue, turning to the occasionally ridiculous technicalities of the court proceedings and finally their dissolution. Why does Szilard fail to answer the question – or does he? I see at least three possible readings of the story.

The first reading is that the story indeed passes the verdict of guilty on Szilard, and to a greater extent on the US politicians. When it comes to the case of "Byrnes", we are told: "Of course, if sentence had been passed and executed, he would have lost his life" (Szilard 114). In appraising the force of the prose, one should recall that James F. Byrnes, to whom Szilard was no doubt referring, was the US Secretary of State at the time the short story was written. It is not unlikely that contemporary readers found Szilard to be blaming Byrnes for war crimes, and blaming himself for collaboration and failure to prevent the catastrophe. Again, we see the theme of the scientist hero, this time failing. The text does not read: "I should have known better". It reads: "I, Szilard, should have known better" – the hero scientist is more knowledgeable than ordinary men, and so has to accept a greater responsibility.

The second reading is to see the story as an allegory of the Nuremberg trials, turning the hypocrisy of the Allies onto themselves: that they only tried war crimes committed by the Axis countries; that they were illogical and inconsistent; and that the US indeed was quite pragmatic when it came to absolving Nazi scientists who could become useful in post-war USA. In this way, when the real issues "fade away", this is just as much a critical comment on the lack of moral strength in contemporary USA and its allied countries.

The third reading is indeed to see the development of the story as a detour that never returns on track, as if the author could not endure the existential weight of the question. In his psychological analysis of Leo Szilard, Frank argues that the key to understanding his remarkable personality is the idea of the exile: always in peril, always ready to go, to move (204-252). A similar point is made by Thompson, who associates Szilard's personality with "angelism" (982-983).

Before passing verdicts on Szilard's personality and the lack of consistency in this short story, however, we should ask rhetorically: how many of the individuals involved in the Manhattan Project and the bombings of Hiroshima and Nagasaki reflected in public about their own guilt as war criminals? I suspect that only a few of them did so. The genius of the story lies perhaps in the dramatic difference of these three readings, which are nonetheless in no way mutually exclusive.

THE TRAGEDY OF SCIENCE

In spite of, or perhaps because of, the existential seriousness of the question, "My Trial as a War Criminal" ends in dark comedy, in incompetence, in irrationality, and in the black and bitter irony that another disaster shifts the agenda so that the trial is cancelled. What then if there were no disturbances, and a fair trial could have taken place? Would the narrator's defence be sufficient? I imagine that it would. Szilard – the real Szilard – did try his best to stop the attacks on Hiroshima and Nagasaki. As for the initiative that led to the Manhattan Project, this was taken in a situation where a possible scenario was that of world domination by a Nazi regime with nuclear arms. Of course that had to be prevented. From this perspective, Leo Szilard was twice a moral hero. The same could be said of Albert Einstein. Judged by their intentions, their motives and their contexts, they excelled as scientists who were aware of their social responsibility.

In the recent television epic *Carnivàle*, the unleashing of nuclear power – "a false sun wrought by the hands of men"[4] – is interpreted as the final victory of Evil. However sophisticated the regimes of arms control and nuclear inspections become, it appears more than imaginable that intentional or accidental uses of nuclear technology will cause extreme suffering in the future. It is likewise imaginable that it will be the final blow to our civilisation. The same could be said of other technological fields developed over the last two centuries. This is not to say that the same technologies and their underlying sciences have not produced tremendous benefits for mankind. The existence of these benefits, however, does not make the risks disappear. It shows the capacity of Szilard's intellect that he was immediately able to see that it is these risks, and not the benefits, that essentially redefine the condition of civilisation: that the world was indeed "headed for sorrow".

The tragedy of science is this: the scientific villains are not the greatest threat to civilisation; the villains and their bizarre excesses are important only in so far as their monstrosities can teach us something about the barely visible aspects of normal science. The tragedy resides in the fact that it is the scientific heroes whose ground-breaking research has unleashed new hidden forces and new forms of destruction. They are heroes, then, exactly because of their intellect, their creativity, their best intentions, and because our civilisation so far has been unable to understand and govern their activity as anything other than the production of Truth, which is a Good. This is why temperance in science is absurd: temperance may be a virtue, but not with regard to the Good. The Good should be embraced unconditionally.

Is there a way out, or at least a way forward? Charles Taylor noted the need to escape from "the epistemological prison" – the epistemological modelling of our understanding of science. As long as scientific and technological practice is conceived as nothing but a truth machine to describe the world, its agency of changing the world remains unmanaged. In recent decades, scholars of science and technology studies, as well as historians,

---

4   http://www.hbo.com/carnivale/episode/season2/episode13.shtml, accessed 25 March, 2009

sociologists and philosophers of science, have made thousands of contributions to understandings of scientific and technological practice that are not epistemologically modelled. Indeed, it has been shown how scientific practice is influenced by its historical, cultural and political context; how sociological and psychological mechanisms are operative within scientific communities, affecting their work and results; and how apparently "pure and basic" research may stand in close relationships with specific demands for technology. Although I do not in any way underestimate the intellectual effort made by these scholars – to whose community I belong – it is amazing how close the individual scientist may be to a more reflexive understanding of the tragedy of his practice. To keep it at a distance, discipline is required. This can be a matter of work discipline, always being laborious, energetic, dutiful and useful, such as in Szilard's case, or ideological discipline, such as the implicit teachings of the epistemological model in natural science education.

It is fashionable, and rightly so in my opinion, to call for scientists' social responsibility (Badash, European Commission). The question is what exactly one is calling for. The kind of social responsibility that outlaws and controls the villains and encourages the heroes will not change the tragic state of affairs. What is required, if such a change is called for, is a reappraisal of science itself along with its heroes. If we require scientists to have a more reflexive understanding of the tragedy of their practice, we are in euphemistic terms asking them to allow themselves to fall into despair.

Among the positive aspects of the difference between literature and reality is the experience that doubt, despair and loss of control can be lived through in literature without necessarily disrupting life. In "My Trial as a War Criminal" the narrator-author sets out on a walk down such a road, but stops midway. With this observation we may conclude by recalling our initial contrast between Victor Frankenstein and Leo Szilard. The interesting difference between them is perhaps in fact the obvious one: Victor Frankenstein never lived, so he may express his deepest despair. Leo Szilard lived; lived to see, as he said, the world heading for sorrow. Being alive, his choice was to act rather than fall into contemplation. Contemplating in fiction was a way to act in the world. Where, in Mary Shelley's *Frankenstein*, the tragedy is written into the story, in Leo Szilard's fiction, the tragedy is that it is not.

WORKS CITED

Bacon, Francis. *Novum Organum*. Chicago: Open Court Publications, 1994 (1620).

Badash, Lawrence. "American Physicists, Nuclear Weapons in World War II, and Social Responsibility." *Physics in Perspective* 7 (2005). 138-149.

Bernstein, Barton J. "Introduction", in Szilard, Leo. *The Voice of the Dolphins and Other Stories. Expanded edition*. Stanford: Stanford University Press, 1992. 3-43.

Bush, Vannevar. *Science: The Endless Frontier. A Report to the President by Vannevar Bush, Director of the Office of Scientific Research and Development*. Washington: US Government Printing Office, 1945. Last accessed 25 March 2009 at URL http://www.nsf.gov/od/lpa/nsf50/vbush1945.htm.

Esterer, Arnulf K. and Luise A. Esterer. *Prophet of the Atomic Age: Leo Szilard*. New York: Julian Messner, 1972.

European Commission. *Code of Conduct Commission Recommendation of 07/02/2008 on a Code of Conduct for Responsible Nanosciences and Nanotechnologies Research, C(2008) 424*. Brussels. Accessed 25 March 2009 at URL http://ec.europa.eu/nanotechnology/pdf/nanocode-rec_pe0894c_en.pdf.

Frank, Tibor. "Ever Ready to Go: The Multiple Exiles of Leo Szilard." *Physics in Perspective* 7 (2005): 204-252.

Lanouette, William and Bela Silard. *Genius in the Shadows: A Biography of Leo Szilárd: The Man Behind The Bomb*. New York: Charles Scribner's Sons, 1992.

Rosenheim, Edward Jr. "The Voice of the Dolphins and Other Stories by Leo Szilard." *The University of Chicago Law Review* 29,1 (1961): 214-217.

Szilard, Leo. *The Voice of the Dolphins and Other Stories. Expanded edition*. Stanford: Stanford University Press, 1992.

Szilard, Leo, Helen S. Hawkins, G. Allen Greb, and Gertrud Weiss Szilard. *Toward a Livable World: Leo Szilard and the Crusade for Nuclear Arms Control*. Cambridge: MIT Press, 1987.

Taylor, Charles. *Overcoming Epistemology. Philosophical Arguments*. Cambridge: Harvard University Press, 1995.

Thompson, Phillip. "Thomas Merton and Leo Szilard: The Parallel Paths of a Monk and a Nuclear Physicist." *Zygon* 39 (2004): 979-986.

PRIMO LEVI'S MOON

Margareth Hagen, University of Bergen

The feeling of awed wonder that science can give us is one of the highest experiences of which the human psyche is capable. It is a deep aesthetic passion to rank with the finest that music and poetry can deliver. (Dawkins x)

Primo Levi (1919-1987), known to most readers mainly for his essays and novels on the Holocaust and his account of his time in Auschwitz, wrote in a continuous dialogue with the natural sciences – his scientific disciplines being first and foremost material sciences such as chemistry and biology, with the related fields of zoology and ethology. Levi's two autobiographical books on the Holocaust experience were followed by two collections of scientific short-stories entitled *Storie naturali* (1966) and *Vizio di forma* (1971), in which biology and technique are the main motives, while the collection *Il sistema periodico* (1975) is entirely dedicated to chemistry. Even though he was preoccupied with and fascinated by "pure" sciences like mathematics, physics and astrophysics, he rarely made these fields themes in his writings. Among the exceptions, however, are a few essays, inspired by the early moon voyages, about man's renewed relationship to the moon and to astronomy. Here Levi questions the human and poetic consequences of the lunar conquests and the astronomic discoveries.

The purpose of this chapter is to ask whether these astronomic essays that reflect on how the poetic tradition has encountered new knowledge about space can illustrate and perhaps distil the thoughts and techniques used by Levi to connect science and poetry. Since Levi brings up the concept of marvel as an integrated part of poetry, the role of marvel, or wonder, in his scientific writing will also be considered.

PRIMO LEVI'S SCIENTIFIC TERRITORIES

To write about the moon not only meant writing about one of the most powerful poetic metaphors of all times, it also meant joining a long line of Italian authors and poets – such as Dante, Ariosto, Galileo, Leopardi, and Levi's contemporary Italo Calvino, who also took a strong interest in the intertwining of literature and science. In an article in *The Times Literary Supplement* (1967), Calvino described his poetic ideals as a *ménage à trois* between science, literature and philosophy (*Saggi* 188-96), while Levi, partly due to his upbringing in fascist Italy, where mainstream philosophy was old-fashioned idealism or religious thought, never ceased to be sceptical towards philosophy. Levi's choice to study chemistry was also a political one: the accusations and descriptions of the British education system made by Charles Snow in his famous essay on "the two cultures" were very close to the situation in Italy during the fascist decennium. Fascist culture was indeed anti-rationalistic, as it cultivated myths, irrational intuition and individualism. Giovanni Gentile, minister of education and official ideologist of the fascist regime, had created a reform that favoured the traditional, humanistic and aesthetic disciplines rather than the natural sciences. Looking back on his years as a student much later, Levi recollected that his Italian teacher claimed that only literary studies had a formative value, while scientific texts had a purely informative function.[1]

Levi repeatedly referred to himself as a technician. The bridge between literature and science in his writings was built during thirty years of practice as an industrial chemist and manager of a paint factory in Turin. Much has been written by scholars and by Levi himself about the frame of mind he developed in his work as an industrial chemist, and on how this influenced his writings. His texts were imbued not only with deductive schemes but also with the day-to-day work procedures and reports from the laboratory, the constant mental disposition to measure and distinguish every human experience, the beautiful work of distilling, for example, and more generally, the ability to contemplate while using the hands and the eyes. To him, creativity and imagination, the intrinsic qualities of literature, were a necessary supplement to science, as he writes in his essay "Thirty Hours on Castoro Sei": "The history of technology demonstrates that, when it is faced by new problems, scientific education and precision are necessary but insufficient. Two other virtues are needed, and they are experience and inventive imagination" (186).[2]

---

1 "It was the Gentile conspiracy. I too had an excellent relationship with my Italian teacher, but when she publicly said that literary subjects have a formative value and scientific subjects have only an informative value, my hair stood on end. This confirmed in me the idea that conspiracy existed. You young Fascist, you young Crocian, you young men grown up in this Italy must not approach the sources of scientific knowledge because they are dangerous" (*Dialogo* 14).

2 *Other People's Trades.* Hereafter abbrev. OPT in parenthetical references.

Levi's scientific tales and essays can be roughly divided into three thematic classes, or motifs, entitled Darwin, Lucretius and Huxley, all of which Levi subjects to philological and etymological questioning. The first major class consists of the tales that Calvino in 1961 described as "fantabiological", and that deal with evolution and biology (*Lettere* 695).[3] Darwinism is also part of the basic world view in Levi's first novel on Auschwitz, a novel that studies human behaviour as partly motivated by biology, and where the narrator appears as a lucid observer of human nature amidst the concentration camp atrocities. Darwin's importance for Levi also appears in his texts not only in the terms of ethology and evolution, but also in his conception of humankind as *homo faber*, or the animal with hands – the hand being a recurring motif in his narratives.

The second part of Levi's scientific narratives is inspired by chemistry, and like many chemists he has a special affection for the Roman poet Lucretius. This thematic nucleus of atomic divisions, motions and compositions naturally also presents autobiographical as well as allegorical stories. According to the scholar Cecare Cases, on a deeper level Levi's chemistry signifies materialism, atomism and a poetic version of hylozoism – the idea that material entities possess life and that life is inseparable from matter (Cases). Levi's hylozoism implies a thorough and continuous anthropomorphisation of the elements.

Levi's third scientific class of narratives is made up of stories in the manner of Huxley's rather pessimistic fiction, the dystopias linked to technique, to the temptations of science and to the dangerous inventions which may come into being in the wake of scientific progress. These texts in particular explore the relationship between science and ethics, the hypocrisy of ethically and politically "neutral" sciences, and the impact of technologies on human social life. Many of these texts in fact illustrate Foucault's thoughts on the mechanisms of power, where technology is primarily a danger to human society.

Several of Levi's short stories cross the conventional borders between genres, moving between autobiography, essayism, realism and fantasy. The stories are populated by scientists and technicians who work with, and investigate, chemistry, neurology, biology, zoology or ethology. Once more it seems interesting that only two of his short stories deal with astronomy, namely "Visto di lontano" ("Seen from Afar"), written at the end of the 1960s

---

3   Levi included a chapter from the *Origins* in his personal anthology, *The Search for Roots* (1981), which he called "Why are Animals Beautiful?"

and included in *Vizio di forma*, and "Una stella tranquilla" (1978), published in the collection *Lilít e altri racconti* (1981).[4]

COMING TO TERMS WITH THE NEW MOON

Reading Levi's texts means reading scientific poetry; and scientific culture is always somehow involved, either as a technique of observation and a pattern of reflection that structure the texts, or more explicitly through the main motif. This view of science's poetical potential was surely also shared by Italo Calvino.

In 1967 Italo Calvino participated in a debate in the national Italian newspaper *Corriere della Sera* with the author Anna Maria Ortese on the poetic consequences of man's lunar conquest. While Ortese lamented the loss of this major poetic figure, Italo Calvino rejected her argumentation with the claim that even if it is true that the moon since time immemorial has signified a relationship with the extra-human universe, with the unreachable: and that even if it is difficult to see how the new images transmitted by the lunar conquest will have anything in common with the moon of past poetry, this is hardly a reason to be sad and despondent. Calvino agrees with Lucretius, who wrote that real piety is to observe the universe with a quiet mind: "he who really loves the moon, cannot be satisfied by contemplating it as a conventional image ... but urges the moon to say more" (*Saggi* 227).[5] Calvino would always assert that our poetic imagination could arise from any kind of suggestion, and that science holds an important reservoir of poetic images and new myths. As he writes in *Six Memos for the Next Millennium*: "Reading even the most technical scientific book or the most abstract book of philosophy, one can come across a phrase that unexpectedly stimulates the visual imagination" (89).

The relationship between Levi and Calvino was one of profound and reciprocal respect. They were both adherents of the Enlightenment and

---

4   "A Tranquil Star." *A Tranquil Star. Unpublished Stories of Primo Levi*. Trans. A. Goldestein and A. Bastagli. London: Norton & Co, 2007. 156-162.

5   My translation. When Calvino spoke of his enthusiasm for the lunar conquests, he had completed his *Cosmicomics,* a stringently composed collection of short stories, which comprises scientific fables spun around the metamorphic being Qfwfq, who narrates his role in the history of the universe. His cosmicomical project was inspired, inter alia, by the work of Giorgio de Santillana, author of *Hamlet's Mill* (1969), on the connections between ancient mythology and natural sciences.

shared the ideals of a neo-encyclopaedic literature. But while Levi, as already mentioned, was chiefly attracted to the materialist and biological sciences, Calvino was more inspired by formal sciences, like mathematics, geometry, astronomy, linguistics and (structural) anthropology, and was also associated with the Parisian Tel Quel group. Moreover, Calvino's fictional texts, particularly in the 60s and 70s, may be interpreted as an endeavour to escape human characters and the naturalistic mode of writing, with its dominant anthropocentric perspective.

Levi no doubt agreed with this view on science as a reservoir for literature; but, being a technician, his language and inspiration also came from practice, from concrete observation and action. As he explained in a dialogue with Tullio Regge:

> I find myself richer than other writers because to me words like "bright", "dark", "heavy", "light" and "blue" have a more extensive and more concrete gamut of meanings ... I mean to say that I have had in my hands materials that are not of current use, with properties outside the ordinary, that have served to amplify my language precisely in a technical sense. Thus I have at my disposal an inventory of raw materials, of tesserae for writing, somewhat larger than that possessed by someone who does not have a technical background (Levi and Regge 59)

Levi did not participate in the debate in *Corriere della Sera*, but in those years he wrote three essays on man's new relationship with the moon and the cosmos: "The Moon and Man", "The Moon and us" and "News from the Sky". Later on, in the 1980s he published two brief essays in *La Stampa,* "We See no Other Adam in the Neighborhood" (1981) and "What was it that Burned Up in Space?" (1986). These five essays illustrate how Levi's writing is always somehow grounded in experience and observation, as they are inspired by recent events: Apollo 8 and 11, Pioneer 10 and 11, and the tragic failure of the Challenger mission in 1986. The negative and pessimistic sentiments on the consequences for literature of man's space adventures seem strangely opposed to Levi's own poetic. Levi's poetics are indeed characterised by a search for new metaphors based on scientific practice and description, along with the technician's or scientist's confrontation with real matter. Despite this paradox, could it be that these reactions to the moon exploits are deeply grounded in Levi's ethics and poetics?

"The Moon and Man" was published in December 1968, shortly after Apollo 8's return from its voyage around the Moon. The text seems strongly inspired by the amazing photos of Earth seen from space, and probably also by the Christmas Eve broadcast from the spacecraft, when James Lowell, one of the three astronauts, exclaimed: "The vast loneliness is awe-inspiring and it makes you realize just what you have back there on Earth" (Williams). At the end of the broadcast the astronauts took turns reading the first ten verses of the Book of Genesis while the magnificent first pictures of Earth taken from space were shown.

The author of "The Moon and Man" is an unusually optimistic Levi, who struggles to find the right words to describe the accomplished mission. The bulk of the essay is a Darwinian and humanist celebration of the excellence and adaptability of *the naked ape*, the "terrestrial animal, son of an everlasting dynasty of terrestrial or marine creatures", which could also make us capable of fighting the wars against earthly "hunger, misery and pain". The image of the tiny Earth offered man an alienating, Copernican gaze, and at the same time a proof of our common ground, as humans, being part of the same tiny ecosystem. "We are at once similar and different: the bravery from which the lunar adventure originated is different, it is Copernican, it is Machiavellian. It defies other obstacles, other dangers, less bloody but longer and heavier" (*The Moon and Man* 90). The experience of our Earth's vulnerability, of human smallness and alienation, has ethical implications. We have all become astronauts, as Michel Serres puts it in *Le Contract Naturel*, where he indulges in the fact that we are completely deterritorialised, as we gaze towards our Earth: "For the first time, philosophy can say man is transcendent: before his eyes, the whole world is objectifying itself, thrown before him, object, bond, gear, or craft; man, for his part, finds himself thrown outside, totally cast off from the globe" (121-122).

Six months later, on 21 July 1969, only a few days before man's first steps on the Moon, Levi wrote the short essay "The Moon and Us". Here, too, he primarily questions what forces man to explore the universe, to travel to the moon, the most foreign ambient, and ends up answering as an ethologist and evolutionist:

> So we are about to take a great step: whether or not it is too long for our legs for the moment escapes us. Do we know what we are doing? It is permissible to doubt it from many signs. Certainly we know, and tell each other the literal, I was about to say the sporting, significance of the exploit: it is the most daring,

but at the same time the most meticulous exploit ever attempted by man; it is the longest voyage, it is the most alien environment. But why we do it, we do not know: the reasons cited are too many, too closely intertwined and at the same time mutually exclusive. At the basis of them all an archetype can be glimpsed; beneath the intricacies of the calculations lurks the obscure obedience to an impulse born with life and necessary to it, the same one which impels the seeds of poplars to wrap themselves in fuzz, to fly away in the wind, and frogs after their last metamorphosis to migrate obstinately from pond to pond at the risk of their lives. (OPT 25)

The comparison of the space voyages with frogs jumping from one pond to another, indicating how, beneath all scientific motives, we find (human) nature, also emphasises the smallness of man in the vast universe, as our planet and satellite are compared to the frog's ponds. The lunar conquest had to take place sooner or later, as a natural impulse, since man is genetically disposed to move on and make new discoveries. This does not in the least interfere with the greatness of the enterprise, as astronomic investigations are also a sign of the intrinsic value of man, in a humanist sense. To Levi man is simply repeating the same extreme voyage as that undertaken by Ulysses, the prime example of human dignity in Levi's work on Auschwitz, *If this is a Man*. In the central chapter of Levi's memoir, he recites to a fellow prisoner Dante's version of the Ulysses figure, who, having returned to Itacha, leaves once more and passes the Pillars of Hercules. Dante changed Homer's tale, sending the hero on further adventures beyond Gibraltar, but on this final voyage Ulysses loses sight of well-known constellations and drowns with his crew. Dante's Ulysses had to go on: "Consider then the race from which you have sprung: / You were not made to live like animals, / But to pursue virtue and know the world" (*Inferno*, XXVI: 118-120). To Levi humankind's dignity lies in the biologically rooted Faustian striving for knowledge.

Biological evolution and etymology are profoundly related discourses to Levi, forming part of the same humanist project, a search for roots. In much of his writings Levi insists on the origin of the names of the elements. Allowing us to grasp the historical traces and roots present in the naming, etymology also helps us comprehend language and the interaction between humanity and matter. Words change through usage and history, because our knowledge of the world changes. The basic structure of the bridge between literature and science is a common language, and to Levi the dialogue is threatened if everyday language, including its metaphors, is unable to keep pace with the development of scientific culture, even though they can never overlap completely.[6] It has been said that the destiny of any language is to start as poetry and end as algebra: Levi's texts can be read as a struggle to preserve poetry also in the realm of algebra, and to never let go of the effort to describe any entity or reality.

Encyclopaedic contemplation of an object, an animal or a piece of matter is found in many of Levi's essays, where the minute descriptions are followed by ethical and poetic reflections. This urge for precise descriptions makes him reflect on words – also when he writes about astronomic topics. "Even our lexicon has become inadequate", he exclaims in the opening of "The Moon and Man", and he continues: "to call it a flight, 'cavalcade' or navigation would amount to diminishing it and depriving it of colour" (89). The same weighing of words appears in the short story "A tranquil star", about a star that becomes a supernova. The story begins with a discussion of language and the difficulties of describing scientific, astronomic concepts, given the fundamental anthropocentric nature of language: "There is, of course, the slim and elegant language of numbers, the alphabet of the powers of ten; but then this would not be a story in the sense in which this story wants to be a story; that is a fable that awakens echoes, and in which each of us can perceive distant reflections of himself" (125).[7] Levi's struggle to domesticate and "humanize" scientific language seems to take place in-between our prosaic everyday life's lexicon of worn-out words that risks being all too familiar and therefore opaque, and the abstract numbering of hard science. In this context the moon metaphor represents a quite different and almost opposite challenge to the poets of our time: familiar through secular poetical tradition, it now has to be filled with new emotional and epistemological content.

TOO CLOSE AND TOO FAR AWAY

Dealing with the moon, Levi seems to imply that scientific knowledge means more alienation and less poetry; poetry cannot cope with the rapid evolution

---

6   The way in which different languages can represent and cover different qualities of an entity is discussed in the collection *Other People's Trades*, where Levi includes two essays on the language of the chemists, representing three different modes of expression: The most ancient is the original naming of a newly discovered substance, the second is the chemical formulas, while the third is the image of the molecular structure, which implies a renouncement of part of the symbolism and a regress to illustration, to pictography (OPT 100-110).

7   "A tranquil star" thematises different relations to the sky, and the limitations of human and earthly perceptions – past, present and future.

THE ART OF DISCOVERY

of science. In the wake of the moon landing we are forced to discard familiar metaphors like "the world of the Moon" and "the other side of the Moon" to refer to longed-for and inaccessible worlds and objects – "the paradigm, the customary synonym, for the impossible" (OPT 24). These metaphors have gone from being images of transcending reality, and of longing, to retaining only a historical sense. Eventually they will die out, and in the future be meaningful only to a few experts, Levi insists.

Levi asserts that being forced to let go of old metaphors means a break in the long chain of storytelling and knowledge; it means losing a familiar relationship with a part of our history and humanist inheritance. This makes it a more serious matter than simply discarding the conventional poetical image of the moon. The alienation resulting from the conquest of the moon, together with the novelty of the photos taken from the lunar point of view, are connected to the paradigmatic relativisation of the humanist and earthly perspective – and thereby also opposed to Levi's firmly humanist grounding of poetic images. The moon has always been symbolically close to man, and indeed because it always was a distant object; with its accessibility to man, the traditional poetic image of the moon ceases to be a usable referent, and passes onto the historical bookshelves. This is the theme of the short story "Seen from Afar", which consists of an introduction and a report of the observation of the Earth written by a Selenite and decoded by the FBI. Published in 1967, it starts with the narrator's introduction as he offers the story as a last homage to past Moon authors (Lucian of Samosata, Voltaire, Swedenborg, Rostand, E.A. Poe, Flammarion and H.G. Wells). As man's first step on the moon is soon to come, all the fantasies, famous or less famous, that literature throughout all time has expressed on the Selenites are about to lose their validity (*Opere* III 211-220).

Levi's texts on the natural sciences seek to bridge the gap between the world of science and the world of immediate experience, employing his own experience of struggling with matter in the laboratory, and adopting a clear, but also very descriptive, epithetic, language. In *What is a thing?* Heidegger analyses the difference between the things of our common experience and those same things as explained by science, stating that despite Copernicus the sun still *rises* and *sets*.

> All that the sun is for the shepherd coming home with his flock does not now need to be described, but it is the real sun, the same one the shepherd awaits for the next morning. But the real sun has already set a few minutes before. What we see is only a semblance (*Schein*) caused by certain processes of rays. But even

this semblance is only a semblance, for "in reality," we say, the sun never sets at all. ... Now which of these is the true sun? (Heidegger 12-13)

To Heidegger language is framed in experience, and his preliminary conclusion regarding the different truths could also be a reflection on the role of poetry: "Does one want science even closer to life? I think that it is already so close that it suffocates us. Rather we need the right distance from life in order to attain a perspective in which we measure what is going on with us human beings" (14). Another well-known analogy is John Keats' belief that Newton had destroyed all the poetry of the rainbow by reducing it to the prismatic colours, but this would not be a precise comparison. The moon landing represented not an epistemological shift, but the experience and the implementation of established theories. Nonetheless, to Levi it meant a disenchantment of the moon, and it is an example of the contrast between the "manifest image" and the "scientific image", to use the concepts of Wilfrid Sellars, which should be resolved by the intermediation of philosophy, or of literature as Calvino, or also Levi, understood its role and potential. But in this particular case, to Levi poetic metaphors must die out when they are contradicted by human experience, when the emotional content of the metaphors disappears: metaphors are strictly bound to an anthropocentric imagination and a human perspective, necessary for our ability to wonder and marvel. This is why a voyage to the moon means not only an invasion of poetic territory, but also a risk of losing the human perspective, in the very act of observing Earth from the outside, as experienced in the photos of Earth from the Apollo 8 flight in 1968, shot from a Copernican point of view.

However, it would probably not be unjustified to contend that Levi's thinking in these essays is a bit hasty, leading to too drastic consequences. Even if the literal meaning of a concept (e.g. the world of the moon) has become accessible to human experience, its figurative meaning (the moon as *the unreachable*), still survives. And it will probably survive as long as concepts such as the moon retain their metaphoric value: as long as human beings are earthly bound, the moon will be a far-away and for all practical purposes unreachable object, even if the steps on the moon were a collective, and also emotionally, experienced leap for mankind. As Leonard Cohen puts it: "They'll never ever reach the moon. At least not the one we're after."[8]

While the essays on the moon concern the new, close relationship with

---

8   Leonard Cohen, "Sing Another Song, Boys".

the satellite, the essay "News from the Sky" deals with the universe and a threatening sense of alienation and profound solitude. "One hundred years ago the universe was purely 'optic'; it was not very mysterious and it was thought it would grow less and less so. It appeared friendly and domestic: [...] in the stars there was hydrogen, helium, magnesium, sodium and iron, the raw materials of our home-grown chemists", writes Levi. But now the heaven above us is revealed as unpredictable, violent and strange, because the stars no longer belong to the sky of Dante and Ariosto. It does not "transmit messages of peace or poetry to us, but quite other messages, ponderous and disquieting, decipherable to a few initiates". And: "Now, the sky which hangs over our head is no longer domestic. It becomes even more intricate, unforeseen, violent and strange, its mystery grows instead of decreasing" (OPT 12). The scientific revelations of the sky do not give man certainty. On the contrary, they open new mysterious doors to a universe in which we are strangers, a new kind of frightening wonder where old familiar relationships like the one between the moon and man have no part.[9]

Mysticism, alienation and fear before *the eternal silence of these infinite spaces* are surely not only of recent times. Neither is Levi alone in his troubled relationship with space science; many poets of the last decades seem to be horrified by the knowledge presented by modern astronomy, as astronomer Jocelyn Bell Burnell writes in the essay on "Astronomy and Poetry":

One thing we now know better than ever is that the sheer size of the universe is both startling and incomprehensible. That it is expanding, and maybe even accelerating in its expansion, makes it no easier. That we cannot directly see at

---

9   There is also a more personal reason for Levi's mixed reaction towards space science. For Levi, the alienation effect of the new and menacing sky probably also has to do with the fact that astrophysics has developed away from observation towards pure theory and mathematics. In one of his autobiographical stories in *The Periodic Table*, Levi recalls the conversations with the professor of astrophysics who was one of the few willing to take a Jew as a student assistant. The ironic description of the astrophysicist's abstractions and scepticism towards the more concrete branches of the natural sciences clearly shows Levi's fundamental opposition to any trace of mysticism: "Not only these humble exercises of ours but physics as a whole was marginal, but its nature, by vocation, insofar as it set itself the task of regulating the universe of appearances, whereas the truth, the reality, the intimate essence of things and man exist elsewhere, hidden behind a veil, or seven veils (I don't remember exactly).... Truth lay beyond, inaccessible to our telescopes, accessible to the initiates" (56).

least 95 per cent of it (the dark matter) leaves us floundering. That we, human beings, are made from the stuff of star death, means we cannot ignore it – in an intimate and ultimate way we too are stars. That its future is hostile to life, and will eventually wipe us out, makes us want to ignore it. (136)

In "News from the Sky" Levi writes: "The birth rate of celestial monsters grows immeasurably greater – our everyday language fails to describe them, it is inept" (OPT 12). While old metaphors die and vanish, the new ones may need some time to mature. The poetic images from the starry sky are no longer familiar and consoling, but have become metaphors of inhuman violence, threats and vast, unreachable distances.

A consideration of poetic images in Levi should also take into account his poems, among which there are indeed quite a few inspired by astronomy. One of the recent astronomic figures, the black holes, a term coined by John Wheeler in 1969, is a trope present both in Levi's poems, metaphorising Auschwitz and the annihilation, and in his essays. In fact, the very last article published by Levi in the newspaper *La Stampa* in 1987 is entitled "The Black Hole of Auschwitz". A text on the black holes can also be sampled in the last issue of his personal anthology, *The Search for Roots* (1982), which opens with the *Book of Job* and ends with an article by Kip Thorne, previously published in "Scientific American" and entitled "The Search for Black Holes". Levi gives the article the title "We Are Alone", and in his introduction to Thorne's text the motif of the immense solitude of man is underscored:

> Every year that passes leaves us more alone. Not only are we not the centre of the universe, but the universe is not made for human beings; it is hostile, violent, alien. In the sky there are no Elysian Fields, only matter and light, distorted, compressed, dilated, and rarefied to a degree that eludes our senses and our language. Every year that passes, while earthly matters grow ever more convoluted, the challenge of the cosmos grows keener and more bitter. (214)

"But", asks Levi, "if the human mind has conceived Black Holes, and dares to speculate on what happened in the first moments of creation, why should it not know how to conquer fear, poverty, and grief? (215). The discovery of the black holes is seen in connection with the solitude of Job in his senseless suffering, present as the opening text of Levi's anthology, and the same connection between science and the *Bible* is also repeated in the poem about the Big Bang that bears the first words of Genesis as its title: "In the Beginning". Poetic tradition and language turn out to be a way of fighting alienation, also through the poetic device of estrangement: Levi therefore wishes to make the astronauts repeat the fictional moon voyages of Ariosto's Astolph and of Dante.

MARVEL

Any reader of Levi will see that to him science and marvel are closely linked. The short story "Hydrogen" in *The Periodic Table* can serve as an example. Here he describes one of his first lab experiments. He is sixteen and collaborates with his friend Enrico in electrolysis experiments; but due to their lack of both proper equipment and experience, the story becomes a sort of comic report of hypothesis and failures. At the end of their experiments Enrico expresses his doubts about the result. Levi gets annoyed and to prove that the jar actually contains hydrogen he opens the cathode jar, holding it with its open end down, strikes a match and brings it close. The result is an explosion.

> We left, discussing what had occurred. My legs were shaking a bit; I experienced retrospective fear and at the same time a kind of foolish pride at having confirmed a hypothesis and unleashed a force of nature. It was indeed hydrogen, therefore: the same element that burns in the sun and stars, and from whose condensation the universes are formed in eternal silence. (Levi 28)

Here Levi passes from the apparition of hydrogen, the lightest and most abundant element in the universe, to high poetry and marvel, reaching out and touching the heavens through Lucretius, Dante and chemistry. In fact, this description of marvel, almost awe, recalls the final lines of Dante's *La Divina Commedia*, one of the cornerstones not only of the western canon, but also of the Italian tradition of scientific, encyclopaedic literature, where God is described as "the love which moves the sun and the other stars".

The dangers to mankind, and to life, presented by scientific endeavours are a common theme in Levi's inquiries following the motif of Huxleyan dystopia; but in the astronomy essays something else is also at stake: the essence of poetry itself, which here is taken to be synonymous with marvel. This is how the threat is expressed in "The Moon and Us":

> We the multitude, we the public are by now habituated, like spoiled children: the rapid succession of spatial portents is extinguishing in us the faculty of wonder, though it is unique in man and indispensable in making us feel alive. Few among

us will know how to relive in tomorrow's flight, the exploit of Astolph or the theological astonishment of Dante when he felt his body penetrate the diaphanous lunar matter "shining, thick, solid and clean". It's a pity, but this time of ours is not a time for poetry: we no longer know how to create it, we do not know how to distil it from the fabulous events that unfold above our heads. (OPT 25-26)

How can Levi, in spite of his poetical practice, claim that scientific discoveries and explorations are threatening the human capacity to marvel, that these new explorations are guilty of destroying our ability to wonder? Years later, in *Six Memos for the Next Millennium*, Calvino would express similar worries concerning the immense "pollution of prefabricated images", and its consequences for human imagination: "a fundamental human faculty, the power to create visions with closed eyes … to think through images" (92).

Marvel and imagination are surely related concepts, but also essentially different: while imagination dwells in man, as a propensity to create and to be inspired, marvel signifies the relationship between man and world. Marvel is a trigger. Levi fears the loss of marvel and of poetry as a consequence of the loss of mystery in the human interaction with the universe. This confrontation illustrates again the differences between these two Italian authors: Calvino's view of poetry is not at all related to Romanticism, while Levi's texts are always concerned with man and with the anthropomorphic limitations and essence of language.

The essay "News from the Sky" starts by quoting the famous aphorism, in the conclusion of Kant's *Critique of Practical Reason*, where the philosopher speaks of life's two marvels which "fill the mind with ever new and increasing admiration and awe: the starry sky above me and the moral law within me." To Kant the starry sky represented the perfect, and eternal, order of the universe, invalidated for Levi by the new discoveries of the violent and ever-changing universe. As we have seen, Levi admits the inevitability, and even the nobility of the astronomic discoveries, but the transmission of these new images of a different sky is a message of unrest and seems strangely incapable of spurring on the poetic imagination: "It is a challenge that must be accepted. Our nobility as thinking motes demands it: perhaps the sky will no longer be part of our poetic patrimony, but it will be… vital nourishment for thought" (OPT 13).

In which sense does Levi use the term marvel, *meraviglia*, in these texts? As an aesthetic category, 'marvel' has been subjected to various interpretations related to the concepts of 'awe' and 'wonder', but also related to the fantastic dimension in art. Originally, as Aristotle used it, marvel was considered an expression of the superhuman, of the divine. In *Metaphysics* (I, 2) Aristotle says that marvel gives man the urge to philosophise.[10] Overtaken by the marvel of an incomprehensible phenomenon, man will be driven to search for new knowledge. This could be a fair description of the scientific poetics of Levi as well, where marvel is linked to the eagerness to create order, to scrutinise and to understand, while a completely unknown territory, the black holes of science, is too far from human perception: "The scientist-poet is not yet born and perhaps never will be born who is able to extract harmony from this obscure tangle, make it compatible, comparable, assimilable to our traditional culture and to the experience of our puny five senses made to guide us within terrestrial horizons" (OPT 12).

The wonder of nature's complexity is one of the most precious human-(-istic) gifts. As we have seen, the point of view in Levi's poetics is strictly anthropomorphic, the use of microscopes, telescopes or other sense-extending instruments does not interfere with this, although the risk of alienation when contemplating the sky is growing in the face of the new scientific discoveries. To Levi the opposite of marvel is not alienation, but certainty: marvel is the realisation that our knowledge and dominion of the world is indeed partial. The technical perfections of the spacecraft systems, along with the photos of the dark side of the moon, seem to him too certain, too secure and at the same time too distant; Levi notes that "the marine literature vanished with the disappearance of the sail ships, and a railway poetry was never born and isn't even likely to come into being. The flight of Collins, Armstrong and Aldrin, is too sure, too programmed, not 'wild' enough for a poet to find nourishment in it" (OPT 26). It seems as if Levi's problem with technology in this context is a consequence of reading it as a symbol of the firm, the pure and the definite. To find nourishment in it, technology must be somehow measured for man, as the marvellous machines of the novels of Verne, where the submarine is "packed with wonders", and like Melville's sailors, who are not only sailors but sailing engineers (OPT 186). Uncertainty, or longing, is the trigger of any questioning, also of the encounters between science and literature. In that way marvel is proto-poetical, as well as proto-scientific, and the opposite of

---

10 "For it is owing to their wonder that men both now begin and at first began to philosophize; they wondered originally at the obvious difficulties, then advanced little by little and stated difficulties about the greater matters, e.g. about the phenomena of the moon and those of the sun and of the stars, and about the genesis of the universe" (*Metaphysics*).

science and poetry is therefore surely not the quest for knowledge itself, but safe, inert, defined and secure knowledge.

CONCLUDING REMARKS

Levi's poetics are a struggle never to give up the human perspective and to preserve the poetic tools to describe and give access to new discoveries. From our reading of his texts on astronomic topics, we can conclude that Levi's concern is strictly humanist, in the sense that one may humanise any topic. This makes him confront two kinds of alienation: the loss of a poetic motif or dimension, a set of metaphors (what used to be far removed is turned into something reachable), and on the other hand reflections on the violent and unpredictable vastness of the universe (the familiar sky is perceived as being violent, totally unpredictable and unknown). Among the tools used by Levi to fight alienation are etymology and literary tradition, while his consideration for the human propensity to marvel turns out to be a common denominator for science and literature, finding common ground in the lack of complete certainty.

Levi's worried confrontations with the sky are indeed quite contrary to Calvino's optimism, and the only possible conclusion seems to involve different views on poetic imagination on the part of these great modern Italian writers, and perhaps also quite different personalities. For both poetic images are linked to epistemology, but Levi's view that poetry and marvel are synonymous is not echoed by Calvino, who considers marvel primarily as the playful and fantastic dimension of literature, more connected to language itself, and not always to ethics. For Levi, on the other hand, marvel and poetry always seem to be closely linked to a human point of view, human being the measure of all things, even though his humanism is struggling against any anthropocentric narcissism (Porro 130). This, then, means that the bond between poetic imagination and scientific deliberation ought never to be untied. The same could be said about the link between the poetic concepts of wonder and epistemological questioning. In this respect he is a traditional and true humanist.

WORKS CITED

Aristotle. *Metaphysics*. Trans. W.D. Ross. Raleigh, N.C. Alex Catalogue, 2000. Accessed 20 Aug. 2009 at URL http://ebooks.adelaide.edu.au/a/aristotle/metaphysics/.

Belpoliti, Marco. *Primo Levi*. Milano: Bruno Mondadori, 1998.

Bunnell, Jocelyn Bell. "Astronomy and Poetry." *Contemporary Poetry and Contemporary Science*. Ed. R. Crawford. Oxford: Oxford University Press, 2006. 125-140.

Calvino, Italo. *Saggi. 1945-1985*. 2 vols. Ed. Mario Barenghi, Milano: Mondadori, 1995.

—. Italo. *Six Memos for the Next Millennium*. London: Vintage, 1996.

—. Italo. *Lettere. 1940-1985*. Ed. L. Maranelli, Milano: Mondadori, 2001.

Cases, Cesare. "L'ordine delle cose e l'ordine delle parole" (1987). *Primo Levi: Un'antologia della Critica*. Ed. E. Ferrero, Torino: Einaudi, 1997, 7-33.

Cohen, Leonard. "Sing another song boys" *Songs of Love and Hate*. New York: Amsco Music Publishing Company, 1972.

Dante. *The Divine Comedy*. Trans. C.H. Sisson. Oxford: Oxford University Press, 1993.

Dawkins, Richard. *Unweaving the Rainbow*. Boston-New York: Mariner, 1998.

Heidegger, Martin. *What is a Thing?* Trans. W.B. Barton, Jr. and Vera Deutsch, Chicago: Henry Regnery Company, 1967.

Levi, Primo. *La ricerca delle radici. Antalogia personale*. Torino: Einaudi, 1981.

—. *The Periodic Table*. New York: Schocken Books, 1984.

—. "La luna e l'uomo". *Il fabbricante di specchi*. Torino: La Stampa, 1986. 128-130.

—. *Other People's Trades*. Trans. R. Rosenthal, London: Michael Joseph, 1989.

—. "The Moon and Man." *The Mirror Maker. Stories and essays*. Trans. Raymond Rosenthal, New York: Schocken Books Inc., 1989. 89-92.

—. "Visto di lontano." *Vizio di forma*. In *Tutti i racconti*. Ed. Marco Belpoliti, Torino: Einaudi, 2005. 211-220.

—. *Ad ora incerta*. Torino; Einaudi, 1990.

—. *Opere*. III. *Racconti e saggi*. Torino: Einaudi, 1990.

—. *Il sistema periodico*. Torino: Einaudi, 2nd ed., 1994.

—. *L'altrui mestiere*. 2nd ed., Torino: Einaudi, 1998.

—. *The Search for Roots. A Personal Anthology*. Trans. P. Forbes. Chicago: Ivan R. Dee, Inc., 2003.

—. *The Black Hole of Auschwitz*. Ed. M. Belpoliti, Trans. S. Wood, Cambridge: Polity Press, 2005.

—. "A Tranquil Star." *A Tranquil Star. Unpublished Stories of Primo Levi*. Trans. A. Goldestein and A. Bastagli. London: Norton & Co, 2007. 156-162.

Levi, Primo and Tullio Regge. *Dialogo*. Trans. R. Rosenthal. Princeton: Princeton UP, 1989.

Levi, Primo and Tullio Regge. *Dialogo*. Ed. E. Ferrero. 3rd ed., 2005.

Porro, Mario. *Letteratura come filosofia naturale*. Milano: Medusa, 2009.

Sellars, Wilfrid. *Empiricism and the philosophy of mind*. Cambridge Mass.: Harvard U Press, 1997.

Serres, Michel. *The Natural Contract*. 1990. Trans. E. MacArthur & W. Paulson. Michigan: University of Michigan Press, 2008.

Williams, David. "The Apollo Christmas Eve Broadcast." Accessed 20 June 2009 at URL http://nssdc.gsfc.nasa.gov/planetary/lunar/apollo8info.html.

THE BIG BANG OF THE NEOBAROQUE: FRAGMENTS OF RELATION OR OF UNITY?

Hans Jacob Ohldieck, University of Bergen

With the collection of essays titled *Barroco* (1974), the Cuban theoretician, poet and novelist Severo Sarduy (1936-1993) explicitly sets out to look for the epistemology underlying the mechanisms of the baroque; by doing so, he seeks to throw light upon the recurrence of baroque traits in the 20th century. In his scrutiny of parallels between the 17th century and his own, he recurs to the cosmological theory of the ellipse to explain the episteme of the former, and to the theory of the Big Bang to explain the re-emergence of baroque elements in the 20th century. According to Sarduy, the cosmological theories constitute emblematic images of the epochs in which they are formed, images that emerge within an *echo chamber*, where they take part in a dialectical movement with other expressions within the period, such as the symbolical fields of art and literature, expressions that Sarduy denominates the *retombée* of the cosmological theory, its "acronic causality" (Sarduy 1975, 14). The *retombée* constitutes a symbolical analogy to the dominant cosmological theory within an epoch, legitimising it through its work on signs.

In this chapter I will focus on Sarduy's investigation of the baroque epistemology in order to contrast two important interpretations of his use of the Big Bang theory within the literary field, one by Yale professor Roberto González Echevarría, and the other by professor Peter Hallward from Middlesex University. As a means of illustrating this contrast, I shall examine their respective interpretations of Sarduy's novel *Maitreya* (1978), one of the most highly acclaimed neobaroque works. What interests me in such a comparison is the way contrasting views on Sarduy's Big Bang image lead us to what Hallward, in *Absolutely Postcolonial – Writing between the Singular and the Specific* (2001), calls "the most salient characteristic of contemporary literature and philosophy", that is: "the assertion of an essential heterogeneity or plurality of subject positions" (2001, 1). Hallward asks: "Are these positions to be read as so many specific perspectives defined in some sense through their relations with each other? Or are they to be understood rather as the singular modes of one self-differing force – fragments, that is, of a single immanent unity, without constituent relations among themselves?" (2001,1). The comparison between González Echevarría and Hallward will centre on this question.

Through their different opinions of what the heterogeneity produced by the Big Bang represents in its literary version, it will be evident that González Echevarría supports a reading based on "specific perspectives", while Hallward aims at showing how the elements that constitute Sarduy's work are "singular modes of one self-differing force". Hallward sees Sarduy's approach as typical of today's postcolonial field, which he criticises for supporting a "logic of self-constituent creation" (2001, 24), implying an "effort to equate subject and object in a term Creative or transcendent of both" (2001, 330). The problem with this approach in a postcolonial setting is that it erases the differences between subject positions by voiding the individual traits, and by voiding the relations between the characters and their specific environments. This makes it hard for readers to identify with characters and to perform an *active valuing* on the basis of their actions. Consequently, the voiding of specific traits makes it difficult to form a collective resistance against the colonial, or neocolonial, oppressors, as territorial specificities are undermined. In addition to Sarduy, Homi Bhabha, Gayatri Spivak, Édouard Glissant, Wilson Harris and Gilles Deleuze are among the theoreticians and philosophers on trial in this book.

Contrary to the singular logic of these authors, what we need in a postcolonial setting, according to Hallward, is a *specific* approach which "maintains the relation between subject and object (and between subjects) *as a relation* in the strict sense" (2001, 330), because "only a specific configuration provides for *decision* as such" (2001, 333), as opposed to "singular inherence" (2001, 330). His critique is directed against immanent traits of the baroque and the so-called neobaroque, affirming that "the 'revolutionary' quality of the baroque lies in its refusal of conservation, of communication, of responsibility" (2001, 275),[1] and that the ellipse, which is a fundamental baroque figure, implies a "refusal of relation" (2001, 304). His critique thus concerns

---

[1] When Hallward writes "revolutionary", he uses Sarduy's own term, a designation Hallward does not agree with. The term is also counter-intuitive to most scholars of the art of the baroque period, generally considered to be a hegemonic and conservative art form, aimed at preserving traditional society, for example in Antonio Maravall (1986). However, in its Latin American offspring it has been regarded as a rebellious, decolonial "art of counter-conquest" (Lezama Lima 1988, 230).

what a number of scholars consider the emblematic expression of Latin America, in which "the baroque ... reappears to bear witness to the crisis / end of modernity", a baroque which constitutes "the very condition of a continent which could not incorporate the project of the Enlightenment" (Chiampi 2000, 17). Is Hallward himself guilty of ignoring the specificity of a Latin American tradition here? This question will constitute the centre of the last part of the chapter.

In Sarduy's work, the relevance of cosmology is not restricted to his essays. The poetry collection *Big Bang* (1974) carries an obvious cosmological influence, and more or less explicit references to this field can also be found in his major novels *De donde son los cantantes* (1967), *Cobra* (1972) and *Maitreya* (1978). Following Friedrich Nietzsche, he believes all language to be metaphoric, as even "science doesn't use a literal, denotative, dry language, but a language of figures, imagined, weaved of metaphors" (quoted in Hallward 2001, 303), including white dwarves, red giants, red shift, light fatigue, black holes, and so on. What a novel like *Cobra* does, then, is to "take the metaphors of scientific discourse ... and make them literal. Of each scientific metaphor it makes a character, that is, it creates an absurd universe parallel to the supposedly real universe" (quoted in Hallward 2001, 303). Pup, one of the characters of the novel, is thus named after a star and appears as a white dwarf, and another, Little Dwarf, has been named after a category of stars. Red giants appear as great fat transvestites covered in henna. Following the same source of scientific influence, *Barroco* presents a coherent theory of the baroque and neobaroque epistemes based on cosmological notions, and thus constitutes a theoretical background for Sarduy's own fiction, and for neobaroque art and literature as a whole.[2]

THE ELLIPSE AND THE EPISTEME OF THE BAROQUE

The analogy Sarduy traces between the baroque age and his own starts with Johannes Kepler. Kepler discovered that the planet Mars did not move in circles around the sun, but rather in ellipses, contradicting the theory of Galileo, who had affirmed, and continued to affirm, the circular movement of the planets. The belief in circular movement was based on a conviction of

2   In a Latin American context, the term neobaroque has been used with reference, among many others, to José Lezama Lima, Alejo Carpentier, Reinaldo Arenas, Guillermo Cabrera Infante, Ernesto Sábato, Fernando del Paso, Octavio Paz, Luis Rafael Sánchez and Haroldo dos Campos, in addition to Sarduy.

the perfection of the circle that had been maintained since Plato and even before. According to this belief, which, in Sarduy's view, was in essence the same for Galileo as it was for the Greeks, there was an hierarchically organised correspondence between the human body and the celestial bodies, following "the authority of resemblance" (Sarduy 1975, 75).[3]

The *retombée* of this celestial circular movement adopts the form of a concentric worldview, and follows the logic of what Foucault calls "the age of resemblance", characterised by interdependence between the world and the words. Following the same cosmic harmony as in the quote above, "the metaphor is the 'retombée' of the circle" (1975, 86) within the literary field of the pre-baroque era, because the metaphor functions as an ornament which does not alter the meaning of the stable and unique centre: The *signifier* always maintains the same distance to the *signified*, because its orbit is that of the circle. This relation changes dramatically after Kepler's discovery of the elliptical movement of the planets. Sarduy affirms: "The passage from Galileo to Kepler is one from the circle to the ellipse, the passage from what is traced around the one, to what is traced around the plural: from classicism to baroque" (1975, 36). The circle with one centre has been replaced by a deformed circle with two centres, of which one is elided. Kepler thus modifies "the scientific support of the epoch's total knowledge" (1975, 88), and the ellipse introduces an epistemic break, producing a decentring movement, of which the consequences in the symbolic fields are evident.[4] Restricting ourselves to the literary field, the cosmological ellipse finds its counterpart in a figural ellipse: "The ellipse, in both of its meanings, is drawn around two centres: one of them visible (the marked signified / the sun), in daylight, and shining in the baroque phrase; the other one is covered (the hidden signified / the virtual center of the planetary ellipse), elided, excluded, dark" (1975, 112).

Contrary to the concentric metaphor following from the Galilean circle in the pre-baroque era, which remained in its representative daylight and never explored any "hidden signified", the elliptical signifier has included

---

3   The translations from French and Spanish are my own where not otherwise indicated. I quote from the French edition of *Barroco*, translated by Sarduy and Jacques Henric, because it is more extensive than the Spanish edition released the year before.

4   Foucault's influence on *Barroco* is important, but Sarduy's emphasis on the *retombée*, according to Irlemar Chiampi, "goes much further than what Foucault postulates, because the epistemic break (from Galileo to Kepler) is legitimized by the change in textual rhetorics, as its necessary counterpart" (Chiampi 2000, 95).

an absent or excluded Other in its orbit. What the baroque ellipsis does, then, is to explore "the cultural unconscious, hidden beneath the naturalizing process" (Sarduy 1975, 117), that is, what the naturalising process of the circle and of "the age of resemblance" has repressed. Consequently, "the metaphors [...] lose their metaphorical dimension: the sense does not precede their production, but is the emerging product" (1975, 118). The signs have no identifiable reverse side corresponding to the signifier, but in its absence, in the void, we experience the *hidden* signified.

THE BIG BANG AND THE EPISTEME OF THE NEOBAROQUE

According to Sarduy, the theory of the Big Bang in the 20th century is analogous to the theory of the ellipse in the 17th century. The latter described the elliptical movement of the planets in the solar system, while the former describes the creation of the universe. The universe is the result of an initial explosion which set the particles that compose it into motion, and the universe is now "in violent expansion, without limits, without any possible form: an insane race of galaxies towards nowhere" (1975, 15). Sarduy finds the *retombée* of the Big Bang in "the phonetic and graphic material in expansion", that is, a "neobaroque of explosion, where the signs turn and flee towards the limits of the support, without any formula permitting us to follow their production towards the limits of thinking: to the image of a universe which explodes all the way to exhaustion ..."[5] (1975, 20).

Despite the break with "the age of resemblance", there was still a harmony within the baroque, both in the thinking of the principal philosophers of the time, Gottfried Leibniz and Baruch Spinoza, and in Kepler's own *Harmonices Mundi*. After Nietzsche and the death of God, the elliptical movement of the baroque has accelerated, and the dispersion of signs knows no limits in the neobaroque; we have moved from "a harmonic closure to the opening into a polytonality, or, in the words of Boulez, 'a polyphony of polyphonies'" (Deleuze 1988, 112), according to another influential study on the baroque, *Le pli – Leibniz et le baroque*, by the French philosopher Gilles Deleuze.

I have just argued how the elliptical movement of the baroque explored

---

5   The parallel between the celestial bodies and the linguistic signs finds important precursors in the Latin American baroque; in both Carlos de Sigüenza y Góngora (*Occidental planeta* and *Libra astronómica*) and Sor Juana (*Primero sueño*) we find the image of the universe as a combination of signs (like stars) in movement, thus creating a language to be interpreted.

"the cultural unconscious" and "the hidden signified". In our epoch, the Big Bang finds its *retombée* in psychoanalysis or *schizo*analysis, depending on which interpretation is emphasised (González Echevarría's or Hallward's). According to the former, the movement of the stars forms a planetary system that covers the void left by the initial explosion. In the psychoanalytical version, the subject is based upon a *repression*, the suppression of an origin, which is experienced as a lack, and this lack produces a desire to cover it; we thus build our defence against it in the form of writing and by means of literary figures (González Echevarría 1986, 149). Hallward, on the other hand, emphasises the *incessant expansion* of the universe ensuing from the Big Bang. In the schizoanalytical equivalent to the cosmological theory, the Big Bang does not leave a void to be covered but constitutes, on the contrary, our desire itself, understood as a surplus rather than a lack. Consequently, we do not need to recover anything; we should rather dissolve fixed entities that halt the incessant expansion of the pure intensity of desire. This expanding movement corresponds to the baroque trait *par excellence*: "the fold which moves to eternity" (Deleuze 1988, 5). The incessant folding produces an endless series of images that do not represent any repressed signified, but rather explore territories that cannot be interpreted, because they have never been trodden. Such an exploration is a fundamental schizoanalytic trait; it is not a matter of covering up some lack, but of finding "a link with the origin" (Hallward 2001, 301), the initial explosion, understood as the endless creative power of desire. In this process, desire will release what the individual has repressed by setting it in motion and by liberating its power to connect and create. The force of the Big Bang can thus pass through the human subject-become-creative with as little resistance as possible, making of desire the factory it essentially is, according to Hallward, rather than the representative theatre of lack as perceived in González Echevarría's view.

According to Hallward's interpretation, Sarduy's Big Bang metaphor thus points towards a homogeneous principle, *one matter energy*, which is immanent in all life. Hallward finds support for his view in *Barroco*, where Sarduy emphasises "the homogeneity of matter", and consequently the extension of "an undefined universe without regions", a space without territories, and with a single creative principle, with which one must find an expressive connection through a "counter-actualisation" of all separate, *individualised* unities (Hallward 2001, 301). Whereas the initial explosion understood as the primacy of a repression in González Echevarría's psychoanalytical approach necessarily resonates in a number of historical and specific Big Bangs or events that create a desire for recuperation, for Hallward the Big Bang thus constitutes the creative, univocal force itself.

THE BIG BANG: LACK OR ABUNDANCE?

The question of whether desire is driven by lack or abundance is important for the two scholars' contrasting approaches to Sarduy's writing. For González Echevarría, something specific needs to be recovered, and the strategy is therefore figural interpretation. For Hallward, however, the movement is one of continuous expansion, where the reader should literally *go with the flow*, in order to follow the deactualisation and dissipation of all fixed reality, and thus come as close as possible to the principle which is Creative of all that is. In this version, neobaroque literature implies "a presence acting directly on the nervous system, which makes representation ... impossible", to quote Deleuze's description of Francis Bacon's paintings (Deleuze 2005, 37). In a similar manner, the question of desire as lack or abundance has consequences for the scholars' respective approaches to the question of metaphors and ellipses in Sarduy's fiction, two figures constantly referred to in the essays of the neobaroque author. González Echevarría emphasises the metaphor through its relation with the metonym in Sarduy's works:

> The act of covering [the void on which life arises] has a metonymical function through the creation of chains of signifiers. Because these figures – like the symptoms which the analyst interprets – include, although erased, the absence, its function is eventually metaphorical, not metonymical. The reason for this is that the memory of the repressed points towards that which is represented. (1986, 151)

For González Echevarría, the memory of specific events is decisive for the form which the representation of the repressed adopts, and therefore there is a metaphorical *relation*. He continues: "The baroque metaphorical system hides a repressed signified which can be released through a reading of signifiers that, although apparently alluding to something else, points towards it" (1986, 151). According to this view, the metaphor is capable of releasing the repressed signified. This is different in Hallward's view, because "language can only be included as part of this univocal matter-energy ... It can only provide a literal image of it (in Lezama's sense) or actualisation of the universe, rather than a representation of it" (2001, 300). He also states: "The relation that governs the literal immediacy of a single textual plane can only be an elliptical non-relation, both as elision of a referent (as voiding of the given) and as invitation to an unrestricted and entirely contingent continuity" (2001, 304). When Sarduy writes about metaphors in his essays, it is thus only as part of a process of metamorphosis, of a *becoming*, in Deleuzian terms, where a "virtual double... gradually [will] besiege and surround the original, undermining it with imitation, with parody, until it is supplanted" (Sarduy 1989, 50). The metaphors form a chain, or a *line of flight*, where the ornaments end up consuming what they set out to describe. In this way, by voiding all specific elements – individual traits, historical moments – or by sending them off along elliptical lines of flight, the infinite speed of the univocal force can pass more smoothly, as all history and individuality are nothing but hindrances that halt the passing of this force. The lack humans might feel as constitutive of their desire, radicates in nothing but contingent historical obstacles restraining the abundant power within us.

MAITREYA AS BIG BANG

In Sarduy's opinion, Lezama Lima is to neobaroque literature what Luis de Góngora is to the baroque: they constitute their respective apotheosises. In Lezama, "the distance between signifier and signified ... is maximum" (1989, 51). The same characterisation is valid for *Maitreya*, "the most emphatically other-worldly of Sarduy's novels" (Hallward 2001, 295), where Sarduy's debt towards Lezama is not restricted to its style, but is also evident in the adoption of a secondary character from Lezama's masterpiece *Paradiso* (1966), the Chinese cook Luis Leng. As the title indicates, Buddhism is a central reference in this novel (Maitreya is the future Buddha), which begins with the death of a master, who predicts his own rebirth: "we emerge from noncreation, and we return to it in the twinkling of an eye" (1987, 7). Then Chinese gunshots are heard, indicating the Chinese invasion of Tibet in 1950. The reincarnated Maitreya is later kidnapped by the Leng sisters and brought to Colombo in Sri Lanka, where he soon loses sight of his mission. He subsequently leaves for Cuba with Leng's niece, where he dies having lost all interest in the kingdom of this world. Part two begins with the birth of identical twins, who become healers. After losing their power when entering puberty, they become soprano singers, known as "Ladies Divine and Tremendous", the former being a duplication of the latter. They are joined by Luis Leng, the Chinese cook from *Paradiso*, and followed by a dwarf they become members of the bourgeoning sex sect, Fist Fuckers of America (F.F.A.) in Miami, whose explicit objective is total chaos. They later move to New York, where the musical success of "Ladies Divine and Tremendous" is threatened by The Gloomy Gals, who try to thwart their success with dirty tricks, and Tremendous sees no other way out than to make a new duplication of herself to fool their pursuers. The Lady T then moves to the Middle East, where she is free to focus on "the apotheosis of the fist", assisted by plenty of vaseline and the dwarf. After a bad fist-fucking experience with a sheikh, they are accused of violating "the anals of the empire" (1987, 133). The dwarf is forced to flee, but after crossing the desert he meets Lady T again, this time with her Iranian driver, in Grand Hôtel de France, where they dedicate themselves to proving "the emptiness of everything" (1987, 158). The Iranian driver loses his mind, while Lady T gives birth to a monstrous child, her "anal son".

Maitreya thus begins with the death of the master, whose disciples "hurled the bones into the void" (Sarduy 1987, 9), repeating analogously what Lezama has said is the fundamental scene of *Paradiso*, where some pieces of the Cuban children's game *yaquis* are thrown in a similar manner, forming the face of the father figure which the protagonist José Cemí seeks to overcome. The scene is of course also an illustration of the formal movement of the novel: the signs are thrown into the air like the stars after the Big Bang, as I've already commented upon when discussing the *retombée* of the cosmological theory. After the dispersion of the master's bones, Sarduy writes:

> The head, like a planet torn from its order and which upon falling would turn back into lava, lime or mother-of-pearl, in a luminous, spiral unwinding, became a giant iridescent conch which when blown by the wind emitted a muffled, un-changing sound, the charred vibration of a remote explosion. (1987, 9)

González Echevarría interprets this scene in the following manner: "The convergence and dispersion of the yaquis in Lezama and the bones in Sarduy point towards the rupture and continuity of the received tradition. The yaquis-bones are like the syllables of a major text that we restore and dissemi-nate at the same time – *corpus* on which we restitute the head" (1986, 195). In González Echevarría's interpretation, "a remote explosion" or Big Bang leads to the dispersion of the bones or pieces of the master *narrative*, which takes the form of an origin; these are the pieces Sarduy has at his disposal when constructing his work, this is his inheritance, to a large extent in line with the "anxiety of influence" theory propagated by González Echevarría's colleague at Yale, Harold Bloom. Those strong enough manage to overcome the anxiety towards their master by creating new images with his or her "bones" (that is, under his/her influence), and Sarduy succeeds, according to González Echevarría, after explicitly adopting a character from *Paradiso* to build the "master-piece" of *Maitreya*. In González Echevarría's psycho-analytical approach, Lezama's work is thus a symbolical expression of "the body of the mother" (1986, vi), which Sarduy has to penetrate. Lezama does not only represent his own literary *corpus*, however, because the adoption of Luis Leng constitutes "the expansion of a passage from *Paradiso*, a sacred text which here *represents the received tradition*" (1986, 192, my emphasis). What Sarduy brings forth in this novel is therefore "a renovated recovery of *lo cubano*, of the Cuban tradition" (1986, 12). Following the analogy between the scientific and symbolical fields, this tradition takes the form of a void that Sarduy's writing encircles with its figural and intertextual complexity. The tradition is fundamentally a void because it is without essence and, consequently, its "ultimate meaning" is always and necessarily deferred. This void or *absence* is experienced as a lack, and despite the impossibility of reaching the object of desire, *the essence*, Sarduy attempts to penetrate *lo cubano* through *Maitreya*, which becomes a "renovated recovery" of the country's tradition through this effort; that is, it becomes another layer in the superposition of interpretations that cover the void of Cuba.

According to González Echevarría, the recuperation does not stop here, however, because "at the historical level, the cataclysm for Sarduy is the Revolution" (1986, vi). Behind the Revolution is, once again, the body of Cuba. Just as the death of the master leaves an absence which has to be covered, so do the revolutions around which *Maitreya* is organised: "*Maitreya* is created through the relation which it stretches out between these moments of dispersion", these "*Big Bangs*, explosions that set history in motion" (1986, 176), and more precisely:

> The characters always exist on the borders of the historical explosion, in its *après coup* or countercoup. In exile.… China, Tibet, Cuba, Iran: we begin with the Chinese Revolution, which is communist and forces the gods into exile, we then move to the revolts in Tibet, that are religious, against the ideology of the occidental origin; we then move to the Cuban Revolution, which ends in the crowning of marxist-leninism, and we end in Iran, where they create a religious revolution against the occidental interference. (1986, 188)

The historical level of González Echevarría's conception of the Big Bang metaphor is evident in this quote: The Big Bangs of revolutions and revolts provoke a dispersion of historical elements that subsequently circle a void, leaving everyone in exile, either internal or external or both. The revolutions and the death of the master are events that serve as historical cogwheels, through the vacuum or opening they create in our relation to other beings, and to our historical surroundings. The events pave the way for new *relations*, new constellations and collective action. The new possibilities are, however, accompanied by an anxiety to *capture the moment of explosion* and maintain the *original* moment, in González Echevarrías's view; these explosions create a desire to include the outside of history, the sacred eternity, within history itself: "The signs of the fallen present are magnetized by the anxiety to be sacred", where *the sacred* refers to both the image of the religious East and the revolutionary event itself, which is a momentary suspension of history. But this desire always ends up frustrated, because "the signs lack permanence, they are empty, hollow forms" (1986, 203); the event they seek to express will always be deferred, it cannot be captured. For González Echevarría, this effort is a personal one for Sarduy, who was an active revolutionary during the first couple of years of the Cuban Revolution, before leaving the country for good; in *Maitreya* he returns to this historical explosion, to recover *lo cubano*.

For Hallward, all this is seen from a different point of view. To begin with, he emphasises the importance of the Buddhist elements of the novel, not in terms of pointing towards historical revolts, but by taking into account the words of the master: "I didn't squander knowledge. I marked its empty nomadic place" (1987, 49). For Hallward, *Maitreya* is such a nomadic place, and it is therefore "the most opaque, the most resistant to theological interpretation as such" (2001, 296) of all of Sarduy's novels. Liberated from "aboutness" as it is, "the text gives free reign to a vision-revelation beyond perspectival constraints" (2001, 296). The series of images do not refer to a pattern of signifieds to be recovered, as they do for González Echevarría. They are *emergent* images, implying a voiding of the individual traits of fixed characters and of the reader in this game of excess. That is why *Maitreya* is nomadic: the images have no concrete references, they are "beyond perspectival constraints" (Hallward 2001, 296), dispersed in the air after the initial explosion, which left each element with its share of the energy implied in the Big Bang; they do not point towards any specific referent, but enfold the Creative principle as it expands.

The focus of *Maitreya* is thus not on the characters, who are merely historical contingencies, but on the environment which resists the subjects, the "passing impressions, random sounds, while contours blend and soften

in a post-impressionist confusion (steam, diffuse, formless, smoke, veils) …
The description writes a space which excludes the merely 'mobile' subject, a
space become composition on its own strictly a-subjective terms" (2001, 297).
Hallward quotes Sarduy when saying that "enlightened, we see that 'the One
is none other than the all, the All none other than the One'", before affirming
that the Buddhist One "enfolds an infinite intensity that invites comparison
with Deleuze's univocal cosmology" (2001, 285). Of course, the Buddhist
One also corresponds with the dominant version of the Big Bang theory, as
"the big bang posited by most contemporary cosmologists is a singularity
in the strict or technical sense: rather than an explosion occurring within
an already unfolded field of time and space, it takes place as an 'inflation'
creative of its own ongoing space of expansion" (2001, 2). This quote, which
contradicts González Echevarría's historical and recuperative perspective,
strengthens Hallward's interpretation of the Big Bang as a metaphor. This
interpretation is further fortified by the focus on the nomadic element in
Sarduy's work, which finds its counterpart in the incessant expansion of the
universe.

Hallward focuses neither on the "anxiety of influence", nor on the Big
Bang of revolutions which González Echevarría emphasised, because the
"extraordinary intertextual dimensions of Sarduy's work should be understood above all as a celebration of this still more fundamental univocity"
(2001, 264). Instead, Hallward quotes the master, who just before dying
said: "We emerge from non-creation, and we return to it in the twinkling
of an eye", and then, the master's own quote from *Heart Sutra*: "The void
is the form. The form is the void …" (1987, 7-8). As we know by now, in
Hallward's opinion, "Sarduy's only ultimate goal" was the "articulation of the
void" (2001, 282), a void that is "beyond thought or representation, forever
empty of actuality yet incomprehensibly full of intensity. It is the seat of
pure Creative energy, the purely implicated source of all explicated expression" (2001, 282). The real aim of *Maitreya* is thus to reach "the zero degree
of the face … that singular, pre-individual face common to all humanity"
(Hallward 2001, 264). That is why Lady T's "face was falling" at the end of
the novel; the scarce individual traits she had were lost along a line of flight
which has as a consequence that "she spreads all over the place", before dis-
solving completely into the topography (2001, 298).

The "zero degree of the face" (Hallward 2001, 264) is that of the master's
head, which is "like a planet torn from its order" (Sarduy 1987, 9), torn from
the order of things, to become an open conch which, without hindrance, is
penetrated by the impersonal wind, carrying that metaphysical "unchang-

ing sound, the charred vibration of a remote explosion" (Sarduy 1987, 9), an explosion that we have seen is the univocal creativity which all humanity has in common. Hallward thus disagrees with González Echevarría when the latter affirms that as readers we "restitute the lost head [of the corpus of the major text]" (1986, 195). For Hallward, what happens is exactly the opposite. To the extent that the intertextual relationship is of any importance, what happens here is a voiding of the major text as well; the master who reaches the void is *l'acéphale* in Bataille's sense, the headless principle without individual or hierarchical organisation, where desire is allowed to flow, liberated from what Sarduy in an interview has called the "individual as metropolis – the conscience or soul – with its colonies: the voice, the sex, etc" (Fossey 1976, 24). As readers we do not restitute the head, which is "the house of logos" and "sign of identity" (González Echevarría 1986, 195), quite the contrary: liberated from restraint and desire for figurative reading, we can feel the vibration of a remote explosion, of the Big Bang, by identifying ourselves with the headless principle, with the "dissolution of the self" (Fossey 1976, 24). That is why we should *not* read *Maitreya* if we want to change our world, according to Hallward.

A LATIN AMERICAN BAROQUE TRADITION

Hallward's critique is poignant, and as Paul Gilroy has pointed out, it "provides a new bench-mark for all future debate in this field" (Hallward cover). One would expect the postmodern fragmentation to lead to more sensibility towards context, to heterogeneous ways of life, but the dominant postcolonial theoreticians – for all their focus on local colour and context – emphasise the univocal force at the bottom of all reality, thus constructing a "world-without-others", according to Hallward (2001, 19); a world which ultimately becomes exclusive, non-contextual, where specificities and differences are dissolved in the unifying principle, as we have seen through his interpretation of Sarduy.

From my point of view, however, Hallward seems to overemphasise the significance of a univocal force as the source of the postcolonial "hybridising trend" (2001, 23) and, simultaneously, that he underestimates the position of hybridity as perhaps the most salient *historical* characteristic of large parts of Latin America and the Caribbean. In a Latin American context, the baroque tradition has been one of "counter-conquest" (1988, 230), according to Lezama Lima, exactly because its rich ornaments have opened for the inclusion of signs that *deform* the major expressions of the colonisers. An emblematic example for Lezama is the way *el Indio* Kondori included Inca symbols in the construction of the San Lorenzo church in Potosí, creating new connections that *deterritorialised* the whole religious expression of the colonisers (1988, 244). In similar fashion, Sarduy draws on the Cuban Santería religion in his works, the upshot of slave rebellion, where the imported Africans deterritorialised the Catholic saints of the colonisers through the creation of hybrid combinations with saints from their native countries. These examples are characteristic of what the Cuban anthropologist Fernando Ortiz in *Contrapunteo cubano del tabaco y el azúcar* (1940) called *transculturation*, which, for various scholars, has been the emblematic trait of both Caribbean and Latin American culture. In the words of Alejo Carpentier: "Our American world is baroque" (2003, 149), "[t]he *criollo* spirit is in itself a baroque spirit" (2003, 142) and "the description of a baroque world must necessarily be baroque" (2003, 153). That is: The baroque is historically rooted in America, contrary to the discourses of modernity and its subsequent developments [postmodernism, poststructuralism] (Kaup 2006). These roots are implicit in "this American señor Barroco" (Lezama 1988, 230), Lezama's emblematic *criollo*, a confluence of all races and cultural expressions on the continent, and González Echevarría is certainly right when pointing out the following:

> Lezama's señor barroco feels strange, different, new. The aesthetics of the baroque is that of the strange being, that of being a stranger. This is the origin of the American, of the new and secondary being *par excellence*. Sarduy's baroque develops on this background. This explains the genealogical breaks, the mysterious births, the strangeness of his transvestites, the persistent transgression of their actions [...]. The baroque is the strange – eccentric – modernity of the European periphery (1986, 205).

González Echevarría's emphasis on the connection between Lezama and Sarduy in this quote is confirmed by Sarduy in his essay "El heredero" (The heir): "The characters, the situations, the textual and perverse miracles of *Paradiso* should resonnate, be unfolded and reactivated in another room … in order to be given a supplement of life, roots of eternity. This is what I tried to do in the novel *Maitreya*, when I adopted a secondary character, Luis Leng, who scarcely occupies a few lines of *Paradiso*" (Sarduy 2000, 169).

Contrary to González Echevarría, Hallward seems to undermine this historical background of *Maitreya*, especially the one represented by *Paradiso*, the *magnum opus* of the Cuban tradition. On the other hand, however,

González Echevarría's psychoanalytical approach seems to reduce the radicality of *Maitreya*. The novel is not a recovery of Cuba, of the revolution, or of Lezama himself. The way *Maitreya* negotiates with history is not through a recovery of specific partial objects, and it is not by restituting the head as a centre of meaning. It is rather by presenting history and tradition as the "nomadic place" which the master himself projected as the field of all knowledge, a headless body without an organising principle, and in its openness it takes the form of the master's own skull. The skull can be identified as Lezama or *Paradiso*, and thereby as a projection of Cuba, cut off from the historical *telos* which is still present in Lezama's works and opening up for new events or historical Big Bangs.

In this intertextual manner, Sarduy sets fixed elements in motion, partly by juxtaposing his own corporal image with the organic metaphors of the Cuban tradition. In the essay "Our America" (1891), the founder of the republic José Martí wrote: "With … white head and the coloured body of the indians and *criollos* we entered … the world of nations" (Martí 2007, 500), while Lezama's "Señor Barroco" is, as we have argued, the emblematic *criollo*. Sarduy cuts off the head, and makes of the nation an *acéphale*, without the hierarchy that is explicit in Martí's "white head". However, the "zero degree of the face" (Hallward 2001, 264) is not one through which a metaphysical force can pass unhindered, as in Hallward's interpretation, but rather one through which different cultural and historical elements – set in motion through the neobaroque intertextual expansion – can form radically new constellations, like the bones that are thrown into the air in a manner reminiscent of Nietzschean dice throws, affirmative of chance encounters.[6] Consequently, the process of voiding in the neobaroque is never complete; it is rather a way of loosening fixed historical relations, bringing them to the surface, in order to open up for new and dynamic connections, where the intensified pieces communicate in the creation of new images. This is why Sarduy compares his neobaroque to the process of *cancerization*: "the anarchic proliferation of cells without model, without paradigm to regulate this proliferation, without subject, I would say" (quoted in Hallward 2001, 322).

What Hallward considers a neglect of territorial sensibility through a voiding of specific relations, is in my view characteristic of the dynamic that

---

6   For an extensive account of the differences between a Nietzschean and a Mallarmean dice throw as an image of a radical event, and thereby also between Deleuze's and Alain Badiou's conception of it, see Badiou (1997), pp. 113-117.

might in fact be the most specific trait in Cuban tradition: what Lezama has called "baroque curiosity" (1988, 229). Such a curiosity explores what the dominant discourse has left in the dark, its Other, and the exploration necessarily takes the form of an *unproductive expenditure*, which gives an experience of what has been excluded. On a rhetorical level, the baroque ellipse is the figure which supports the movement of the Big Bang; the multiplication of ellipses is what makes possible the radical deterritorialisation which is Sarduy's version of the Big Bang: a continuous expansion. The ellipse is simultaneously "shining in the baroque sentence", and moving towards the "elided, excluded, dark" Other (1975, 112). It produces endless folds of ornamental exuberance, but at the same time the folds form an excess to the discursive order, thus exploring what Bataille calls non-knowledge, where new becomings can arise from the dark. It is therefore highly significant that Lady T gives birth to a monstrous child through the anus, contrary to natural reproduction. Here the ellipse's movement towards the elided Other finds resonance on the thematic level: Not only does the birth take place through organs of excrements that are, to a certain degree, excluded from the social sphere through taboos;[7] the new-born was also conceived through an act of unproductive expenditure, of *eroticism*, again contrary to the reproductive act: by means of Lady T's devotion to the Iranian driver's fist. A new becoming thus arises from the dark, a stranger, conceived in defiance of the reproductive order of things; it is, however, a *new* and at the same time a *secondary being* because of the negotiations with tradition that bring it forth, deforming historical elements through its transformative work on signs. I thus agree with González Echevarría that "the essence of the neobaroque is this transmutative capacity of forms, never the abolition of these" (1986, 224). The neobaroque is not incompatible with a focus on territory, quite the contrary: The continous flux of deterritorialising and reterritorialising movements is in itself constitutive of the Cuban territory and its tradition. As Lezama famously stated: "Perhaps we could say that the firmest Cuban tradition is that of the future" (González 1994, 56).

---

7   Bataille writes in *L'érotisme*: "Excrements are not object of taboos expressed through strict social rules to the same degree as those concerning the corpse or the menstrual blood. But through their contiguities, a general field of excrements, putrefaction and sexuality has been formed" (Bataille 1957, 65).

WORKS CITED

Badiou, Alain. *Deleuze – "La clameur de l'être"*. Paris: Hachette Littératures, 1997.

Bataille, Georges. *L'érotisme*. Paris: Les Éditions de Minuit, 1957.

Carpentier, Alejo. "Lo barroco y lo real maravilloso." *Ensayos selectos*. Buenos Aires: Corregidor, 2003. 123-155.

Chiampi, Irlemar. *Barroco y modernidad*. Mexico City: Fondo de Cultura Économica, 2000.

Deleuze, Gilles. *Le pli – Leibniz et le baroque*. Paris: Les Éditions de Minuit, 1988.

—. *Francis Bacon*. London/New York: Continuum, 2005.

Fossey, Jean-Michel. "Severo Sarduy: Máquina barroca revolucionaria." *Severo Sarduy*. Ed. Julián Ríos. Madrid: Editorial Fundamentos, 1976.

González, Reynaldo. *Lezama Lima: El ingenuo culpable*. Havana: Editorial Letras Cubanas.

González Echevarría, Roberto. *La ruta de Severo Sarduy*. Hanover: Ediciones del Norte, 1986.

Hallward, Peter. *Absolutely Postcolonial – Writing between the Singular and the Specific.*Manchester and New York: Manchester University Press, 2001.

Kaup, Monika. "Neobaroque: Latin America's Alternative Modernity." *Comparative Literature* 58 / 2006. 128-152.

Lezama Lima, José. "La curiosidad barroca." *Confluencias*. Havana: Letras Cubanas, 1988. 229-247.

Maravall, José Antonio. *Culture of the Baroque – Analysis of a Historical Structure*. Minnesota: University of Minnesota Press, 1986.

Martí, José. "Nuestra América." *Obras escogidas, tomo* 11. Havana: Editorial de Ciencias Sociales, 2007. 497-505.

Sarduy, Severo. *Barroco*. Paris: Gallimard, 1975.

—. *Maitreya*. Hanover: Ediciones del Norte, 1987.

—. *Written on a Body*. New York: Lumen Books, 1989.

—. "El heredero." *Antología*. Mexico: Fondo de cultura económica, 2000.

THE RIGORS OF SUN, THE CLEMENCY OF THE SHADOW: FROM EAKINS TO BUFFON – WITH LOVE?

Željka Švrljuga, University of Bergen

> … history is not simply a science but also and not least a form of remembrance <Eingedenken>. What science has 'determined,' remembrance can modify. Such mindfulness can make the incomplete (happiness) into something complete, and the complete (suffering) into something incomplete. (Benjamin 1999a, 471)

By juxtaposing history *qua* science and remembrance, the theory of historiography and the theory of the real course of events, or more precisely, the official records of history and personal documents of lived experience, Walter Benjamin advocates concern for the subject of experience before historical events, for a particular destiny (an individual) before the history of mankind (1999b, 255). This understanding is the ideological premise for Patricia Eakins's 1999 novel *The Marvelous Adventures of Pierre Baptiste, Father & Mother First & Last*, which she ideationally and stylistically grafts on Georges-Louis Leclerc, Comte de Buffon's *Histoire naturelle*.

Like so many scholars of his time, Buffon (1707-1788) started off as a generalist. Although he had already made a name for himself in mathematics, he is best remembered as a natural historian who provided a paradigmatic 18th century descriptive model of studying nature as a system, as opposed to the Linnean taxonomy which was inspired by man's need for systematising nature (Roger 84-85). Darwin himself acknowledges Buffon as the first naturalist to treat evolution scientifically, but circumvents further discussion because of the inconsistency of Buffon's argument (xiii). Considered one of Darwin's precursors, Buffon is articulate in his claim: "Nature … has neither classes nor species; it contains only individuals. These species and classes are nothing but ideas we have ourselves formed and established" (Buffon 3: 326). His *magnum opus* is a history and theory of the natural world, and its 36 quarto volumes are the 18th century master narrative in natural history. Despite Darwin's high commendations of Buffon the scientist, one can challenge or even dispute the link between history *qua* science and natural history on the grounds that Buffon's work belongs to natural philosophy rather than to science proper. Eakins's textual politics doubly inflects Buffon's scientific treatise: not only does the author thematically and narratively transform this treatise into the eponymous character's alternative history to Buffon's master narrative; she fashions it on its 19th century slave-narrative prototype.[1] Thus the master-slave dialectic becomes an informative and formative impetus for the novel.

ONCE UPON A GENRE...

Eakins's choice of narrative design may concurrently be motivated by her subject matter: the first-hand experience of and escape from slavery relayed by the subject of experience. Originally devised for abolitionist purposes, the slave-narrative proper, which was both a hermetic and prolific genre, focused on the who, what, and where of slavery, yet offered little or no space for reflection or cultural commentary, lest they be related to personal experience of the abominable institution. Thus, when the protagonist in Eakins's novel claims difficulty in mastering the letter Y of the alphabet, it is evident that he alludes to its homophone – why – since he is caught "composing in the dust, an inquiry into a moral question" of the whites' urge "to master the world" (Eakins 20). Although the *Urgenre* and its transformations have an explicit race-political agenda, its latter adaptations tend to explore the undercurrents of the institution of slavery: European expansionism, colonisation, and cultural and economic exploitation that have led to racialisation and racism. Eakins shores up this agenda with the scientific thought of the 18th century, and highlights the ensuing science/fiction nexus by means of parody as a critical prism through which slavery and its historical backdrop are scrutinised by way of Buffon. The traffic between literature and science, and the parodic and its "target" text, offers analytical commentary and aesthetic revaluation of the novel's hypotext.[2]

---

1 Although the slave-narrative originates in the 18th century, and its advent concurs with the publication of Buffon's *Histoire naturelle*, it was originally "an exercise in creative hearing" in the hands of a white amanuensis-editor (Andrews 8). With the slave literacy on the march in the 19th century, and despite its still obligatory white hallmark of approval, the genre bespoke its number one political concern: writing as a trope for freedom.

2 Gérard Genette's concept of hypotext refers to a subtext upon which another text is grafted (5). With no space to develop a comprehensive discussion of parody, I will employ the term in a broad and inclusive sense that, based on the prefix *para* as in the Greek original *parodia*, becomes a doubly encoded message: besides denoting

There is no doubt that the novel follows and amends the slave-narrative requirements, but its contemporary perspective pushes it to and beyond its boundaries. Ashraf Rushdy's oft-quoted definition of the neo-slave narrative, implying a direct, linear descent from the slave narrative with regard to form and narrative conventions (3), begs a reformulation that would grant the recent form a chance to further free itself from the constraints of its generic template.[3] For, as Jacques Derrida maintains, the law of genre apparently demands a "vow of obedience" (225), while its limits incite challenge, opposition and transgression. The law assumes a counter-law, a law unto itself, which Derrida's conundrum "the law of the law of genre" sees as "a principle of contamination, a law of impurity, a parasitical economy … a sort of participation without belonging" (227). The implied shift from *belonging* to a genre (entailing closure and "ownership") to *participation* in the genre (alluding to openness and agency) notionally ties up with the fictional and/or authentic narrator-protagonist's change in status from slave (chattel, property) to free agent or self, and the novel's generic encapsulation to its coveted manumission.

The literary concept of genre that Derrida discusses under the rubric of typology (the non-natural or *technē* of the arts) is secondary to the notion of genre, whose origin is in nature or *phusis*. By way of word play, Derrida brings together biological genre and human genre (224), but also gender, as social and grammatical categories. The polyvalence of the word and its numerous derivatives that bring to light its multifaceted potential – from engendering to degenerescence, generation, and genealogy – resemble Buffon's understanding of the law of genre as a "right of nature, power founded on unalterable laws" (5: 89), despite man's attempt to interfere:

Men have had no influence on independent animals, but they have greatly altered, modified, and changed domestic ones; therefore, we have made physical and real generas [sic], greatly different from metaphysical and arbitrary ones, which have never existed but in idea. These physical genera, are in reality composed of all the species, which by our management have been modified and

---

a contrast, *para* also purports complementarity (Hutcheon 32). It is in this second sense that our understanding of the contemporary parody lies, which, in turn, subsumes the carnivalesque (Bakhtin), palimpsests (Genette), and intertextuality (Bakhtin; Kristeva).

3   For a systematic discussion of the slave-narrative genre see James Olney, especially 50-52.

changed, and as all these species so differently altered by the hand of man, have but one common origin in Nature, the whole genus ought to form but one species. (8: 69-70)

The nominal difference between their respective designations aside, Derrida and Buffon recognise in the genera/genre nexus a nature/culture dichotomy that Eakins draws on, subverts and expands. If genres are man-made taxa (comprising a group of a genus or species), and species are determined by their ability to reproduce themselves within a genus and still retain their natural characteristics as a common trait, then genres mix – through human intervention. The initial decree *qua* prohibition that the law of genre issues – "Genres are not to be mixed" (Derrida 223) – is an inspiration to Eakins to defy it. She mixes genres/genders and species as the title of the novel suggests. The author flouts the Law's "No!" with her fictional experiment that triumphs with Pierre's celebratory "yes" at the end of the novel. This final celebration confirms Pierre's generic duplicity and hermaphrodism in his signature: "Pierre, Mère et Père,/Premier, Dernière, yes" (249), with which the novel ends. While the French version of the signature pertains to the novel's declared status as a testament, which the opening sentence of the novel proclaims it to be, it uncannily blurs the notions of *genre* in a generic enigma. Pierre's uniqueness that joins the sexual gender (Mére et Pére) and the grammatical gender (Premier, Dernière), which grammatically inverts the gender of the parent, defies the gender symmetry as much as the novel defies generic taxonomy. Gender like genre redefines itself by way of performativity and transsexuality, which in turn enable Pierre Baptiste to engender and give birth to his progeny, as much as they enable Eakins to further inflect her multigeneric narrative. Or, to say it with Derrida, "The genders/genres pass into each other … [and] this mixing of genders … may bear some relation to the mixing of literary genres" (245).

Pierre's conception and parturition that crowns his "marvelous adventures," which the title heralds and the novel's Overture confirms, offers yet another generic twist upon which the novel metamorphoses into the genre of magical realism. Even though the particulars of the event are revealed in the third and final part of the novel, the reader is duly forewarned: "'*La plus grande merveille,*' said the great Buffon, '*c'est dans la succession.*' All the greater the marvel when the succession were untoward" (1-2), with which the novel opens, prepares the ground for the existence of the protagonist's progeny.[4] Or, as the Buffon of *Histoire naturelle* continues, "It is in the succession, in the reproduction, and the duration of species that nature becomes inconceivable … the depth of which we are not enabled to fathom" (2: 257). While this ambiguous formulation cancels an essentialist reading of species as lineal descendants of an original pair, it in no way clarifies their creation and succession but declares them a marvel. This, in turn, inspires Eakins's marvellous narrative turn. Pierre miraculously gives birth to four marvellous offspring to whose idiosyncrasies we will return.

THE SCIENCE/FICTION TRANSFER

Although Eakins's novel is by no means the first to ponder the institution of slavery through the prism of science, it is the most experimental and consistent neo-slave narrative to date to incorporate scientific experiment at the level of content, method, and form and language. Following Buffon, the author's concern is with generation, species, cultures and varieties in human population. She deliberates the effect of white ideology via Buffon's unfortunate slips of the pen when he writes: "White then appears to be the primitive colour of Nature" (4: 324), which literally haunts the text of the novel.[5] Eakins's position is unambiguous: whiteness as the historical norm inspires hierarchical thinking and needs to be examined, questioned, indeed replaced and repealed, which is what the novel does by "rewriting" Buffon's *Histoire naturelle* into Pierre's "*Shadow Histoire*" (33). In so doing, Eakins transforms the official natural history (science) into a personal and cultural response (history *and* story), crafting her novel on a parodic (parasitical) principle. Injustice would be done if we overlook broader ideological implications of Buffon's work in Eakins, who in a grand yet coherent sweep moves from species in general, to the science of man and, finally, to the Savant's

---

4 For Antoine Cazé, the "untoward" suggests "a narrative strategy of mis-direction, or … re-direction" (16), which I read as generic shifts that closely follow narrative developments.

5 The extent to which Eakins has read Buffon is uncertain. What is certain, however, is her familiarity with Jacques Roger's study of Buffon, which she duly acknowledges. Unlike the more modern translation that we find in Roger, which proclaims whiteness "Nature's primary color" (175), the wording in Barr's Buffon is a direct translation of the original "la couleur primitive de la Nature" (3: 502), where the attribute "primitive" denotes "original; essential, fundamental" ("Primitive"). In its own way, each rendition highlights Buffon's understanding of the origin of human species as degenerating from the white original to folk groups or races.

creation of the earth. All of these are glossed at some length for, as the extended one-page title of the novel declares, Pierre's is both a *"Cyclopedish Histoire"* and a *"Commonplace Book"* (v), which allows Eakins to move deftly between different discourses and still remain true to her overall project.

The setting of the novel is the imaginary island of Saint-Michel in the French Anduves, where the white master, Messieur Dufay, collects, draws and describes nature for the venerable Comte de Buffon.[6] His ambition is to amend the French scholar's taxonomy with the species from the colonies and make himself a name in the sciences of the Enlightenment. Following the practice of the period, nature is "institutionalised" and its specimens seem to be collectibles through taxidermy and drawing, which are shipped to the Cabinet of Natural History at the Royal Botanical Garden in Paris to be described, classified and exhibited. The reference to the Botanical Garden that "quotes" and displays nature in a tableau eventually becomes a trope of arranged and denaturalised nature, as opposed to nature as an ecosystem, which Pierre's narrative ponders. Although Buffon conceived *Histoire naturelle* as a study of species or genera of quadrupeds, birds and fish, he never completed his project. What he left out – the fish, which his follower Bernard-Germain-Étienne de Lacépède investigated – is what Master Dufay studies with his slave's help. Pierre is forced into the sea to collect specimens for his master to describe and draw. As his name – Pierre Baptiste – suggests, his immersion into the sea becomes a baptism, following which he is converted into a naturalist. A cradle of all life on earth, the sea is, according to the native and African traditions, "the salty tear-drenched garden of the dead" (7), into which the deceased are launched to their final rest. Signifying on the Middle Passage and the slaves' arrival in the New World, the passage which in many ways literally transformed the Atlantic into this "garden of the dead," Eakins seems to suggest that the slaves' funeral ceremony portends a wilful return home, just like traditional stories of flying Africans suggested a spiritual flight and homecoming. Pierre's reluctance to enter the sea is thus predicated on his fear of disturbing his ancestors; but, instead of their scattered bones, he discovers a "garden of fishes" (4), whose life, and

---

6   In a parodic turn that characterises the narrative as a whole, the master's name echoes the name of Buffon's predecessor as the intendent of the Jardin du Roi – Charles de Cisternay DuFay. Although a physicist and chemist by profession, DuFay initiated collections that Buffon would later expand (Roger 59), even though the collection of specimens from the colonies predates DuFay. However, his retouched name brings in not only the colonies but also the economic system that they relied on.

variety of species, colours and movement transform the sea (the garden of the dead) into (a garden of) Eden. In line with the 18th century practice of studying nature in the institution called garden, and aware that the garden is *of* nature but does not stand *for* nature, Eakins inverts the nature/culture paradigm by proclaiming a natural environment a garden, highlighting its dual status with cultural connotations ("the garden of the dead," paradise) and "natural" referencing ("the garden of fishes"; "the garden of sand," 185). Not only does the author obliquely critique the Enlightenment's constructed/homey environment where nature was studied; she also emphasises the arbitrariness of language and our ideological approach to it.

This *natural* paradise of the underwater world is not available to the master, who shuns the water and dismisses what he does not see, thus refusing to acknowledge that a slave knows more than the master.

> [M'sieu] did not revere the fish, and his stiff fillets, dull eyes already rotting, were not his truest portraits. He never even saw the hermaphrodite plants, with thick stalks and bright-petaled flowers, yet with roots, emerging from the calyx, squirming and grasping at tiny fish, which they did feed into the calyx as hands would stuff a mouth. For M'sieu did not believe Pierre when Pierre spoke of them, and offered to bring one up, though it might be a pet of the dead. M'sieu did not believe a slave-man could discover creatures a master had not. "Tut tut!" he said. (8)

The master's claim to the knowledge of nature is consequently partial since what he draws is a still life. Pierre, in turn, knows that the essence of life is movement, variety and versatility, which is what he admires in nature. While the master freeze-frames Pierre's catch, Pierre witnesses that fish are "impossible to catch and hold, their form their movement, their movement one with the water" (7), except for catching a glimpse of their shape and movement in their natural habitat. What is lacking in Dufay's drawings, then, is life itself, and the shadow that guarantees it and suggests movement, which is one of the reasons why Pierre tags his narrative "shadow histoire." While the novel's dependence on Buffon is incontestable, as a (hi)story of the slave community which lives in the shadow of the Anduvian sugarocracy of which Master Dufay is one of the ruling specimens, the narrative is in many aspects deserving of its name. Pierre's intent is "to shadow M'sieu in the philosophic project he had undertaken with the Sage of Montbard" (45-46), and eventually to overshadow Buffon and correct his fallacies. But as the project's designation indicates, shadow is predicated on the sun, whose rigour is declared "a terrible stasis, the paralysis of [its] merciless glare" (13), which is the effect it produces in Dufay's drawings. The sun's inclemencies play a significant role in Buffon's science of man and the varieties in the human population, to which the discussion will eventually turn.

The initial training in observation is the first step in Pierre's becoming a naturalist. By perusing books, he learns that the Buffonian method of studying nature consists of "OBSERVATION, AND PHILOSOPHIZING UPON OBSERVATION" (213, upper case in the original), which becomes the protagonist's (and the novel's) principal narrative mode in sections that parody Buffon. The politics of observation is contingent upon the subject of perception, whose status and training prompt specific ways of seeing. Whereas the master marvels over the colour and glory of the local fauna and flora, the slave protagonist discovers the marvellous in nature – in the insignificant, and in places/natural elements that the master ignores: "fishes & orchids, vermin & shadows & slaves" (15). The master/slave dialectic determines the politics and ethics of reading, implying what should be studied and how. Eakins contrasts Dufay's selective and superficial vision with Pierre's visual acuity and analytical ability, which put him ahead of the master (and his intellectual model Buffon) in matters related to the reading of nature. Her fictional "historical subject" is not only the object of her attention, but also her mouthpiece with which she critiques Buffon's hierarchical structuring of nature. Speaking from the obverse of power structures, Pierre is fascinated with the power of nature as well as being amazed by its subversive potential, which serves Eakins as an analogical pattern for the reading of slave culture. Thus Pierre's preoccupation with the underwater world, the island's vermin, and the putrefaction which invades the master's campaign chest and destroys his drawings, which are intended for Buffon. Eakins employs a baroque and ideologically laden language which mixes the 18th century "scientific" jargon, military terminology, and aspects of the concurrent gothic genre. This miscellany of styles highlights the abject invader's scope and force, which supersede death itself.

> On the pigments of his pages there bloomed a terrible colony of proliferating, stunted monsters, regiments of blue & green & white spoilers, obliterating the limpid symmetries of M'sieu's vision, as if creatures of shadow and orchid-dust mites, obscure, hot vermin and hermaphrodite flora-fauna he had refused to draw, had vengefully mingled their juices and their rage and given birth to generations of vileness so wicked their stench was worse than death. (14)

For the slave population, the study of nature is neither a matter of prestige nor restrictive in any way, which is why Pierre is a better observer than his master. Pierre receives his education in an open-air classroom which eventually proves to be a better place of study than the comfortable room of the planter's house. His tutoring through the open window allows him to earn a double major in nature and in culture, with the window as a threshold chronotope where the two spheres meet. Eakins highlights this spatio-temporal encounter and crisis with yet another of Pierre's discoveries: a new species that he terms "CHANGELING" (20), and the master eventually names after himself – "*Metamorphosa dufayensis*" (21). The name punning is unambiguous: what the master can claim, the ostensible and intellectual ownership, a slave as chattel cannot. Not only is the naming policy predicated on Buffon's practices of retaining the popular name besides its Latinised version; it equally suggests that the latter, although nominally sophisticated and empowering and morphologically clarifying in terms of the species' particularities, implies universality because it conceals its geographical origin (Roger 275). Pierre explains that if we, the readers, have never come across a reference to this animal, it is because "Buffon does not always acknowledge" (22). Also, the politics of font that provides a visual hierarchy stresses the author's preference in terminology, which is consistent with Eakins's overall political project. But the Latinate name under which this new species figures, with its popular etymology as a notional support, reflects the master's own position as a "CHANGELING" or a "PARASITE" (20), which resembles, lives on its host organism – the bee – and lives off its work. Eakins's analogy seems to parody Buffon's understanding of organic transmutation, according to which the environment shapes the species, which will ultimately culminate in the new species that Pierre creates.

EXPERIMENTUM CRUCIS

It is not difficult to establish that Eakins's grand fictional design entertains several experimental sub plots, the original one being Pierre's role as object of study in his master's research project. Dufay's naturalist orientation to observe, describe, show and explain is broadened at the point when he switches from theory and philosophy to practical experimentation, such as when he forces his slave to learn to swim by hypothesis. The master's approach to the practice of swimming is theoretical, whereas the slave develops his theory from practice itself. When, in the second stage of the master's experiment, Pierre is taught to read and write, the master seems to be inspired by the same passage from Buffon's *Histoire*, which later inspires Pierre to write his own "shadow histoire." The novel quotes this crucial passage at greater length than we do here:

> Even though Negroes have little intelligence, they do not fail to have a great deal of feeling; they are gay or melancholy, hard working or idle, friends or enemies according to the way they are treated, they are happy, joyful, ready to do anything and the satisfaction of their spirit is written all on their faces; … They have the seed of all virtues, and I cannot write their history without being moved by their state. Are they not unhappy enough at being reduced to servitude, at being obliged always to work without ever being able to acquire anything? Is it also necessary to exhaust them, strike them, and treat them like animals? Humanity revolts against these hateful treatments that a greed for profits has created…. (46-47)

Dufay's educational experiment with Pierre is a test of the black man's learning abilities and intelligence, which eventually becomes a lucrative investment when the master entrusts the business of the plantation to his slave to pursue his study of nature. Yet the master's profit is marginal since what he saves (wages which would have gone to a white bookkeeper) is what Pierre invests in the wellbeing of the slaves by cunningly moving around the ciphers in the master's books. As a classical trope of freedom in all slave narratives, literacy literally transforms Pierre from a cipher (the price in the master's book and a "mere nothing") to man, from object (a marketable commodity) to subject (a speaking, thinking, and writing being), and, finally, from slave to free man. Pierre's transfer from field work to office work in the master's library gives him access to books which he eagerly peruses, and which increase his educational and intellectual appetite and develop his taste. His preference for Buffon is immediate, as is his desire to amend him with his own "ENCYCLOPEDIA OF THE CUSTOMS AND INDUSTRIES AND TRUE RELIGION OF SLAVES TRANSPORTED FROM GUINÉE, WITH FABLES AND MAXIMS, THE COLLECTED ENTIRETY PROVING US WORTHY OF THE STATUS OF FREE MEN" (53; upper case in the original). In an endless process of renaming and transforming itself, Pierre's narrative ostensibly claims a typical format of the Enlightenment, which enables it to examine Western thought and ponder different aspects of knowledge. Diderot, whose presence is registered in the list of authors and genres that Pierre furtively studies, becomes an explicit generic and intellectual reference. The new direction that the narrative assumes from this point on enables Eakins to insert African and native folktales and creation myths, which emphasise the politics and aesthetics of double consciousness and double-voicedness that are so central to her project. While narrative templates change and proliferate, they ideologically follow a humanist and egalitarian principle that Pierre endorses:

> And in my cyclopedish histoire I inscribed an account of the world reflecting the TRUE condition and experience of ALL its denizens, in the heretofore despised animal kingdoms and the neglected human realms, among persons of diverse & varying parts, to instruct and delight ALL MANKIND. (144)

In making Pierre compose an alternative, ethnic yet universally valid and non-discriminatory encyclopaedia, Eakins talks back to the white racial paradigm of the Enlightenment. The island microcosm of Saint-Michel brings together peoples from three different continents, cultures and languages: the French landed aristocracy, the native Xuacomac, and the imported slaves from Africa. Eakins puns on Buffon's maxim that "climate, food, and manners" (4: 324) determine the formation of races, even though the French Savant seldom employed that term, but used "varieties of human species" (4: 190) or "race of men" instead (4: 238, 264, 271). His division of the "nations of the globe" according to horizontal climatic zones translates into the novel's racial paradigm whereby the shade of skin colour and the alleged adaptability to work in hot and humid climate determine the group's position in the hierarchy. Accordingly, Pierre's dark skin would place him at the bottom of the scale, also in terms of his intellectual abilities.

Eakins's parodic take on Buffon gains momentum at the point when Pierre flees the plantation and sends himself to Buffon as a specimen of black intellectual worthy of Buffon's company and title *philosophe*. The paradox of his deed is obvious: on the one hand he wants to reach France and gain his freedom, whereas on the other he turns himself into an object – a collectible item for the Royal Botanical Garden and Buffon. With the rum keg as a means of escape, Eakins signifies on Henry Box Brown's 1849 slave narrative, which recounts Brown's escape to freedom (in a box), as much as highlighting Europe's dependence on her colonies in economic terms, sugar cane and its derivatives in particular. The barrel as a means of transportation with Buffon's name and address on it written in Pierre's hand highlights the role of literacy in the slave escape plot, at the same time as making him aware that all free men have a family name. Of the two options that immediately come to his mind – Dufay and Buffon – he decides on the latter since the former associates him with property and slavery. Pierre's wooden "envelope" thus joins three referents under the sign "Buffon": the black Buffon as sender of the message, Pierre Baptiste Buffon as message-cum-specimen, and the white Buffon as receiver. "Buffon," consequently becomes a synonym for scholar and free thinker, regardless of the colour of the skin.

Eakins's strategy of punning and allusion, however, never loses sight of the text's underlying buffoonery. The arbitrariness of naming as well as Pierre's different names indicate different aspects or stages of his identity: from the pejorative slave moniker Goody, to his white name Pierre Baptiste that his godmother gives him (yet he must relinquish it should another white family want it for their son), and finally to the enigmatic African name he is supposed to grow into, the name his mother would have given him at puberty had she not been sold away from the estate. Unable to learn his intended name, the second-best solution is identity by choice.

Pierre's escape serves as the novel's narrative passage from the realistic mode to the fantastic or marvellous. As he aimlessly spins in his keg in the sea (of improbabilities) and spins his scheherazadian stories in his "cranial conjure house" to keep himself alive (194), so does Eakins's narrative spin off in another "untoward" direction at the point when Pierre is swallowed by a sea monster and ejected on a desert island. Just like the narrative that produces and reproduces itself, Eakins transforms Pierre into a hermaphrodite, who gives birth to four marvellous offspring born of his mouth just like words, look like fish yet possess human qualities of reason and intelligence, and are indeed his "untoward" succession:

> Did not their existence call into question the very notion of *species*? Mayhap his offspring would give birth to creatures as unlike themselves as they were unlike Pierre. Mayhap a NEW FORM OF LIFE had sprung from Pierre's mouth as heroes had sprung from the forehead of Zeus-God in days of old. (199)

Asserting that reality is a product of language, which makes everything possible, Eakins suggests that reality is as fishy as language is slippery. Thus, the worlds of myth and magic (magical realism included) no doubt have their basis in reality – if not always literally, then in some sense figuratively, and stand for the human need that mandates survival and regeneration. Eakins's novel aptly demonstrates that a revision of thought requires a rethinking of language, and expresses a need for an alternative vocabulary, which is more adequate to the complexity of our reality and which also speaks in tongues.

Consequently, she labels Pierre's progeny "FILOSO-FISH" or "FILOSO-FISH SAVANTS" (215), signalling that naming is a symbolic act.

Even though Pierre ponders the shape of his progeny, there are textual cues that may account for their fishy appearance. Pierre's most private part, which is referred to as "Johnny Fish" (5), is one possible explanation; another being his rescue by his fish-friend Amie,[7] who nurtures him back to life by vomiting her fish gruel into his mouth, thus possibly impregnating him. Neither, however, accounts for the "father and mother" of the title, which suggests Pierre's unique hermaphroditic self-sufficiency – something which he earlier admired in sea plants and orchids, and discovers in his progeny. Hermaphrodism joins opposites in harmony and becomes Eakins's trope for equality, balance and dualism with which she, through her mouthpiece Pierre, tries to cure the world from hierarchical binary thinking. For, as the extended title of the novel claims and Eakins's emendation of Buffon's seventh epoch of nature confirms, Pierre indeed establishes "A REALM of Equality & Freedom & Bounty, in Which No Creature Lives from Another's Labor" (v, upper case in the original).

Pierre's philosophical proviso thus draws on his progeny's existence in relation to – themselves, which his "*Sunt, ergo sunt*" highlights. Yet he also suggests that thought and imagination guarantee existence to his offspring by turning around the Cartesian premise of "Cogito, ergo sum" into "*Cogitent, ergo sunt*" (203): They are thought, therefore they are. Thought becomes the epitome of freedom, which in turn does not depend on privilege or rank, thus on notions of hierarchy, but is an inalienable condition of life and movement that nature affords all her creatures.

The paradox of Pierre's conception and parturition comes as a surprise to Pierre himself since he deliberately chose a barren wife in order *not* to father children and participate in the perpetuation of the abominable institution. Now, however, that he is marooned and free, and his offspring born of him are not only free by birth, but are free floating signifiers in search of their signifieds, Pierre is able to take issue with his slave past and the system of oppression under which he was born. However, his passage from slave to philosopher reveals that he has unwittingly adopted western ideology at the moment when he decides to brand his children in order to be able to differentiate them from other "pupils in a school of fish" (205).

---

7   Declared abbreviated from "ma bon amie" (193), the name is a spelling variant of the French name Aimée, or "beloved." Eakins no doubt plays with sound proximity by transforming the friend into a girlfriend or sweetheart.

Knowledge-seeking Pierre seems to have forgotten that branding is the white man's writing on the black body that signifies ownership, and that he, too, bears Dufay's signature on his own body. Stigmatisation, taxonomy and the writing of history entail power and ownership through naming, something which the already mentioned *Metamorphosa dufayensis* has illustrated. But just as the changling changes its form, so does Eakins's novel continuously change its shape and narrative course and becomes, by analogy, a generic "crosster" (203) – to use one of Eakins's many coinages – or, a *Metamorphosa eakinsensis*. With the narrative that metamorphoses into different genres, and science that morphs into fiction – and fiction into science – but also species that ostensibly reproduce outside of or across their genera, Eakins confirms the novel's heliotropic dependence on Buffon in both senses of the word. When most critical of her model, Eakins targets Buffon's article of faith that concerns the superiority of man over other creatures, for which she sees a solution in nature – in the sea, in which "all creaturely conception floats" (215), and where equality of all life is the maxim:

> Yet if, in The Eighth Epoch, men learn to dwell as one family with all other creatures, then we shall have a new histoire to write together, more compendious than any conceived before. From the honest labor of this conception will be born forms of language and thought, and thus of life, that were not present in the rock and fire of Creation. This Pierre believes. For, after much reflection, he does not hold with the Christians, that all that man may be, already is. Rather he submits, all that may be is not yet born. (245)

The new histoire that Eakins proposes will replace Benjamin's two avenues to the writing of history, but until this utopian moment sees the light of day, we will have to content ourselves with a historical-materialist approach that, like Eakins's "CYCLOPEDISH HISTOIRE," will continue to challenge history's official documents (of science) like *Histoire naturelle*. As long as science attempts to outshine or be equal to nature instead of trying to explain and understand it, it may suffer the same destiny as the gigantic maps in Jorge Luis Borges's "Of Exactitude in Science": destruction due to the "Rigors of Sun and Rain" (141).

Andrews, William L. "The First Fifty Years of the Slave Narrative, 1760-1810." *The Art of Slave Narrative: Original Essays in Criticism and Theory*. Eds. John Sekora and Darwin T. Turner. Macomb: Western Illinois University, 1982. 6-24.

Benjamin, Walter. *The Arcades Project*. Cambridge, MA: Belknap-Harvard University Press, 1999a.

—. "Theses on the Philosophy of History." *Illuminations*. Ed. Hannah Arendt. London: Pimlico, 1999b. 245-58.

Borges, Jorge Luis. "Of Exactitude in Science." *A Universal History of Infamy*. Trans. Norman Thomas di Giovanni. London: Allen Lane, 1973.

Buffon, Georges Louis Leclerc. *Histoire naturelle, générale et particulière, avec la description du Cabinet du Roi*. Tome Quinzième. Paris: L'imprimerie royale, 1767. Accessed 18 Feb. 2009.

—. *Buffon's Natural History. Containing a Theory of the Earth, a General History of Man, of the Brute Creation, and of Vegetables, Minerals Etc*. Vol 2. London: Barr, 1792. Accessed 16 Apr. 2009.

—. *Buffon's Natural History. Containing a Theory of the Earth, a general History of Man, of the Brute Creation, and of Vegetables, Minerals Etc*. Vol. 3. London: Barr, 1792. Accessed 20 Apr. 2009.

—. *Buffon's Natural History. Containing a Theory of the Earth, a general History of Man, of the Brute Creation, and of Vegetables, Minerals Etc*. Vol. 4. London: Barr, 1792. Accessed 20 Apr. 2009.

—. *Buffon's Natural History. Containing a Theory of the Earth, a general History of Man, of the Brute Creation, and of Vegetables, Minerals Etc*. Vol. 5. London: Barr, 1792. Accessed 20 Apr. 2009.

—. *Buffon's Natural History. Containing a Theory of the Earth, a general History of Man, of the Brute Creation, and of Vegetables, Minerals Etc*. Vol. 8. London: Barr, 1792. Accessed 20 Apr. 2009.

Cazé, Antoine. "Reduplication and Multiplication: Split Identities in Eakins's Writing." *Reading Patricia Eakins*. Ed. Françoise Palleau Papin. Orleans: University Press of Orleans, 2002. 13-26.

Derrida, Jacques. "The Law of Genre." *Acts of Literature*. Ed. Derek Attridge. New York: Routledge, 1992. 221-52.

Darwin, Charles. *On the Origin of Species by Means of Natural Selection, or, the Preservation of Favoured Races in the Struggle for Life*. New York: D. Appelton, 1882.

Eakins, Patricia. *The Marvelous Adventures of Pierre Baptiste, Father and Mother, First and Last*. New York: New York University Press, 1999.

Gennette, Gérard. *Palimpsests*: Literaute in the Second Degree. 1982. Transl. Channa Newman and Claude Doubinsky. Lincoln: University of Nebraska Press, 1997.

Hutcheon, Linda. *A Theory of Parody: The Teachings of Twentieth-Century Art Forms*. Urbana: University of Illinois Press, 2000.

Olney, James. "'I Was Born': Slave Narratives, Their Status as Autobiography and as Literature." *Callaloo* 0.20 (Winter 1984): 46-73.

"Primitive." OED *Online*. Accessed 28 Apr. 2009.

Roger, Jacques. *Buffon: Life in Natural History*. Ithaca, NY: Cornell University Press, 1997.

Rushdy, Ashraf. *Neo-slave Narratives: Studies in the Social Logic of a Literary Form*. New York: Oxford University Press, 1999.

ECOPOETRY'S QUANDARY

Charles I. Armstrong, University of Bergen

Poetry is not a science – that much seems clear. But can poetry take on board the findings and fascinations of the natural sciences? More specifically, does overly elaborate use, in a poem, of scientific knowledge or methodology entail a reprehensible transgression of poetry's own aesthetic essence? For William Butler Yeats, looking back at the formative years of his generation of poets in the 1936 introduction to *The Oxford Book of Modern Verse*, one of the notable and laudable features of the new poetry of the age was that it had left behind precisely such impurities: "The revolt against Victorianism" included "a revolt against irrelevant descriptions of nature, the scientific and moral discursiveness of [Alfred, Lord Tennyson's] *In Memoriam*" (Yeats 183).

The insights or productive dogmas of yesteryear, though, are far from invulnerable, and the tendencies dismissed by Yeats have often resurfaced, in different guises. Given the enormity of the ecological challenges with which we are faced today, it is especially hard to dismiss "scientific and moral discursiveness" out of hand. Would it not be blatantly culpable of a poet not to make use of all the means necessary in order to impress upon his or her readers, as forcefully as possible, the utmost importance of the current environmental crisis? Given the conflicting impetuses of literary integrity and ecological responsibility – one autonomous to the poetical endeavour, the other heteronomous but perhaps equally compelling – a quandary becomes evident.

Beyond the rather tidy either/or opposition of aesthetic versus practical exigencies, this chapter will gradually approach the possibility of moving beyond such a dichotomy. Although a measure of culpability is hard to avoid, it is not impossible to conceive of a poetical practice that would transcend this well-worn duality. This issue will come into view after an introductory addressing of the concepts of *ecocriticism* and *ecopoetry*, which shows that the latter term especially involves contemporary poetry in rather conflictual relations to practical exigencies, the heritage of Romanticism, and the use of science. Subsequent to the elucidation of these relations, the second half of this chapter will move to more concrete examples of ecopoetry, drawing on a recent anthology titled *Wild Reckoning* and a poem by Alice Oswald.

During the last ten or fifteen years, concerns with the environmental crisis have made an increasing impression on both literary studies and literature itself. Within literary theory, the term *ecocriticism* has been used as a common denominator for approaches to literature that concentrate on how texts either overtly or more implicitly relate to the environment. Cheryll Glotfelty has provided a wide definition of ecocriticism:

> [A]ll ecological criticism shares the fundamental premise that human culture is connected to the physical world, affecting it and affected by it. Ecocriticism takes as its subject the interconnections between nature and culture, specifically the cultural artifacts of language and literature. As a critical stance, it has one foot in literature and the other on land; as a theoretical discourse, it negotiates between the human and the nonhuman. (Glotfelty xix)

By mainly addressing literature on the basis of a thematic concentration on a particular concern, ecocriticism is comparable to many other theoretical movements that have been in the ascendancy during the last couple of decades. Unlike most of these movements, though, the very nature of the subject matter of ecocriticism brings it into close contact with the natural sciences. According to William Howarth, ecocriticism's willingness to engage with the natural sciences distinguishes it from most other movements within contemporary literary theory. In his essay "Some Principles of Ecocriticism," he claims that it "seeks to redirect humanistic ideology, not spurning the natural sciences but using their ideas to sustain viable readings." In doing so, it is taking into account recent scientific changes that have been overlooked by much literary criticism: "Today science is evolving beyond Cartesian dualism toward quantum mechanics and chaos theory, where volatile, ceaseless exchange is the norm. While some forms of postmodern criticism are following this lead, many humanists still cling to a rationalist bias that ignores recent science" (Howarth 78).

Within the more encompassing scope of ecocriticism, the term *ecopoetry* designates a more particular field of enquiry. It is not, however, always used in the same way. One of the critics who has done most to propagate the term, J. Scott Bryson, claims that any "definition of the term *ecopoetry* should probably remain fluid at this point because scholars are only beginning to offer a thorough examination of the field" (Bryson 5). He describes it via "three overarching characteristics – ecocentrism, a humble appreciation of wildness, and a skepticism toward hyperrationality and its resultant over-reliance on technology" (Bryson 7). This last trait he also characterises as "a skepticism that usually leads to an indictment of an overtechnologized modern world and a warning concerning the very real potential for ecological catastrophe" (Bryson 6).

So far so good, but we enter into more contentious territory when Bryson claims that ecopoetry is only of a relatively recent date, and that it is to be clearly distinguished from Romantic poetry. This distinction is followed up by Roger Thompson – in the essay collection *Ecopoetry: A Critical Introduction*, edited by Bryson – who contrasts the contemporary ecopoet with Emerson's transcendentalist conception of the poet. For Thompson, "the ecopoet might be called cause-centered, declaring the natural world as center to societal reform". Ecopoets, he claims, "are, in fact, ecocritics themselves, shelving notions of nature as solely metaphoric divinity in favor of a conception of nature as potential action, possible location of human reform" (Thompson 36). His main exemplar is the contemporary American poet W.S. Merwin, and towards the end of his essay he claims that "the ecopoet might be called uniquely American or, at least, uniquely democratic, because ecopoetry is less about specialized, priestly incantations and more about accessibility to people whom the poet hopes to call to action, not simply contemplation" (Thompson 37).

I will return to the issue of Americanness, but for now it's more important to pause at the notion of ecopoetry's resisting "specialisation". Here brief reference is being made to the fact that many understandings of the essence of poetry – as a "specialised" discourse, in a manner of speaking – would seem to resist the kind of directness Thompson is endorsing. One obvious stumbling block for poetry's engaging too closely with both ecology and the natural sciences is the way modern poetry typically conceives itself as resisting instrumental uses of language. If an environmentally sustainable planet is the final goal of poetic utterances, does this not entail a manhandling of the muse – as anticipated in Yeats' poem "The Fascination of What's Difficult," when the poet complains of how practical exigencies force Pegasus to "Shiver under the lash, strain, sweat and jolt / As though it dragged road metal" (lines 7-8)? Dominic Head has addressed such a concern, claiming that "a new ecological grand theory – the planet as limit – must provoke the postmodernist's incredulity. But of course there is nothing new about this limit (you would have to be on another planet, quite literally, not to accept it). Moreover, prescriptions for the best action, from an ecological point of view, are necessarily provisional, continually refashioned as the scientific ideas on which they are based are contested and transformed" (Head 28). This argument, then, would hold that the holistic perspective of ecology is not too absolutist or objectifying. It is saved from such a damning state either due to its functioning merely as an implicit, regulatory idea, or as a result of its links to concrete action being based upon principles that are subject to verification and revision (as in Popper's conception of science). While the latter point might actually be counter-productive for some poets, who would be unwilling to champion particular causes because these causes were felt to be too temporary or of uncertain long-term importance, the former point is more classical. Since Kant, it has always been possible to argue that art has an implicit or symbolic relation to ethical or epistemological ideals, and that this is perfectly acceptable as long as the link is a tacit one.

The latter position underlies Jonathan Bate's understanding of ecopoetry, which has had considerable influence in Britain. Unlike American theorists such as Bryson and Thompson, Bate has always stressed the continuity between contemporary ecopoetry and Romanticism: his 1991 book *Romantic Ecology: Wordsworth and the Environmental Tradition* paved the way in this regard. His study from 2000, *The Song of the Earth*, further strengthens this link through readings of figures such as Byron, Keats and John Clare. *The Song of the Earth* is also notable for articulating a conception of ecopoetry that is far removed from the ideals of the two mentioned American ecocritics. Building on the thought of Martin Heidegger, Bate conceives ecopoetry as essentially a matter of stance rather than statement: "ecopoetics," he writes, "should begin not as a set of assumptions or proposals about particular environmental issues, but as a way of reflecting upon what it might mean to dwell with the earth. Ecopoetics must concern itself with consciousness. When it comes to practice, we have to speak in other discourses" (Bate 2000, 266). Later, Bate goes so far as to claim that "When ecopoetics is translated into political system, its case, too, is hopeless.... Whatever it becomes, it ceases to be ecopoetics" (Bate 2000, 268).

The consequences of Bate's resistance to linking an environmentally engaged poetry to a concrete political programme should not be overstated, though. He does not, for instance, sever the link between poetry and its surroundings: the Romantic poet John Clare is important to Bate precisely for this reason. Clare is said to "disprove an argument much favoured by disenfranchised late-twentieth-century radical literary theorists, namely that the bond with nature is forged in a retreat of social commitment, that it is a symptom of middle-class escapism, disillusioned apostasy or false consciousness" (Bate 2000, 164). Not only does Clare's poetry reflect clear social relations, it also points to recent developments in the understanding of nature:

THE ART OF DISCOVERY

It is a first principle of scientific ecology that the survival of both individuals and species depends on the survival of ecosystems. Clare foreshadows scientific ecology in his knowledge that, James McKusick puts it, "an organism has meaning and value only in its proper *home*, in symbiotic association with all the creatures that surround and nourish it" (Bate 2000, 167-168).

Other ecologically minded readers of Clare have pointed out the humble attentiveness and observational skill with which he confronts natural phenomena, effectively pitting him against the more self-conscious and idealising practice of Wordsworth (dominant since Geoffrey Hartman's interpretation of the latter).[1] As a result, our view on Romanticism itself has changed in line with recent developments in nature poetry.

The contrast between Bate and the American ecocritics might lead one to believe there is something of a transatlantic divide within the field, roughly similar to the distinction often drawn between practical criticism and American New Criticism, as well as between cultural materialism and American New Historicism. A recent anthology of both English and American poems addressing the environmental issue largely confirms this suspicion. *Wild Reckoning* was published in 2004, marking the fortieth anniversary of Rachel Carson's classic warning against the consequences of the use of pesticides. Seventeen of the poems included in the anthology were specially commissioned, most of them being based on the premise that the poets in question would write a poem out of a cooperative project with a scientist. This dimension of commissioning brought added pressure on the problematical link between poetry's muse and practical projects, and (unsurprisingly perhaps) some of the results reflect this. The editors had planned a series of dialogues between poets and scientists, but this idea was shelved. Instead, there is an appendix with short comments from the poets, many of which reflect rather cursory and half-hearted engagements with the work of the scientists with whom they were paired off. James Lasdun, for instance, describes his poem "A Peeled Wand" as reflecting his own encounter with a beaver. The poem, he states, "is more a collaboration with an animal than with a scientist. I did however have illuminating conversations with Kristine Flones, a Wildlife Rehabilitator here in the Catskills, who confirmed to me that what I had observed was entirely in keeping with the behaviour of beavers" (Lasdun 245-246). If Lasdun's engagement with science appears limited to a time-span

---

1   Bate himself makes a similar point in Bate 2003, 187.

subsequent to the poem, John Burnside's was correspondingly circumscribed to the time period *antecedent* to his writing. Burnside describes the gestation of his poem "Salvelinus Alpinus," during a visit to Tromsø in the north of Norway, as follows:

> I worked with the botanist Elizabeth Cooper, fully intending to write very specifically about sub-Arctic flora, in particular the Arctic poppy (which appears at the centre of the poem). In the end, the Arctic charr made an unexpected appearance, after an eerie encounter in a Tromsø fish market, so the plant references, while still central, gave way, on the surface at least, to fish (something of a pet theme for me). (Burnside 244)

Sure enough, in Burnside's poem, the flower is far less conspicuous, and less important, than a vision of the collective unity of the moving shoal of charrs – which

> wanders with the light
> as one long soul: a unity of eyes
> and movement, centred everywhere at once
>
> and nowhere, as the centre of the world
> is here, and now, in every blade of grass
> or poppy head that shivers in the wind (lines 7-12)

Here the "blade of grass" would seem to be a fairly transparent allusion to Blake, while the more general idea is very reminiscent of the kind of pantheism with which Coleridge flirted (cf. McFarland). Yet it would be wrong to see Burnside as opting for Romanticism in simple opposition to science, since of course Romantic pantheism was a cross-cultural phenomenon that fed not only into poetry but also into the science of figures like Blumenbach and Davy.[2] Romanticism also looms large in the former poet laureate Andrew Motion's contribution to *Wild Reckoning*, his poem "Sparrow" indicating its provenance in the ethical imagination of Romanticism by quoting a letter of Keats as its epigraph: "If a sparrow come before my window I take part in its existence and pick about the gravel".[3]

---

2 This is for instance evident in Roe. For a more encompassing, populist, and recent attempt to revise clichés about Romantic resistance to science, see Holmes.
3 John Keats to Benjamin Bailey, 22 November 1817, cited by Motion 143.

While English poets like Motion and Burnside engage with the Romantics, the American poets featured in the anthology would seem to be more affected by their dialogues with contemporary scientists. The non-commissioned poem that kicks off the volume as a whole, Rodney Jones' "The Assault on the Fields," directly addresses the dire consequences of pesticides – directly linking its poetry to a political cause. The commissioned poems by Linda Gregerson and Allison Funk are more meditative, effectively highlighting the obvious fact that much science is at least as removed from immediately practical concerns as poetry is. Gregerson's "Elegant" spins a web of words around the model organism developed by the 2002 winners of the Nobel Prize in physiology in order to explain "genetic regulation of organ development and programmed cell death" (Gregerson 245). Funk's poem on mayflies, "Ephemeroptera," uses metaphors deployed by her entomologist brother as a kind of trigger for poetic exploration:

Blizzard. Smoke. Interstellar
dust. Even you, an entomologist,
turn to metaphor,

awed by their emergence
over water (lines 1-5)

Both of these poems highlight an obvious common ground between poetry and the natural sciences in the inventive use of figural language and/ or heuristic images. Arguably, though, the rather flat prose of Gregerson's poem also underlines the fact that a precise or insightful understanding of scientific research is far from being a guarantee for imaginative power. Certainly, if ecopoetry is to provide a mere mouthpiece to existing scientific theories it will hardly challenge existing preconceptions, let alone live up to Neil Evernden's description of ecology as "the 'subversive science' [that] undermines … science itself" (Evernden 93).

The English poet Deryn Rees-Jones should be well qualified to address these issues, as she is not only a renowned poet and critic, but has also worked on the links between these two fields at the Centre of Poetry and Science at the University of Liverpool. The mere existence of such a centre is of course symptomatic of the recent appearance of more general, institutional moves to link these two fields. Rees-Jones credits the formative impetus of her contribution to *Wild Reckoning*, "Trilobite," to the palaeontologist Richard A. Fortey's "enthusiasm, his ability to write like a poet while thinking like a scientist," which "left me wanting to know more about these small creatures" (Rees-Jones 247). While it is obviously an imaginative construction, Rees-Jones' poem nevertheless describes a meeting with this now extinct creature in relatively close detail. When its body parts are listed, however, she shows some circumspection, referring to "the three sections of its crossways nature / – *cephalon, thorax, pygidium* / as later, now, I've learned to call them" (lines 10-12). These lines register something of a collision between the generalised, everyday consciousness of the poetic self that one usually finds in contemporary British poetry,[4] and more specialised anatomical vocabulary. An avant-garde British poet such as J.H. Prynne would not flinch at the overlap of these two dimensions, but in the more mainstream voice of Rees-Jones there is something of a standoff between the specialisms of poetry and science.

This opposition can be interpreted more broadly as reflecting a conflict between an embodied, perceiving self akin to that postulated by the philosophies of phenomenology and hermeneutics, on the one hand, and the less grounded representations of explorative natural sciences on the other. Thus while Linda Gregerson's poem is attracted to "something less congenial to the seeing / eye, the microscope," that of Rees-Jones is firmly rooted in the experiencing self: she traces "how it came to me, this trilobite" (line 6). Accordingly, these conceptions of ecopoetry seemingly bolster, rather than challenge, the separation of what Snow called "two cultures". Yet it would be wrong to see this divide as absolute, even within the field of contemporary poetry. Ever since Romanticism, of course, there has been a spate of claimed transcendences of the subject-object dichotomy that arguably looms in the background here.

The work of the English poet Alice Oswald certainly demonstrates that excellent poetry is being written at present that refuses to settle for received opinions or dichotomies. Oswald is a former gardener, whose book *Dart* won the T.S. Eliot prize for the best poetry volume of 2004 in Great Britain, and who has also edited a volume entitled *The Thunder Mutters: 101 Poems for the Planet*. An inspection of "Otter Out and In," a poem from the first of her three poetry volumes proper to date, will serve to illustrate how she relates to the issues discussed so far.[5] This text fits with the mainstream of

---

4   On subjectivity in contemporary poetry, see "Poetry as memory: the autobiographical lyric in contemporary British and American poetry," in Middleton and Woods.

5   "Otter Out and In," in *The Thing in the Gap-Stone Stile* 29. (The volume was first published in 1996, by Oxford University Press.)

romantically inclined verse in that it insists upon a grounded, observing subjectivity. The dynamic and elusive otter only comes to light for a situated audience: "The whole river transforms upon an otter. / Now and gone, sometimes we see him / swimming above the fish" (lines 9-11). The audience of two may share a sense of togetherness, but they view nature from the outside: as line five points out, they are "arm in arm" but only appear as representations "apart upon the water".

Yet the poem will not leave things at that, refusing to unequivocally embrace the aesthetic distance that Timothy Morton has claimed insidiously undercuts the worldview of most ecological literature (cf. Morton). Rather than simply affirming the mind's solitude or intersubjectivity's own self-sustaining dialogues, it seeks to attain an attentive solicitude towards the natural event. As line nine points out, "The whole river transforms upon an otter". This moment of revelation is arguably linked to the most ecologically informed aspect of the poem, as the otter's centrality to the entire ecosystem of the river here embodies the notion of "keystone species" developed in the Harvard biologist Edward Wilson's book *The Diversity of Life*. Yet this idea is not commented upon or used as an external epigraph for Oswald's poem: it's integrated into its very texture. It's also an idea that "Otter Out and In" plays around with on several levels. Not only does the otter's continued disappearance and reappearance (in line 8) mirror the fragility of its existence, but this double movement is also echoed by its audience. In the final line, the line "out and in and disappear into darkness…" may describe both spectacle and spectators. By integrating the human subjects into the ecosystem of the river, Oswald makes them dependent upon the otter, and effectively negotiates with the legacy of Romantic subjectivity. It would be wrong to say that this is a dismissal of Romanticism, since English Romanticism consistently questions what Keats called the "egotistical sublime": rather, it represents an exploration of a sidelined but important strand of Romanticism, bringing it into line with current ecological thought.

In this manner, the poetry of Alice Oswald can be said to combine the Romanticism of someone like John Clare with the contemporary, ecological biology evident in the work of Edward Wilson, effectively straddling the very divides that have been so insistent in this paper. It would be precipitate to see this as a lasting solution or final synthesis, though: Oswald's poetry is certainly troubled by these oppositions, and her acts of transcendence are just as vulnerable to critical scrutiny as those found in the various philosophies and theories that have trodden similar ground before her. For one thing, her poetry avoids being overtly prescriptive in the way favoured in

American conceptions of ecocriticism. In a short prose essay she writes: "We have a problem with our fields, with our weather, with our water, with the very air we breathe; but we can't quite react, we can't quite get our minds in gear" ("Wild Things"). But once one moves to her poetry, the form and the content of the literary text are to be as interdependent as the living entities of an ecosystem: no straightforwardly prescriptive statements, where form is bruised to pleasure sense, are included.

In general, then, the quandary seems to be not fully solvable, as ecopoetry is arguably more the name of a problem, or ongoing discussion, than an established phenomenon. The transcendence of the dichotomy between autonomous and heteronomous conceptions of poetry does not take place: ecopoetry is the meeting place of these two exigencies, rather than their annihilation. Poets can share something of the imaginative liberty underlying much scientific endeavour, and they can also be inspired by the ecological insights provided by modern science. This does not mean, however, that poetry is easily converted into a vehicle for discursive truths about man's troubled dealings with nature – however laudable or urgent such truths may be. But at its best, the kind of poetry called ecopoetry can combine excellent poetical craftsmanship with an attentive curiosity about the natural world around it. As such this literary phenomenon is, in glimpses at least, thrillingly responsive and acutely responsible to one of the most important challenges of our time.

WORKS CITED

Bate, Jonathan. *The Song of the Earth*. Cambridge, Mass.: Harvard University Press, 2000.
—. *John Clare: A Biography*. London: Picador, 2003.
Bryson, J. Scott. "Introduction." *Ecopoetry: A Critical Introduction*. Ed. J. Scott Bryson. Salt Lake City: The University of Utah Press, 2002.
Burnside, John, and Maurice Riordan (eds.). *Wild Reckoning: An Anthology Provoked by Rachel Carson's 'Silent Spring'*. London: Calouste Gulbenkian Foundation, 2004.
—. On "Salvelinus Alpinus." *Wild Reckoning: An Anthology Provoked by Rachel Carson's 'Silent Spring'*. Eds. John Burnside and Maurice Riordan. London: Calouste Gulbenkian Foundation, 2004.
Evernden, Neil. "Beyond Ecology: Self, Place, and the Pathetic Fallacy." *The Ecocriticism Reader: Landmarks in Literary Ecology*. Eds. Cheryll Glotfelty and Harold Fromm. Athens and London: The University of Georgia Press, 1996.

Glotfelty, Cheryll. "Introduction." *The Ecocriticism Reader: Landmarks in Literary Ecology*. Eds. Cheryll Glotfelty and Harold Fromm. Athens and London: The University of Georgia Press, 1996.

Gregerson, Linda. On "Elegant." *Wild Reckoning: An Anthology Provoked by Rachel Carson's 'Silent Spring'*. Eds. John Burnside and Maurice Riordan. London: Calouste Gulbenkian Foundation, 2004.

Head, Dominic. "The (Im)possibility of Ecocriticism." *Writing the Environment: Ecocriticism and Literature*. Eds. Richard Kerridge and Neil Sammels. London and New York: Zed Books, 1998.

Holmes, Richard. *The Age of Wonder: How the Romantic Generation Discovered the Beauty and Terror of Science*. London: Harper Press, 2008.

Howarth, William. "Some Principles of Ecocriticism." *The Ecocriticism Reader: Landmarks in Literary Ecology*. Eds. Cheryll Glotfelty and Harold Fromm. Athens and London: The University of Georgia Press, 1996.

Lasdun, James. On "A Peeled Wand." *Wild Reckoning: An Anthology Provoked by Rachel Carson's 'Silent Spring'*. Eds. John Burnside and Maurice Riordan. London: Calouste Gulbenkian Foundation, 2004.

McFarland, Thomas. *Coleridge and the Pantheist Tradition*. Oxford: Clarendon Press, 1969.

Middleton, Peter, and Tim Woods. *Literatures of Memory: History, Time and Space in Postwar Writing*. Manchester: Manchester University Press, 2000.

Morton, Timothy. *Ecology Without Nature: Rethinking Environmental Aesthetics*. Cambridge, Mass.: Harvard University Press, 2007.

Oswald, Alice. *Dart*. London: Faber and Faber, 2002.

—. "Wild Things." *The Guardian*, 3 December 2005.

—. *The Thing in the Gap-Stone Stile*. London: Faber and Faber, 2007.

Rees-Jones, Deryn. On "Trilobite." *Wild Reckoning: An Anthology Provoked by Rachel Carson's 'Silent Spring'*. Eds. John Burnside and Maurice Riordan. London: Calouste Gulbenkian Foundation, 2004.

Roe, Nicholas, (ed.). *Samuel Taylor Coleridge and the Sciences of Life*. Oxford: Oxford University Press, 2001.

Thompson, Roger. "Emerson, Divinity, and Rhetoric in Transcendentalist Nature Writing and Twentieth-Century Ecopoetry." *Ecopoetry: A Critical Introduction*. Ed. J. Scott Bryson. Salt Lake City: The University of Utah Press, 2002.

Yeats, William Butler. *Later Essays*. Ed. William H. O'Donnell. New York and London: Charles Scribner's Sons, 1994.

METAPHOR AND COGNITION IN SCIENCE, POETRY AND THEOLOGY

Jostein Børtnes, University of Bergen

To speak of metaphoric processes in science and theology is a fairly recent development in cognitive theory. Metaphor's link with philosophical argument, with questions of truth and reality, so clearly set out by Aristotle, had been lost. Metaphor had been reduced to one of the figures of speech, an improper term replacing the proper term which the reader had to identify in order to establish the correct meaning of the expression.

One of the first works to bring about a change in the understanding of metaphor in the natural sciences is *Models and Analogies in Science* by the English philosopher of science Mary Hesse, published in 1966. In her book, Hesse proposed to supplement the prevailing hypothetico-deductive interpretation of scientific explanation with a metaphoric one, arguing that models and analogies are central both to scientific understanding in general and, in particular, to the understanding of how scientific theory is extended and how theories generate genuinely novel predictions. More recently, the importance of metaphor and analogy for scientific thought has been further elaborated by a number of scholars, for instance by Richard Boyd, to whom metaphors are important because of their ability to provide alternative or new ways of viewing the world, whereas so-called literal language may be too restrictive because of its inability to provide these perspectives (Boyd 1993).

A similar re-evaluation of metaphor and analogy has taken place in theology, not least thanks to the works of Paul Ricoeur, who in his influential study, *The Rule of Metaphor: Multi-disciplinary Studies of the Creation of Meaning in Language* (1977), has retrieved for contemporary scholarship Aristotle's insistence on the truth of poetry and metaphoric speech. This insight can, according to David Tracy, also be extended to biblical hermeneutics (Tracy 103-4 & 137 n. 18). A similar argument is put forward by Sallie McFague. In her important contribution to metaphoric theology she writes:

The *primary* context then, for any discussion of religious language is worship. Unless one has a sense of the mystery surrounding existence, of the profound inadequacy of all our thoughts and words, one will most likely identify God with our words: God *becomes* father, mother, lover, friend. Unless one has a sense of the nearness of God, the overwhelming sense of the way God pervades and permeates our very being, one will not find religious images significant: The power of the images for God of father, mother, lover, friend will not be appreciated. Apart from a religious context, religious language will inevitably go awry either in the direction of idolatry or irrelevancy or both. (McFague 2)

In the following, I will try to show how metaphors, far from being an ornamental device poets superimpose on ordinary language in order to make it poetic, constitute the very basis of scientific and religious thought and language.

WHAT IS METAPHOR?

In their trailblazing study, *Metaphors we Live by*, first published in 1980, George Lakoff and Mark Johnson give the following definition of metaphor: "The essence of metaphor is understanding and experiencing one kind of thing in terms of another" (Lakoff and Johnson 5).

In literary theory, the thing named by the metaphor is sometimes called the "vehicle," and the abstract concept understood and experienced the "tenor" of the metaphor. Cognitive scientists call them the "source (domain)" and the "target (domain)" respectively.

In "God is love" – a metaphor I shall come back to – "love" is the "source domain" or vehicle, while "God" is the "tenor" or "target domain" we try to fathom by way of *mapping* or *projecting* onto it the source domain.

METAPHOR IN EVERYDAY SPEECH

Metaphor is conventionally thought of as a figure of speech, a device associated with rhetoric and poetic imagery, in contrast to the literal use of non-poetic language. However, research into the nature of metaphor carried out in the last decades of last century has shown that metaphor is much more than a poetic device. According to the restatement of the key ideas brought forward in *Metaphors we Live by*:

Metaphors are fundamentally conceptual in nature; metaphorical language is secondary.

- Conceptual metaphors are grounded in everyday experience.
- Abstract thought is largely, though not entirely, metaphorical.
- Abstract thought is unavoidable, ubiquitous, and mostly unconscious.
- Abstract concepts have a literal core but are extended by metaphors, often by many mutually inconsistent metaphors.
- Abstract concepts are not complete without metaphors. For example, love is not love without metaphors of magic, attraction, madness, union, nurturance, and so on. (Lakoff and Johnson 272)

A great number of our everyday metaphoric expressions are variations of *conceptual metaphors* such as ARGUMENT IS WAR or LOVE IS A JOURNEY or LIFE IS A CONTAINER, to name but a few that we all know from our own experience: "She was totally defeated in the debate"; "their relationship seems to have come to a halt"; "he led such an empty life." Conceptual metaphors are not poetic *per se*, but they may, of course, be used poetically.

The general conclusion in *Metaphors we Live by* is that "conceptual metaphors are grounded in *correlations* within our experience;" and that these "experiential correlations may be of two types":

> The first is described as *experiential co-occurrence*, as in, for example, MORE IS UP, a metaphor grounded in an experience like seeing milk rising higher and higher as it is poured into a glass. But this experience cannot explain more complex metaphors, such as LIFE IS A GAMBLING GAME. This kind of metaphor is grounded in *experiential similarity*. Actions in life are like gambles with winning or losing as the possible outcome. When such a metaphor is extended, we may experience new similarities between life and gambling games. (Lakoff and Johnson 155)

In his very constructive critique of Lakoff and Johnson's theory of conceptual metaphor, Steven Pinker argues that "you can't think with a metaphor alone," as the authors of *Metaphors we Live by* seem to maintain. Taking their LIFE IS A GAMBLING GAME metaphor as an example, he claims that here it is the abstractness of an idea like "gamble" that "is doing all the work": "The abstract ideas define the dimensions of similarity [...] that allow a conceptual metaphor to be learned and used" (Pinker 251).

In more general terms, Pinker argues that "metaphors are useful to think with to the extent that they are *analogies* – that they support reasoning in the form 'A is to B as X is to Y'" (Pinker 253). Pinker bases his argument on the research of the psychologists Deidre Gentner and Michael Jeziorski. In their study, "The shift from metaphor to analogy in science," they view *metaphor* "as a rather broad category, encompassing analogy and mere appearance, as well as a variety of other kinds of matches" (Gentner and Jeziorski 452). In their definition, conceptual metaphors like those analysed by Lakoff and Johnson in *Metaphors we Live by* are "examples of systematic relational metaphors, that is, metaphors that could also qualify as analogies" (Gentner and Jeziorski 452). Apart from such systematic relational metaphors, there are those that "could not qualify as analogies," such as "attributional metaphors – mere appearance matches, based on shared object descriptions." They give as an example "her arms were pale swans," and metaphors like e.e. cummings' "the voice of your eyes is deeper than all roses." These metaphors "are not bound by the one-to-one-mapping constraint and can include mixtures of several bases, as well as thematic and metonymic relations" (Gentner and Jeziorski 452). Steven Pinker follows Gentner and Jeziorski, claiming that the more useful metaphors "allude to the way the source of the metaphor is assembled out of parts":

> The source (for example a journey) is stripped down to some essential compo-
> nents (A, B, and C). The metaphor puts these components into correspondence
> with components of the target (such as a romantic relationship): A is to X, B to
> Y, C to Z. Then some concept related to A in the source, such as B, is used to
> pick out an analogously related concept in the target, such as Y. In a journey, one
> sometimes has to pass over bumpy spots to reach a destination. The way love is
> like a journey is that the experience of the relationship is like the relationship
> of travel on the road, and the couple's shared goal is like the traveller's destina-
> tion. Ergo, one may deduce, for a couple to achieve a shared goal, they should
> be prepared to endure periods of conflict. (Pinker 2008:253)

METAPHOR IN SCIENCE

Pinker's insistence that metaphors are useful to think with to the extent that they are analogies and "can power sophisticated inferences" (Pinker 253) is important for our understanding of the role of metaphor in science. But it is important to keep in mind that analogies are not necessarily there before the metaphor has created them. As Aristotle writes in his *Poetics* 1459a6: *to gar eu metaferein to to homoion theôrein estin* (to metaphorize well is to see the similar). The point is that to perceive similarities is a creative cognitive act.

Gentner and Jeziorski suggest that the *analogy* in the modern sense it is understood in science today emerged in the period roughly 1570-1670. "The shift from metaphor to analogy is one aspect of the general change in the style of scientific thought during that period" (Gentner and Jeziorski 475).

In their studies of metaphors in science and technology, the theologian Mary Gerhart and the physicist Allan Russell take a different view, insisting on a distinction between metaphor and analogy. Their examples are "the Copernican Revolution," verbally expressed in the formula "The Sun (not the Earth) = the Center," and "the Newtonian Synthesis," put across as "The Laws of Heaven = The Laws of Earth."

In *De Revolutionibus Orbium Coelestium* (1543), Gerhart and Russell point out:

> Copernicus claimed that the Sun rather than the Earth was the center of the universe (solar system). To the best of our knowledge the claim was made on the basis of no definitive observational evidence whatsoever. The "facts" – i.e., the observations that had been made of the motions of the sun – were as completely accounted for by Ptolemaic theory as they were by Copernican. [...] We understand the Copernican assertion as deriving from a metaphoric act based on his understanding of the relations among the heavenly bodies [...]. The negative reaction reached its climax in 1633 with the Italian church's house arrest of Galileo Galilei (who *did* have observational evidence to support his teaching the Copernican system). (Gerhart and Russell 23-4)

From Copernicus' *De Revolitionibus Orbium Coelestium* (1543) Gerhart and Russell move on to a discussion of Newton's equation of the laws of the heavens and the laws of the earth. Claiming that "Copernicus' metaphor changed the way we see ourselves as related to the rest of the universe," they argue that "the metaphoric process that caused Isaac Newton to equate the mechanics of the heavens with the mechanics of earthly objects had perhaps an even more profound effect on our lives":

> The Newtonian synthesis combined the Galilean laws of terrestrial motion and Kepler's law of planetary motion using a new form of mathematical analysis – the calculus – to create analytical mechanics, arguably the most powerful scientific system up to the twentieth century. (Gerhart and Russell 26)

Gerhart and Russell understand both the Copernican and the Newtonian equations as "cognitive disruptions." In their view, it is this disruptive force that characterises metaphor in contrast to analogy and simile: An "analogic act" expands meanings within fields without distorting the fields, whereas the "metaphoric act," which "also involves the recognition of similarities," creates the similarities by a "disruptive cognitive act" which "*forces* an uncalled for analogy between the fields of meaning – a distortion of one or both of these fields – in order to achieve the required analogy. When the distortion is productive, it creates new understandings and meanings" (Gerhart and Russell 29). Gerhart and Russell's third example of metaphoric process in science, which I shall not go into, is Einstein's metaphoric act of insisting that "the concept of (Galilean) relativity applied not only to mechanical phenomena, but to electromagnetic phenomena as well" (Gerhart and Russell 42).

Let me conclude this discussion of metaphor and analogy in science by quoting the philosopher Richard Boyd:

> [T]he use of metaphor is one of many devices available to the scientific community to accomplish the task of *accommodation of language to the causal structure of the world*. By this I mean the task of introducing terminology, and modifying usage of existing terminology, so that linguistic categories are available which describe the causally and explanatory significant features of the world. (Boyd 483)

Steven Pinker, in his comment on this passage, understands Boyd to the effect that "metaphor in science is a version of the everyday process in which a metaphor is pressed into service to fill gaps in a language's vocabulary":

> But they aren't shackled by the content of the metaphor, because the word in its new scientific sense is distinct from the word in the vernacular (a kind of polysemy). As scientists come to understand the target phenomenon in greater depth, they highlight the aspects of the metaphor that ought to be taken seriously and pare away the aspects that should be ignored. (Pinker 2008: 257-8)

METAPHOR IN POETRY

I have already quoted a metaphor from the poet e.e. cummings, "the voice of your eyes is deeper than all roses," an example of metaphors that, according to Gentner and Jeziorski "are not bound by the one-to-one-mapping constraint and can include mixtures of several bases, as well as thematic and metonymic relations" (Gentner and Jeziorski 452).

THE ART OF DISCOVERY

E.e. cummings' "the voice of your eyes is deeper than all roses," is an example of the *image* metaphor, a type of metaphor frequently encountered in literary texts. The cognitive linguist Raymond Gibbs observes that poets "often write for the express purpose of creating disturbing new images that result from the mappings of image structures from widely disparate knowledge domains." But, in principle, metaphoric image mappings "work in the same way as other metaphoric mappings by mapping the structure of one domain onto the structure of another. But in image metaphors the domains are mental images" (Gibbs 258-9).

Gibbs gives as an example a line from the opening lines of André Breton's *Free union*, taken from George Lakoff and Mark Turner's *More than cool reason* (1998): "My wife […] whose waist is an hourglass." The line "describes the superimposition of the image of an hourglass onto the woman's waist by virtue of their common shape." We notice that only a part of the hourglass, its middle, is mapped onto the woman's waist, and Gibbs concludes that in most image-mapping metaphors "there is a mapping of the part/whole structure of one image onto aspects of the part/whole structure of another" (Gibbs 259).

One remarkable example of a poem combining image mapping and instantiations of two metaphors that are central to our conceptualization of life is Alexander Pushkin's "Телега жизни" ("The Cart of Life" 1827):

ТЕЛЕГА ЖИЗНИ

Хоть тяжело подчас в ней бремя,
Телега на ходу легка;
Ямщик лихой, седое время,
Везет, не слезет с облучка.

С утра садимся мы в телегу;
Мы рады голову сломать
И, презирая лень и негу,
Кричим: пошел!.......

Но в полдень нет уж той отваги;
Порастрясло нас: нам страшней
И косогоры и овраги:
Кричим: полегче, дуралей!

Катит по-прежнему телега;
Под вечер мы привыкли к ней
И дремля едем до ночлега,
А время гонит лошадей.

"Although its load is heavy at times, | The coach is easy on its move; | The reckless coachman, gray time, | Drives on, will not get off his seat. | In the morning we sit down in the cart; | We're glad to break our necks | And scorning indolence and comfort, | We cry: Off you go! … | At noon it's no longer the same bravery; |We're shaken about: We're more afraid | of the steep slopes and of the gullies; | We cry: More careful, you fool! | The coach rolls on as before; | By evening we're used to it. |And dozing we approach our night lodgings, / While time urges the horses on."

The most easily recognisable conceptual metaphor in the poem is probably A LIFETIME IS A DAY, in which morning equals birth, noon the prime of life, and evening old age. In "The cart of life" these stages are sequentially developed in the second, third and fourth stanza respectively. As we see, the mapping of *day* from the source domain onto the concept of *life* in the target domain corresponds to the mapping of *night* from the source onto the concept of death or afterlife in the target (day:night::life:death).

In "The cart of life," Pushkin has combined A LIFETIME IS A DAY with two other basic metaphors: LIFE IS A JOURNEY, and LIFE IS A CONTAINER. The first of these two, the conceptual metaphor LIFE IS A JOURNEY, generates the story told in the poem. The second, LIFE IS A CONTAINER, is a type of metaphor often referred to as *image-schemas* (e.g. in Lakoff and Turner 97-100). Here, this schematic image of a bounded space with an interior and an exterior is mapped onto another, the much richer image of the Russian *telega*, or *cart*, in the poem's title and in the first, second and fourth stanza. Closely associated with the cart-of-life metaphor is the metaphor "time is a coachman," in which the image-schema TIME IS A MOVER is mapped onto the image of the *jamshchik*, which sounds just as arch-Russian as the *telega* (even though none of the words is etymologically Russian). Both image metaphors – "life is a *telega*" and "time is a *iamsh-chik*" – give the poem a *couleur locale* that nationalise the almost universal conceptual metaphors and image-schemes underlying the verbal texture of the poem. This combination of metaphoric universality with culturally dependent image metaphors is conducive to the aesthetic reception of the poem.

In his book *The Language and Imagery of the Bible*, the biblical scholar, George Caird, writes that "all, or almost all, of the language used by the Bible to refer to God is Metaphor" (Caird 18). We need only think of Christology to see the point of Caird's assertion. In the New Testament, Jesus is seen as "Son of Man," as "the Word made flesh," as "Son of God," "the Second Adam," and "the Messiah." His life and death have been conceived in atonement theology as "ransom," "sacrifice," "redemption," or "substitution."

In the early church, Jesus was understood metaphorically *as a parable of God*. As Henny Fiskå Hägg observes, Clement of Alexandria (c.150-211/216) describes the incarnation "as the parable *par excellence*. The Lord came in the likeness of what he was not: 'Wherefore also the Lord, who was not of the world, came as one who was of the world to men' (*Strom.* 6.126.3)" (Hägg 146). In a more general statement, John Dominic Crossan maintains that "Jesus proclaimed God in parables, but the primitive church proclaimed Jesus as the Parable of God" (Crossan xiv).

In recent years, a number of scholars, both Catholic and Protestant, have tried to revitalise this metaphoric understanding of Christian theology, often to the strong disapproval of the ecclesiastical authorities.[1] Here, I would like to discuss two instances of this renewed metaphoric understanding: the metaphor "God is love" in 1 John 4:8, and Paul's juxtaposition of husband and wife with Christ and the Church in Ephes 5:31-2. The first – "God is love" (*ho theos agapê estin*, 1 Joh 4:8) – is one of the key metaphors of the Christian faith. In his discussion of "God is love," David Bentley Hart comments that the phrase

> provides within the context of the discourse to which it belongs a moment of extreme semiotic resistance, the richness of an irreducibility that calls out for a constant energy of addition and deferral, an eruption of analogical additions proportionate to and determined by its intensity. To say this differently, the "successful" theological metaphor is one that is not analytic, but is, so to speak, a kind of synthetic a priori: It says more than can be said, it is somehow logically prior to all its efficient causes – or, rather, it exhibits its final cause first. (Hart 304)

---

1 The clearest example is Roger Haight's *Jesus: Symbol of God*, Maryknoll, NY: Orbis Books, 1999. Haight, whom the Vatican has now forbidden to teach theology, was criticised in a Notification of the Congregation for the Doctrine of the Faith of 13 December 2004, in which it is claimed that his book contains "serious doctrinal errors regarding certain fundamental truths of faith".

This "extreme semiotic resistance" is caused by the forceful distortion that occurs when "love" as the source domain is mapped onto God as target domain. Crucial to the equation is the "disruptive cognitive act" (Gerhart and Russell 29) that produces the tensive character of the analogy, its "is and is not" quality, which refuses all literal interpretation. There is a tension between this particular equation and a range of alternative, often contradictory metaphors for God in the New and Old Testaments as well as in the Christian tradition: God is "king," "shepherd," "father," "rock," "light," "truth," and "wisdom," but God is also "omnipotence" and "wrath," the latter a concept seemingly incompatible with the concept of "love." And it is the mapping of the source domain "love" onto the target domain "God," associated with all the other attributes, that prompts the disruptive, meaning-generating process of understanding the metaphor "God is love." This metaphor changed God from being the projection of our fear to the object of our desire, challenging us to imagine a new relationship between God and ourselves, as it foregrounds an agapic aspect of God that is new and revolutionary in the Christian kerygma.

The "is and is not" of metaphor is particularly interesting against the background of the traditional Christian distinction between an apophatic or negative theology, in which God is described by the way of negation or ignorance, and the cataphatic theology of affirmation. What Hart asserts about analogy also holds true for metaphor. It is "that form of discourse that is apophatic and cataphatic at once":

> Between the desert of absolute apophaticism and the immobile hypotaxis of absolute cataphaticism stands the infinity, the unmasterable parataxis, of analogy, at home in an endless state of provisionality and promise. Analogy differs and defers, as a licit and yet infinitely insufficient act of predication, and as an aesthetic and moral reply to the divine address. (Hart 306, 311)

In the history of Christian theology, various forms of literal readings and univocal interpretations have all too often superseded this aesthetics of analogy. I would like to briefly mention a fairly recent example of how biblical metaphors can be literalised and deprived of their polyphonic openness, Pope John Paul II's use of Paul's locution "the church is the bride of Christ" in Ephes 5:31-2:

> 31 This is why a man leaves his father and mother and becomes attached to his wife, and the two become one flesh.

32 This mystery has great significance, but I am applying it to Christ and the Church.

To the innocent reader, this looks like a straightforward quadratically proportional analogy, in which the relation between "man" and "wife" in the first part corresponds to the relation between "Christ" and "Church" in the second: A:B::C:D.

In official Catholic theology this is not so, however. John Paul II discusses the analogy in *Mulieris dignitatem*, his apostolic letter "On the dignity and vocation of women," issued 15 August 1988, in which he uses it as a final argument against women priests:

> Since Christ, in instituting the Eucharist, linked it in such an explicit way to the priestly service of the Apostles, it is legitimate to conclude that he thereby wished to express the relationship between man and woman, between what is "feminine" and what is "masculine." It is a relationship willed by God both in the mystery of creation and in the mystery of Redemption. It is the Eucharist above all that expresses the redemptive act of Christ the Bridegroom towards the Church the Bride. This is clear and unambiguous when the sacramental ministry of the Eucharist, in which the priest acts "in persona Christi," is performed by a man. This explanation confirms the teaching of the Declaration Inter Insigniores, published at the behest of Paul VI in response to the question concerning the admission of women to the ministerial priesthood. (*Mulieris dignitatem* § 26)

So, what has happened here? The answer is that the pope in the course of his discussion chooses to disregard the metaphorical character of the analogy by reading it descriptively – "Christ" *is* "the Bridegroom," and "the Eucharist, in which the priest acts 'in persona Christi' is performed by a man." It not only *is*, it *must* be performed by a man. This is the gist of the whole letter, the final argument preventing women from being ordained ministers in the Catholic Church. In this univocal identification of the priest with Christ, the tensive "is-is-not" of metaphor has been obliterated in a way that verges on idolatry.[2]

In its biblical context, the Pauline locution has to be interpreted differently. Here, the components of the source, the bridegroom (A) and the bride (B), and the relationship between them, are not identical with, but corre-

---

2 For an extended discussion of this problem, cf. Børtnes 2007.

spond to (are like) the relationship between Christ (C) and the church (D) in the target: A:B::C:D. In order to understand the analogy theologically, we have to remember that between the divine person of Christ and the human person of Paul's Jewish bridegroom "no similitude can be expressed without implying a greater dissimilitude". This formula, introduced in 1215 by the fourth Lateran Council and often referred to as the *maior dissimilitude*, is fundamental to all theological metaphors and analogies between God and his creation. God is always greater (*Deus semper maior*), and within the analogy between God and creation there will always be an "infinite interval":

> Theology's analogical speech should be understood as *epektasis*[3]: Language, drawn on by the beauty of the Word who is the distance containing all the words of creation, traverses the analogical interval between God and creation (of which God himself is the distance), between creation's proportions and the proportion of peace that belongs to God's infinity; and so there can be no end to the progress of language towards God – so long as it is governed by the measure of charity revealed in Christ – nor any "comprehensive" portrayal of the interval. (Hart 301)

SIMILAR, AND YET SO DIFFERENT

This "analogical interval" is the main *differentia specifica* of theological metaphors and analogies compared to their application in science. For, as Pinker points out, scientists "constantly discover new entities that lack an English name, so they often tap a metaphor to supply the needed label: *selection* in evolution, *kettle pond* in geology, *linkage* in genetics, and so on". But when, in the course of their investigations, scientists "come to understand the target phenomenon in greater depth and detail, they highlight the aspects of the metaphor that ought to be taken seriously and pare away the aspects that should be ignored":

> The metaphor evolves into a technical term for an abstract concept that subsumes both the target phenomenon and the source phenomenon. It's an instance of something that every philosopher of science knows about scientific language

---

3   Epektasis is a term introduced by Gregory of Nyssa in the sense of "a stretching out toward an ever greater embrace of divine glory" (Hart 20). From *epekteinomai*: stretch out, strain. Cf. Phil 3, 13: "Beloved, I do not consider that I have made it my own: but this one thing I do: forgetting what lies behind and straining forward (*epekteinomenos*) to what lies ahead."

and that most laypeople misunderstand: Scientists don't "carefully define their terms" before beginning an investigation. Instead they use words loosely to point to a phenomenon in the world, and the meanings of the words gradually become more precise as the scientists come to understand the phenomenon more thoroughly. (Pinker 257-8)

What Pinker calls "our powers of analogy", enable us "to apply ancient neural structures to newfound subject matter, to discover hidden laws and systems in nature" (Pinker 276). This would account for the usefulness of metaphors and models in science. But our powers of analogy also enable us "to amplify the expressive power of language itself" (Pinker 276). This would account for the poetic and rhetorical functions of metaphor. And last but not least, "metaphor provides us with a way to eff the ineffable" (Pinker 277). In theology, Hart maintains, analogy "clarifies" language about God, "not by reducing it to principles of simple similitude, but by making it more complex, more abundant and polyphonic, richer, deeper, fuller" (Hart 310). Whereas scientists deploy metaphors and models in order to arrive at a finality of reference, theological metaphors and analogies can never be converted into stable identities. They must always be open to further refinement and supplementation.

WORKS CITED

Boyd, Richard. "Metaphor and theory change: What is "metaphor" a metaphor for?" *Metaphor and Thought.* 2nd ed. Ed. A. Ortony. New York & Cambridge: Cambridge University Press, 1993. 481-532.

Børtnes, Jostein. "Le Christ époux – métaphore ou idole?" *Amour, violence, sexualité De Sade à nos jours: Hommage à Svein-Eirik Fauskevåg à l'occasion de son 65e anniversaire.* Ed. M. Wåhlberg and T. Koldrup. Paris: L'Harmattan, 2007. 119-132.

Caird, George. *The Language and Imagery of the Bible.* London: Duckworth, 1980.

Crossan, John Dominic. *In Parables: The Challenge of the Historical Jesus.* New York: Harper and Row, 1973.

Gentner, Dedre and Michael Jeziorski. "The shift from metaphor to analogy in science." *Metaphor and Thought.* 2nd ed. Ed. A. Ortony. New York and Cambridge: Cambridge University Press, 1993. 447-480.

Gerhart, Mary and Allan Melvin Russell. *New Maps for Old: Explorations in Science and Religion.* New York and London: Continuum, 2001.

Gibbs, Raymond W., Jr. *The Poetics of the Mind: Figurative Thought, Language, and Understanding.* Cambridge: Cambridge University Press, 1994.

Hart, David Bentley. *The Beauty of the Infinite.* Grand Rapids Michigan: William B. Erdman, 2003.

Hägg, Henny Fiskå. *Clement of Alexandria and the Beginnings of Christian Apophaticism*. Oxford: Oxford University Press, 2006.

Lakoff, George and Mark Johnson. *Metaphors we Live by: With a New Afterword*. Chicago and London: The University of Chicago Press, 2003. (1st ed. 1980.)

Lakoff, George and Mark Turner. *More than Cool Reason: A Field Guide to Poetic Metaphor*. Chicago & London: The University of Chicago Press, 1989.

McFague, Sally. *Metaphorical Theology*. Philadelphia: Fortress Press,1982.

Pinker, Steven. *The Stuff of Thought: Language as a Window into Human Nature*. London: Penguin, 2008.

Ricoeur, Paul. *The Rule of Metaphor: Multi-disciplinary Studies of the Creation of Meaning in Language*. Trans. R. Czerny with K. McLaughlin and J. Costello. Toronto: University of Toronto Press, 1977. Orig. title: *La métaphore vive*. Paris: du Seuil, 1975.

Tracy, David. *The Analogical Imagination: Christian Theology and the Culture of Pluralism*. New York: Crossroad, 1981.

THE ART OF SELECTION: LESSONS FOR RESEARCH POLICY IN *HEDDA GABLER*

Rasmus T. Slaattelid, University of Bergen

Developing and writing up research grant applications takes up a substantial part of the work time for researchers in academia. It involves not only academic staff, but also research administration units, and in some instances hired experts in proposal writing. At the receiving end, the process of assessing the proposals also requires resources in the form of a research bureaucracy, academic assessment panels, and individual reviewers. From time to time, doubts are raised about the wisdom of investing time and effort on work that often does not pay off in the form of funding. Once in a while the frustration curve reaches a peak, and some radical solution is proposed. A recent newspaper article by a prominent Norwegian professor of system dynamics argues that the Norwegian Research Councils should be abolished and funding allocated to applicants according to their scientific output over the last ten years (Moxnes 2009). Others claim that the funding system is unsuitable for many disciplines in the humanities and social sciences, and forces researchers to alter the way they do research in order to comply with the criteria set up by funding agencies. The demand for larger research projects with short time-spans does not fit well with the traditionally small-scale projects found in much of the humanities and the social sciences (Goldsworthy 2008). There is some evidence that this leads to unfavourable conditions for creativity in research also in the natural sciences (Heinze et al. 2009).

The selection process to which applications are subjected is typically governed by standardised selection criteria. Ensuring that the application satisfies each of the selection criteria to the highest possible degree is the way to maximise the chances of success. The underlying assumption is that high scores on the selection criteria, and high-quality research output, are positively correlated. Critics sometimes question this assumption by citing spectacular scientific breakthroughs that would have remained unfunded if subjected to present-day selection criteria (Reichelt; Bie; Vogel; Newman).

Goldworthy's claim that standardised evaluation criteria are changing the way researchers work, and not necessarily for the better, is one expression of how the normative fabric of science is being affected by these selection processes. We know little about what the outcome of the transformations will be, and what implications they will have for our possibilities of developing and producing the knowledge we need in the future. We need to know more about how the evaluation criteria shape the way we think about our own research, and how, in turn, they shape the research we are producing. How do they frame our research questions, and thereby the answers that we are able to produce?

In the following I will look at one of the practices where this normativity is expressed: the practice of selecting young researchers for academic careers. When I say "look at the practice of", I really only mean looking at the framing of a practice, because my only access to this practice is indirect, through explicitly formulated and publicly accessible selection criteria. Empirical research into *how* the selection processes actually work on this level is very limited, which is surprising given the important role they play in contemporary knowledge production.

Metaphorically speaking, this concerns the ways in which the scientific community is reproducing itself – to borrow an expression from Bourdieu (Bourdieu and Passeron 1977). The reproductive technologies available to the scientific community have been designed to favour candidates with certain attributes not possessed by others. Why are these favoured attributes preferred over alternatives? One answer is that these are the attributes that have been found to be predictive of a candidate's success in academia. Alternatively, the sum total of these factors has proved itself to be one way of maximising the candidates' chances of survival in an academic environment. A third answer is that these factors have been seen to foster a maximum of originality and quality in the candidates' future research. Yet another, more sociologically framed answer is that these factors express the different and sometimes conflicting interests of the stakeholders involved in the reproduction of academia. Each of these answers presupposes different normative perspectives on the process that we are looking at. I will not go into any of them in detail, but simply try to show, using Ibsen's *Hedda Gabler* as a "case study", how normative perspectives are embedded in the guidelines for applications for post-doctoral fellowships from The Research Council of Norway (RCN 2009). It should be noted that the RCN guidelines are representative for such guidelines in general. With variations, similar criteria are in use in major funding agencies such as The US National Science Foundation (NSF 2009), and Research Councils UK (AHRC 2009).

The guideline consists of a list of 12 selection criteria according to which the application and applicant will be assessed. The criteria are:

1) Scientific merit
2) Project management
3) Research group
4) Candidate for grant
5) Feasibility
6) International cooperation
7) National cooperation
8) Dissemination of results
9) Relevance and benefit to society
10) Strategic significance
11) Environmental, ethical and gender perspectives
12) Relevance to the call for proposals

There is no explicit indication in the document of the weight of each criterion, except that under the heading *scientific merit* one reads: "The scientific quality of the research is an essential criterion in evaluating applications and, as such, is of considerable importance." In its own peculiar way, this understatement expresses the conflicting interests that have to be negotiated in selecting candidates for funding. In this context the statement has a particular significance in that in qualifying the essential as being "of considerable importance", it opens a space for issues that have traditionally been considered external to scientific research, but are now deemed important, such as questions of ethics, relevance to society, gender perspectives, race, and so on.

What then, can reading *Hedda Gabler* teach us about these selection criteria? In answering this question I will focus on the characters of Hedda's husband Jørgen Tesman, and that of her friend Eilert Løvborg. I think of these two opposing characters as heuristic tools by which the RCN construction of the early-career researcher can be understood. *Hedda Gabler* does not deal with some urgent social question of the day, as many of Ibsen's other dramas do, nor does it take a stand on some burning issue in the public debate of the time. In *Hedda Gabler*, Ibsen claims, "it is the characters that speak, not me" (Koht). When it comes to the two young researchers in the play, however, it is easy to agree with Koht that Ibsen's sympathies lie with Eilert Løvborg, the charismatic, visionary drunkard genius, and not with Jørgen Tesman, the myopic, pedantic, boring, but hard-working "archivist".

In this sense, one could claim that the author does take a stand on the question of which researcher ethos is more valuable.

The action of Ibsen's play starts in the morning following Hedda and Jørgen Tesman's return from their honeymoon abroad, which has lasted almost six months. In their absence, Tesman's aunt and his friend judge Brack have bought a villa on the outskirts of town on behalf of the young couple. It has been financed on the likelihood that Jørgen will soon be appointed professor at the university, a post that "has been as good as promised" to him. The future income from the professorship comes under threat when Eilert Løvborg, a former fellow student of Tesman's, re-emerges as his academic competitor and a likely candidate for the professorship. This potential conflict highlights the differences in character between the two young researchers.

Starting from the description of their physical appearance, and all the way to their academic interests and work habits, the contrast between Tesman and Løvborg is marked: Although they are both working in the same field, cultural history, their research projects seem to have little in common. Tesman's project is to give "an account of the domestic crafts of medieval Brabant", and involves extensive work in archives and libraries around Europe.[1] He has received funding for his research in the form of a "big fellowship" that has helped pay for the young couple's travels around Europe.

The descriptions of the working habits of Tesman in the play, mostly by Hedda and by his aunt Julle, but also by Ibsen in the notes for the play, convey an image of someone who is passionate about his work, especially about searching for material in archives and libraries. According to Hedda: "He's absolutely in his element if he's given leave to grub around in libraries. And sit copying out ancient parchments ... or whatever they are." The fruits of his searches are brought home to be further investigated: "Just think Auntie", Tesman says, "the whole of that [suit]case was crammed full of nothing but notes. It's quite incredible, really, all the things I managed to dig up round about in those old archives. Fantastic old things that no one knew anything about... "

Hedda, who does not share her husband's passion for archives, points out to judge Brack that "Tesman is an academic" in the negative sense that he has been talking to her "about the history of civilization day in and day out" for the six months of their combined honeymoon/research trip (dur-

---

1 The English translations from *Hedda Gabler* are from Ibsen 1998.

ing which Tesman has also earned his doctorate), "and then this stuff about medieval domestic crafts…! That's the most sickening of the lot!" Hedda admits that he is "a most diligent research worker", adding that "he might get somewhere with it in time in spite of everything." Tesman's need for academic journals in the field is insatiable. When Hedda asks if he really *needs* to buy still more academic journals, he replies: "Oh yes, my dear Hedda … can't get too many of those. One must keep up with everything that's written." Tesman's aunt Julle points to his talent for "collecting things and sorting them out" which he has inherited from his father. Towards the end of act four, Tesman promises to devote "his life" to the work of reconstructing Lövborg's lost manuscript from the notes. "And this", he says, "putting other people's papers in order […] that's just the sort of thing I'm good at."

What about Eilert Lövborg? What does the play tell us about his researcher ethos? Eilert Lövborg is Tesman's opposite in almost every respect. He has a history of alcohol abuse and dissolute behaviour that has led to him being rejected by his family relations, and has left his career in ruins. However, after having left town for a couple of years to live quietly in the countryside, he returns with an *opus magnum*. His research project is a "big new book", "dealing with cultural development … sort of altogether". The book has been published only two weeks before and has "sold […] many copies and caused […] an enormous stir". Tesman is impressed and thinks "it's remarkable how soberly he's argued it". Lövborg however, reveals to Tesman that the book has been written in a strategic attempt to build up a position for himself and "start over" his academic career. But this is not all – the sequel that Lövborg has been working on is "the real thing": "I put some of myself into this one," Lövborg says. The new project "deals with the future", with "the social forces involved" and with "the future course of civilization". The difference in character between Tesman and Lövborg is nowhere more evident than when Tesman, upon hearing this, exclaims: "Amazing! It just wouldn't enter my head to write about anything like that".

Lövborg's working habits are also far from anything Tesman would think of doing. Emotionally unstable, he relies on "inspiration" from his female "companion" Mrs. Elvsted to find focus and concentrate his efforts. Towards the end of the play, he admits that it is in fact his book *and* Mrs. Elvsted's – that he would not have been able to write it without her help, support, and inspiration. At the same time, he refers to the manuscript as his "life's work": "I've torn my own life to pieces", he says towards the end, "so I might as well tear up my life's work as well".

And now, let me propose a *Gedankenexperiment*. What if Lövborg and

Tesman were competitors, not only for a professorship in 19th century Christiania, but in applying for funding in one of the standard frameworks for research funding of today – the Personal Post-doctoral Research Fellowship from the Research Council of Norway? Which one of the two would the RCN choose to fund? The question is admittedly anachronistic, but keeping that in mind, who *would* the RCN fund?

Going back to the assessment criteria, the first item on the list is scientific merit. It is divided into four bullet-points, starting with *originality*: "Originality in the form of scientific innovation and/or the development of new knowledge". Originality is one of the key values in the normative structure of science, Merton has taught us (1973), and on the issue of originality something can be said for both of our candidates. Tesman, who seems to be the weakest candidate in this respect, has nevertheless made some "discoveries" in the archives, where he has found "[f]antastic old things that no one knew anything about". At least in his documents and data there is original new material that will perhaps lead to the development of new knowledge. In Lövborg's case, the originality is of a different kind: he has written a work that surprises and impresses the scientific community, as well as the reading public. Tesman's informal "peer-review" suggests that the work is something quite out of the ordinary. After having heard Lövborg read from his manuscript, he tells Hedda: "you've no idea, it's going to be ever so good! One of the most remarkable books ever written, I'd almost say. Think of that!" Løvborg's score on originality is outstanding, while Tesman's, even in the most favourable view, would be merely good.

Regarding the remaining bullet points under "scientific quality", the clear formulation of objectives, research problems and hypotheses, it is difficult to give anything approaching an accurate assessment. The same goes for the strength of the theoretical approach, operationalisation and the use of scientific method. Nevertheless, it seems that Lövborg's "cultural development sort of altogether" project is in need of narrowing down in order to be manageable in a scientifically responsible way, while Tesman's project, "domestic craft in medieval Brabant", seems better focused and more manageable. There is also evidence in the play that Tesman has a firm grip on scientific method, and his appetite for academic journals tells us that he is well informed on the state of the art in his field.

What about the second criterion: Project management?[2] The description

---

2   The second and fourth criteria have been conflated since these will normally refer to the same person in the case of personal postdoctoral grant applications.

THE ART OF DISCOVERY

states that the evaluation should focus on the applicant's general qualifications for directing and organising the project. Here there seems to be a distinct difference between the two candidates. Ibsen writes in his notes for the play that: "The despair of Eilert Lövborg stems from the fact that he wants to control the world, but cannot control himself" (1928). His dependence upon others for inspiration and moral support, as well as his history of an interrupted career and debauched life, would not give him a high score on this criterion. Tesman, on the other hand, seems to be perfectly able to plan and to lead research projects to their successful conclusion, and is clearly the stronger of the two in this respect.

The third criterion concerns the research group, or the learning environment. The little evidence that I have found in the play indicates that Lövborg's learning environment was virtually non-existent, apart from his muse and secretary, Mrs. Elvsted. He is working alone, in relative isolation. Tesman, on the other hand, seems to have an extensive network of connections abroad and at home, given that he has earned a doctorate abroad, and has a position as a professor at the university "as good a promised to him", presumably by someone who is in a position to give such a promise, and has the influence and power to fulfil it.

Regarding the feasibility criterion, the RCN requires that the project should be realistic and feasible scientifically, organisationally, and within the stated budgetary and timeline parameters. Again, a project that treats the "history of cultural development sort of altogether" leaves something to be desired in terms of focus and scientific feasibility. Also on this point, Lövborg's project comes out second to the more focused project of Tesman. When it comes to budgetary and timeline parameters, Løvborg's history of career lacunas and of squandering his inheritance would not convince a review panel of the feasibility of his project. Tesman, on the other hand, seems to have a proven record of completed projects, although the budget of his latest research trip/honeymoon with Hedda seems to have been overstretched. Overall, Tesman again turns out to be the stronger of the two.

The sixth and seventh criteria, international and national cooperation, are clearly points for which Tesman should receive high scores, because of his travels abroad to academic institutions and archives, as well as the fact that he earned his doctorate abroad. In this respect Tesman fully lives up to the ideals of the funding agency.

The eighth criterion concerns plans for communicating results. Both candidates have plans for publishing results in monographs – which is still the preferred format in most of the humanities. Lövborg has also planned a series of public lectures in which he will present his results – a nice example of public outreach, which gives him a slightly higher score on this criterion than Tesman, although his motivation for lecturing – to outshine Tesman in reputation – is hardly in keeping with the academic virtue of humility.

The ninth criterion asks for the project's relevance and benefit to society. Here, again, it is difficult to compare the two projects, because comparatively little is revealed about the content of Løvborg's project in the play itself. However, thanks to Eivind Tjønneland's work on this topic (2001), and Ibsen's notes for the play (1928), we know a little about what topics Ibsen had in mind while writing, even though these topics are not explicitly mentioned in the play. Tesman takes up the topic of domestic crafts [husflid] in medieval Brabant, one that seems surprisingly up-to-date from our retrospective point of view. The choice of topic can be interpreted as an attempt to bring new phenomena, until now ignored, into the light of research, and to raise awareness about the value of domestic crafts both in academic circles and in the public sphere. In addition, the topic will inevitably be focused on the often ignored work of women, and as such it could contribute to a raised awareness of the role of women in history and in society. On both counts, Tesman's work has potential political implications and obvious social relevance, and could also, at least from a gender perspective, be beneficial to society. Løvborg's project is also politically charged, but in a much more direct sense, in that he, through his work, envisions a future where a new form of relationship between man and woman is possible, that of companionship, out of which the true spiritual human being can arise. This vision of the future is intended as an intervention in the public debate with the aim of changing contemporary views of morality (in addition to the aim of outshining Tesman in reputation). None of the projects can be said to lack relevance and benefit to society, although Tesman probably deserves a higher score by virtue of being less polemic and more balanced.

I have had difficulty in finding any sensible application of the criterion of strategic significance for the home institution, as well as for relevance to call. This leaves us with the last criterion: environmental, ethical and gender perspectives.

Both projects have at least a strong *potential* for a gender perspective, although it is not possible to determine the extent to which this is incorporated into the actual projects. In Løvborg's case, however, there are some obvious ethical issues to be addressed. Although he admits that the project is his *and* Mrs. Elvsted's work; that "Thea's soul is in that book"; even that she *wrote* the text, he does not seem to find it problematic that he alone should take credit for the work. A question mark from the reviewer is to be expected on this criterion.

It is time to sum up our findings. By now, it should come as no surprise that Tesman's project is the one that gets the highest overall score and is selected for funding by the RCN. Løvborg, in spite of his many talents and his originality, will not convince any funding agency with an adequate system of quality assurance in place.

This story tells us a few things about the selection criteria and the way they may work in concrete cases. Firstly, they are normative in the sense that they single out and select in favour of properties that are considered desirable or "good" and against properties that are undesirable or "bad". This leads to further questions: Whose interests do the selection criteria serve? Where do the norms and ideals embedded in the selection criteria originate? To what extent are they adequate for selecting candidates for scientific research?

Secondly, on the basis of the criteria it is possible to construct an idealised "model candidate" that fulfils all the criteria to the highest possible degree. Candidates approaching this model candidate will, for example, be combinations of Jørgen Tesman and Eilert Løvborg. These "Tesborgs" are rare: the dream candidates for any research institution or funding agency, combining scientific creativity with the ability to carry through projects on time and as budgeted.

Thirdly, if followed to the letter, the Tesman-Løvborg case shows that the criteria will systematically select the low-risk candidate with a high median score rather than the brilliant high-risk candidate with an outstanding score on scientific merit and a lower score on the remaining criteria, in cases where they are applied to a Tesman-Løvborg alternative. This is a rational choice *given* the selection criteria. The question remains, however, whether the kind of rationality on which they are based is fit to determine who is most likely to take his or her field "substantially beyond the current state of the art" in terms of research questions and problem solutions (ERC 2008). There is a tension in research policy between the drive for well-defined, well-ordered projects with short time-spans and a high probability of being completed on time, and the demand for excellence. In the first case, quality enters into a trade-off with fixed budgets, fixed time-spans and pre-formulated goals. In the second case, the focus is on the quality of the research, not on the completion of the project. The recent "policy of excellence" which has resulted in new research establishments and in new funding opportunities like those of the European Research Council[3] is a sign that this tension is felt and is being acted upon.

Perhaps we are making up a problem here? Is the view that the aim of scientific research is to achieve extraordinary breakthroughs in the frontiers of knowledge simply legend, the expression of an idealised "romantic" view of academic work? Is scientific research better viewed as a *craft* and researchers as craftsmen and women who have acquired their skills to an agreed level of quality? In this perspective the list of evaluation criteria can be viewed as simply a checklist of the various elements of skill and knowledge that define the craft of researching. Writing a good piece of research is in principle not much different from making a good shoe. Choosing the reliable Tesman over the capricious Løvborg makes good sense if you need a reliable craftsman. I would certainly think twice about hiring a visionary risk-loving plumber with ambitions of going "substantially beyond the current state of the art" if all I wanted was another bathroom.

Whatever our view on the nature of scientific research, what we can learn from reading *Hedda Gabler* is that the selection criteria that we use in choosing candidates for academic careers reveal the underlying values of the institution making the selection, and that these values are not necessarily the same as the expressed values of the institution. To reflect upon this mismatch and to understand how it came to be "naturalised" is the challenge that Ibsen confronts us with.

WORKS CITED

AHRC – Arts and Humanities Research Council (2009). *Research Funding Guide*, www.ahrc.ac.uk/FundingOpportunities/Documents/Research%20Funding%20Guide.pdf, section 5.

Bie, Stein W. "Avslåtte forskningssøknader: Visdom i etterpåklokskap?" *Forskningspolitikk* 3/2005 (2005).

Bourdieu, Pierre and Jean-Claude Passeron. *Reproduction in Education, Society and Culture*. London: Sage, 1977.

ERC. *European Research Council Work Programme 2009* (2008). <http://erc.europa.eu>.

---

3   The mission statement of the ERC is a clear expression of the policy of excellence: "The ERC's main aim is to stimulate scientific excellence by supporting and encouraging the very best, truly creative scientists, scholars and engineers to be adventurous and take risks in their research. The scientists are encouraged to go beyond established frontiers of knowledge and the boundaries of disciplines." (ERC 2010)

ERC. *Mission*, http://erc.europa.eu/index.cfm?fuseaction=page.display&topicID=12 (accessed May 11, 2010)

Goldsworthy, Jeffrey. "Research grant mania." *Australian Universities Review* 50.2 (2008): 17-24.

Heinze, T., Shapira, P., Rogers, J.D. & Senker, J.M. Organizational and institutional influences on creativity in scientific research. *Research Policy* (2009) 38, 610-623.

—. "Optegnelser." *Collected Works*. Eds. Francis Bull, Halvdan Koht and Didrik Arup Seip. Centennial edition Ed. Vol. 11. 21 vols. Oslo: Gyldendal, 1928. 496-516.

Ibsen, Henrik. *Four Major Plays*. Oxford World's Classics. Oxford: Oxford University Press, 1998.

Koht, Halvdan. "Innledning [til Hedda Gabler]." *Henrik Ibsen's Collected Works*. *Centennial Edition*. Ed. Halvdan Koht and Francis Bull. Vol. XI. XXII vols. Oslo: Gyldendal norsk forlag, 1934. 261-90.

Merton, Robert K. "Priorities in Scientific Discovery." *The Sociology of Science: Theoretical and Empirical Investigations*. Ed. Norman W. Storer. Chicago, Ill.: University of Chicago Press, 1973. 286-324.

Moxnes, Erling. "Legg ned Forskningsrådet." Chronicle. *Aftenposten* 02.01. 2009, morning edition, sec. 2: 4.

Newman, Melanie. "Curiosity's priceless, argue trailblazers." *Times Higher Educational Supplement* 10 August 2007, sec. News.

NSF – The National Science Foundation (2009). *Proposal and Award Policies and Procedures guide*. Nsf 09-29, Part I, Ch. III.

RCN. "Personal Post-doctoral Research Fellowship." Oslo, 2009. Accessed 1 April 2009. <http://www.forskningsradet.no/servlet/Satellite?c-Page&cid=119559288295 1&pagename=ForskningsradetEngelsk%2FHovedsidemal>.

Reichelt, Karl L. "Eksperters dubiøse rolle." Forskningspolitikk. 1/02.04. (2008).

Tjønneland, Eivind. "Historiefilosofien i Ibsens opptegnelser til *Hedda Gabler*." *Et skjær av uvilkårlig skjønnhet: Om Henrik Ibsens Hedda Gabler*. Ed. Anne Marie Rekdal. Oslo: Cappelens Akademisk, 2001. 149-63.

Vogel, Gretchen. "A knockout award in medicine." *Science* 318 (2007): 178-79.

LIST OF ILLUSTRATIONS

CONTRIBUTORS

Charles I. Armstrong is a professor of British literature at the University of Bergen. He is the author of *Figures of Memory: Poetry, Space and the Past* (2009) and *Romantic Organicism: From Idealist Origins to Ambivalent Afterlife* (2003), both published with Palgrave Macmillan, as well as a co-editor of *Postcolonial Dislocations: Travel, History and the Ironies of Narrative* (Novus, 2006).

Andrea Battistini is Professor of Italian literature at the University of Bologna. He has published numerous books on the history of rhetoric, the history of ideas, on autobiography, the encounters of science and literature, the philosophy of Giambattista Vico, on Galileo Galilei and on Italian prose of the twentieth century. Among his recent books are *Galileo e I gesuiti. Miti e retorica della scienza* (2000), *Vico tra antichi e moderni* (2004) and *Lo specchio di Dedalo* (2008).

Dame Gillian Beer is King Edward VII Professor Emeritus of English literature at the University of Cambridge. Her most important research is on the exchanges between literature and science, and the broader implications and challenges of interdisciplinary studies. Among her books are *Darwin's Plots: Evolutionary Narrative in Darwin, George Eliot and Nineteenth-Century Fiction* (1983, third ed. 2009), *Open Fields: Science in Cultural Encounter* (1996) and *Virginia Woolf: the Common Ground* (1996). She is at present completing a study of Lewis Carroll's Alice books in the context of nineteenth-century intellectual controversies.

Jon Bing is a writer and a professor of law at the Norwegian Research Center for Computers and Law (NRCCL) at the Faculty of Law, University of Oslo. He is considered a pioneer in International Legal Information. Bing has held many positions, both nationally and internationally, including the chairmanship of the Arts Council of Norway. He made his debut as a writer of fiction in 1967 and has been awarded many prizes for his work in the literary field. In 2004 he received the Norwegian Library Association's honorary prize.

Jostein Børtnes is Professor Emeritus at the University of Bergen, where he was professor of Russian literature (1984-2007). His most recent book is *The Poetry of Prose: Readings in Russian Literature* (2007).

Ragnar Fjelland is Professor of philosophy of science at the Center for the Study of the Sciences and the Humanities and Department of Physics and Technology, University of Bergen. His topics of interest include the significance of technology for the acquisition of scientific knowledge, problems of complexity and uncertainty, ethical problems raised by modern science and technology, and the challenge of environmental problems to science.

Christine Hamm is Associate Professor at the Department of Linguistic, Literary and Aesthetic Studies, University of Bergen. She published the monograph *Medlidenhet og melodrama: Amalie Skrams romaner om ekteskap* in 2006 and is the coeditor of *Tekster på tvers: Queer-inspirerte lesninger* (2008).

Margareth Hagen is Associate Professor of Italian Literature at the Department of Foreign Languages and Literatures, University of Bergen. She holds a doctorate on sixteenth century Italian literature and her research interests are Italian Renaissance Studies and the encounter of science and literature in the works of Italo Calvino and Primo Levi.

Holly Henry is Associate Professor of English at California State University, San Bernardino. Her interdisciplinary research focuses on modernist studies, the cultural studies of science, and the history of astronomy and space science. Henry is the author of *Virginia Woolf and the Discourse of Science: The Aesthetics of Astronomy* (Cambridge UP 2003) and has co-authored an essay on the legacy of the Apollo programme in *Space Travel and Culture: From Apollo to Space Tourism* (Wiley-Blackwell/The Sociological Review 2009).

Randi Koppen is Associate Professor of British literature at the University of Bergen. Her research interests are mainly within the fields of British modernism, theatre studies, and literature and science. She is the author of *Virginia Woolf, Fashion and Literary Modernity* (Edinburgh University Press, 2009) and *Scenes of Infidelity: Feminism in the Theatre* (Solum Press, 1997).

Hans Jacob Ohldieck is a PhD scholar at the Department of Foreign Languages and Literatures, University of Bergen. He is currently writing his dissertation on Latin American and Neobaroque literature.

Margery Vibe Skagen is Associate Professor of French Literature at the Department of Foreign Languages and Literatures, University of Bergen. Her doctoral thesis, in French literature, focuses on the poetics of melancholy in Baudelaire's writings. Main research interests are French 19th century supernaturalism, literature and medical history, literature and science.

Rasmus T. Slaattelid is Associate Professor of the philosophy of science and science studies at the University of Bergen. His research is focused on the philosophy of the humanities, visualisations in science, and science policy.

Roger Strand, PhD in biochemistry, is Professor and Director at the Centre for the Study of the Sciences and the Humanities, University of Bergen. Strand's research lies mainly within the philosophy of natural science, environmental science and medicine. In particular, he has been interested in questions about scientific uncertainty and complexity in the interface between science and its use in society. Since 2006 he has been a member of the national research ethics committee for science and technology in Norway.

Željka Švrljuga is Associate Professor of American literature at the University of Bergen. Research interests and publications are divided between the rhetoric of pain in literature and arts, and the neo-slave narrative genre.

Eivind Tjønneland is Professor of Scandinavian literature at the University of Bergen. His most recent work includes the editorship of *Opplysningens tidsskrifter* (2008) and *Holberg* (2008).